Apocaly...
the End

Wolfson College Lectures

Apocalypse Theory and the Ends of the World

Edited by
Malcolm Bull

BLACKWELL
Oxford UK & Cambridge USA

236.3

Copyright © Blackwell Publishers, 1995
Chapter 12 © Edward W. Said 1995

First published 1995
Reprinted 1996

Blackwell Publishers Ltd
108 Cowley Road
Oxford, OX4 1JF
UK

Blackwell Publishers Inc.
238 Main Street
Cambridge, Massachusetts 02142
USA

British Library Cataloguing in Publication Data

A CIP catalogue record for this book is available from the British Library.

Library of Congress Cataloging-in-Publication Data
Apocalypse theory and the ends of the world/edited by Malcolm Bull.
    p.   cm. – (Wolfson College lectures)
    Includes bibliographical references and index.
    ISBN 0–631–19081–3 (alk. paper). – ISBN 0–631–19082–1 (pbk.: alk. paper)
    1. End of the world – History of doctrines.   2. History – Philosophy.
    3. Apocalyptic literature – History and criticism.
    I. Bull, Malcolm.   II. Series.
    BT876.A66 1995
    124 – dc20

200 23587

94–33969
CIP

Typeset 11 on 13 pt Bembo by Best-set Typesetters Ltd., Hong Kong
Printed in Great Britain by Athenæum Press Ltd, Gateshead, Tyne & Wear

This book is printed on acid-free paper

Contents

Contributors

Malcolm Bull is a Lecturer at the University of Oxford, and a Research Fellow of Wolfson College.

Norman Cohn is Astor-Wolfson Professor Emeritus of History at the University of Sussex.

Laurence W. Dickey is Associate Professor of History at the University of Wisconsin – Madison.

Frank Kermode is an Honorary Fellow of King's College, Cambridge.

Krishan Kumar is Professor of Social Thought at the University of Kent at Canterbury.

Bernard McGinn is Naomi Shemstone Donnelley Professor in the Divinity School at the University of Chicago.

Christopher Norris is Professor at the Centre for Critical and Cultural Theory at the University of Wales in Cardiff.

Richard Popkin is Professor Emeritus at Washington University, St Louis, and Adjunct Professor of History and Philosophy at UCLA.

Marjorie Reeves is an Honorary Fellow of St Anne's and St Hugh's Colleges, Oxford.

Christopher Rowland is Dean Ireland's Professor of the Exegesis of Holy Scripture at the University of Oxford.

Edward W. Said is University Professor at Columbia University, New York.

Elinor Shaffer is Reader in Comparative Literature at the University of East Anglia.

Acknowledgements

This book is based on the 1993 Wolfson College Lectures. I am very grateful to the members of the college who made the series possible, notably John Penney, Janet Walker and the then President, Sir Raymond Hoffenberg, and also to Marjorie Reeves, Richard Popkin and Laurence Dickey, who agreed to contribute to the volume at a later stage.

1

On Making Ends Meet

Malcolm Bull

I

In English, an 'end' may be the termination or the goal of action, and it is often both, for no one wants to end up where they have no desire to be. But to arrive and stop at one's destination, to finish at the intended point and go no further, inevitably requires a balance of aspiration and calculation that may be difficult to achieve. If, as in much of everyday life, the goals to which action is directed are provisional and the cessations temporary, the delicate balance between the desirable and the possible can be constantly readjusted. But if it is the totality of experience that is at stake – the ultimate goal, the final ending – there is little room for manœuvre and the limits of hope may be drawn uncomfortably tight.

That the world should have ends, in the sense of a terminus and a telos, is not self-evident. But although the idea of a world without end or purpose is logically coherent, infinite duration is difficult to conceive, and the notion of eternal aimlessness repugnant to the moral imagination. In practice, therefore, most are inclined to attribute at least one end to the world. Someone who perceives no shape in the history of the universe may posit its termination as a result of cosmic collapse, and someone who believes in the eternity of the world may argue that history is orientated toward some unrealizable goal. Both of these theories have been seriously proposed – the former in scientific projections of universal catastrophe, the latter in the Kantian dream of unending progress – but most visions of the future fall somewhere between a pure eschatology of unmotivated disaster and a pure teleology of interminable purposefulness.

However, combining the teleological and the eschatological may draw the ends of the world together without allowing them to meet. The world may end before the purpose of history has been realized; time may continue long after meaningful development has ceased. In recent years, both possibilities have seemed conceivable: during the Cold War, Marxists feared that a nuclear war would take place before the dialectic of history had been completed; after the Cold War, Francis Fukuyama argued that although normal life persisted, history had already come to an end.[1] Yet the problem itself is an ancient one. One way to resolve the difficulty is to postulate a cycle in which unrealized objectives are fulfilled, and the time left over from one dispensation becomes the opening of the next. Thus, the doctrine of reincarnation permits meanings to be carried beyond the boundaries of history, and the theory of eternal recurrence accommodates extra time in ceaseless repetition. This move disposes of the excesses of time and meaning, but only by deploying the frustrating logic of supplementarity – objectives are constantly displaced to the next incarnation, the end forever deferred to the next cycle. In consequence, whatever the psycho-social comforts of repetition,[2] the intellectual challenges posed by infinity and aimlessness are not permanently resolved. As Kant noted, eternal oscillation 'amounts to nothing more than if the subject had remained in the same place, standing still'.[3]

Because the prospect of perpetual recurrence may be, as it was for the philosophers of antiquity, 'not a source of consolation, but . . . an additional source of horror',[4] cyclical theories almost always spawn philosophies in which some individuals are able to escape from the circle. But if individuals can be liberated, why is it necessary to have a cyclical theory at all? As Augustine acutely observed, a soul that attains bliss only to return to misery cannot be truly happy, whereas a soul that is able to move irreversibly from misery to beatitude begins in time a movement that ends in eternity; and if the soul can reach a destination beyond time, 'Why not then the world?'[5] Put another way, if the telos of the individual life can coincide with its terminus, there seems no reason why the ends of the world should not also meet.

II

A formal typology of the philosophies of history can be created by determining whether they are teleological or eschatological, and if they are both, whether telos and terminus coincide. A further refinement might be to distinguish between ends that are good and those that are bad.[6] But it is difficult to hold on to the concept of a bad telos or a good terminus: a desirable ending is inevitably transformed into a goal, and outside of an everlasting hell, the teleology of evil is invariably terminal. In the modern period at least, a better way to differentiate theories is to locate them ideologically on the continuum between the religious or secular, and sociologically on the axis between 'high' or 'low' culture. Conjoined, the latter distinctions yield four categories of thought: high-religious; high-secular; popular-religious, and popular-secular. There is no reason why each of these categories should not contain all the ideal types of eschatology and teleology discussed above. But in fact things are simpler. I will discuss each of the ideological and sociological categories in turn.

Within the history of the West, religious belief about the future has primarily meant the eschatological conviction that history will be brought to a close by the coming, or return, of a messianic figure who will vindicate the righteous, destroy their enemies, and rule over a kingdom of peace and prosperity. In Christianity, the near un-intelligibility of the canonical apocalyptic texts outside (and perhaps within) their historical setting ensured that their interpretation was long the preserve of a clerical or scholarly elite. The tradition developed two more or less distinct forms: the spiritual and the historical. In the spiritual interpretation – expounded in the lost work of the fourth-century Donatist, Tyconius, and subsequently developed by Augustine – apocalyptic symbols refer to continuing moral realities in the life of the church and the world.[7] In the historical form, derived from the twelfth-century Calabrian abbot, Joachim of Fiore, the scriptures are interpreted with reference to the sequence of events in religious and political history. Whereas in spiritual readings of apocalyptic the emphasis is on the synchronic differentiation of good and evil, historicist interpreters give history a shape and a direction, a telos as well as a terminus.[8] (Although in pre-millennialism the Second Advent comes before the millennium, while in post-millennialism the Second Coming is preceded by a millennium in which the telos of complete felicity is either gradually approached or enjoyed throughout.)

If high-religious theories of history are always eschatological and only sometimes teleological, high-secular theories are usually the reverse. As the Enlightenment weakened belief in divine intervention, philosophers began to focus on the pattern and purpose of history without reference to its end.[9] From Voltaire to Comte in France, and from Lessing to Marx in Germany, increasingly specific and ambitious philosophies of history were developed. History, it was argued, furnished abundant evidence that mankind was progressing, not only in the arts and sciences, but also in its spiritual condition and social organization. The pattern of the past, whether linear or dialectical, indicated the direction and, by extrapolation, the goal of human development – a goal that was at least partially independent of the efforts of individuals to attain it. This teleological interpretation of history was given added if ambiguous support by the Darwinian theory of evolution; even so, it has not been the only expression of high secular thought on the subject: the late nineteenth century saw the re-emergence of cyclical theories, and in the twentieth, critics of the Enlightenment have often couched their attack on its teleology in the eschatological language of apocalyptic.

At the same time as secular philosophers were developing an interest in the shape of history, religious millenarianism was gaining a popular audience and narrowing its focus on the end of time. Popular millenarianism, which had been a recurrent but often short-lived feature of Christian history, has, since the early nineteenth century, developed a broader and more stable constituency. Unlike high-religious eschatologies, which are often concerned with the past and the distant or indefinite future, popular eschatology is focused on events taking place in the present and immediate future. Contemporary Christian millenarians, such as the North American fundamentalists discussed in Paul Boyer's recent study *When Time Shall Be No More*, see current political leaders (and sometimes also themselves) as major figures in the final drama of history.[10] For them, like their precursors in almost every century of the Christian era, each newsworthy development is a portent of the end giving fresh urgency to the call for repentance.

Popular-secular apocalyptic feeds on the same images of nuclear holocaust, ecological catastrophe, sexual decadence and social collapse that inspire contemporary religious millenarianism. But unlike the religious variety, secular apocalyptic – which is found in many areas of popular culture, but most notably in science fiction, rock music and film – is not usually intended to effect personal spiritual transformation. It may be designed to influence public opinion in favour of social or political objectives such as nuclear disarmament or environmental regulation, but in many cases the language of apocalyptic is deployed simply to shock, alarm or enrage. For example, in *Apocalypse Culture*, a widely read alternative text in the late 1980s and early 1990s, the apocalypse serves as the unifying theme for a collection of writings on bodily mutilation, Satanism, sexual perversion and terrorism. As the publisher puts it: 'Two thousand years have passed since the death of Christ and the world is going mad. Nihilist prophets, born-again pornographers, transcendental schizophrenics and just plain folks are united in their belief in an imminent global catastrophe'.[11] Like their religious counterparts, popular-secular apocalyptics discern little purpose in the world, except in its ending.

The relationships that exist between these categories of eschatological and teleological thought are more complex than might be imagined. To cite just one example, in *Lipstick Traces: A Secret History of the Twentieth Century*, Greil Marcus provocatively suggests that the similarities between John Lydon, a.k.a. Johnny Rotten, the lead singer of the Sex Pistols, and John of Leyden, the sixteenth-century Anabaptist who proclaimed himself 'King of the New Jerusalem', may be more than phonic. Lydon was the creation of Malcolm McLaren, a friend of Christopher Gray – a former member of the Situationist International whose translations of Situationist texts McLaren helped to publish. Led by Guy Debord, the Situationists had drawn directly on *The Pursuit of the Millennium*, Norman Cohn's classic study of popular medieval millenarians (such as John of Leyden), and fused the anarcho-religious impulse with Marxism. In the post-Situationist underground, Debord's 'chiliastic serenity' gave way to the blank apocalypticism of punk as Marx's secular messianism fell away from the nihilistic religious apocalypticism to which it had been joined. So, according to Marcus, when Johnny Rotten sang 'I am an Antichrist' in 'Anarchy in the UK', he was not simply laying claim to a well-established anti-social role, he was also giving a revealing glimpse of punk's intellectual heritage.[12]

As this intriguing connection between the nihilist strain in popular culture and the millenarian tradition suggests, apocalyptic ideas can circulate between, as well as within, sociological and ideological categories. The eschatology of high Christian culture can be said both to have set the agenda for secular philosophies of history and to have provided a detailed framework for popular religious millenarianism. As a consequence, there are surprisingly close parallels between the postmodern theories of posthistory and fundamentalist millenarianism. In their turn, both popular-religious millenarianism and high-secular eschatologies provide languages which can be used, sometimes in combination, to give voice to populist protest in which the redemptive claims of religion and high culture are both absent. This popular-secular apocalyptic is almost an inversion of high-religious eschatology, a rhetoric in which the damned seem to be celebrating their own damnation. As such it may be reappropriated by both high-secular and popular-religious critics of teleology to undermine the complacent belief that all are rejoicing in the benefits of progress.

To the casual observer, this interlacing of apparently incompatible rhetorics may seem nothing more than a curious irony, but for both the user and the interpreter of apocalyptic discourses it is important to determine which are the echoes and which the prophetic voices.

III

In this volume, only some of the many theories and beliefs about the end of the world are examined. The boundary explored is not primarily that between 'high' and 'low' cultures or between contemporary religious and secular ideologies (although both frontiers are repeatedly crossed), but rather that which divides the religious eschatology of the Christian tradition from the secular intellectual strategies that come after it. There is, therefore, little about religious millenarianism after the emergence of its secular counterparts, or about popular apocalyptic, which is discussed chiefly in the context of parallel developments in high culture.

But within these limitations, the coverage is fairly comprehensive. In the first section of the book, devoted to religious eschatologies, all the contributors emphasize the close connection between belief in the imminent end of the world and goal-directed behaviour. Norman Cohn argues that the origins of eschatology are to be found in the latter half of the second millennium BCE in Zoroaster's break with the traditional cyclical world-view. Christopher Rowland suggests that early Christian apocalyptic was not focused exclusively on the termination of the world, but also on 'the present as a decisive opportunity for the transformation of the world'. Bernard McGinn argues that a Christian society was created because and not in spite of the fact that the Last Judgement remained psychologically imminent throughout the early Middle Ages. Marjorie Reeves describes the tensions between eschatological and teleological interpretations of the Joachite tradition, and Richard Popkin reviews the reformist political climate of millennial expectation amongst Protestants and Jews in the seventeenth century.

The history of Christian eschatological expectation reveals that the end of the world has long played a significant role in the generation of meaning. The essays in the second and third parts of this volume suggest that even when divorced from a traditional Christian context, the ends of the world may still form the boundaries, and thus also the shape, tone and perhaps even substance of secular discourse. The essays on secular ends highlight three very different examples of the post-Enlightenment reappropriation of Christian eschatology. Elinor Shaffer argues that critical biblical scholarship allowed the Romantics to assume the mantle of prophecy and create their own form of apocalyptic literature. Laurence Dickey explores the fusion of religious eschatology and secular teleology in Cieszkowski's philosophy of history. Krishan Kumar discusses the 'debased millenarianism' of the twentieth century's prophets of doom.

The final section suggests that, whether they use an apocalyptic tone, belong to a decadent epoch or embody a late style, certain texts can be characterized by their sense of having been written at the end – at the limits of meaning, the close of an era, the end of a life. Christopher Norris discusses the self-consciously 'apocalyptic tone' adopted in Derrida's interrogation of the teleology of the Enlightenment and the eschatology of nuclear strategy. Frank Kermode explores the parallels between Joachim's concept of a transition between two ages and the *fin-de-siècle* concept of decadence, and Edward Said investigates the late styles of Beethoven and Adorno.

IV

The contributors to this book address several issues that are currently the focus of intense scholarly interest. The origins of apocalyptic in the ancient world, the significance of the millennium in early modern intellectual life, the relationship between the utopian and millenarian traditions, and the construction of discourses at the limits of experience

and meaning are all the subject of continuing investigation and contro-
versy. Each of the essays in this volume makes a significant contribution to one or another of these debates. But taken collectively, they
also address an issue that none deals with individually. Implicit in the
organization of this book is the assumption that there are sufficient
connections between the religious and secular versions of both eschatology and teleology to justify their discussion within the same context.
This is far from being a novel suggestion,[13] but at least one version of
this thesis has come under sustained attack in recent years, and it is
now impossible to produce such a volume without clarifying and
perhaps defending the premise upon which it is founded.

The central question in what has become known as the Löwith–
Blumenberg debate is whether or not the development of secular
philosophies of history can accurately be described as a secularization of
Christian eschatology. The idea that the Christian belief in the millennium has been transformed into the secular vision of progress was
given its fullest statement in two books published in 1949: Ernest Lee
Tuveson's *Millennium and Utopia* and Karl Löwith's *Meaning in History*.[14] Although Tuveson's study was devoted to English authors of the
seventeenth and eighteenth centuries, and Löwith's focused on French
and German writers of the late eighteenth and early nineteenth centuries, the argument was the same in both cases. According to
Tuveson, it was accurate 'to speak of "progress" as a "faith", for
it . . . resulted in part from the transformation of a religious idea – the
great millennial expectation'.[15] According to Löwith: 'The irreligion of
progress is still a sort of religion, derived from the Christian faith in a
future goal, through substituting an indefinite and immanent *eschaton*
for a definite and transcendent one.'[16]

Blumenberg seems to have been familiar only with Löwith's work,
which, in comparison with Tuveson's, is both less specific about the
process of transformation and more critical of the result. However, in
the first part of his massive study, *The Legitimacy of the Modern Age*, he
marshalled a battery of arguments against the secularization thesis
which are applicable to any formulation of the theory. According
to Blumenberg, if the secularization thesis is to work it must be on
the basis of an analogy between the secularization of ideas and
the secularization or expropriation of ecclesiastical property. The
secularization theorist must therefore be able to demonstrate 'the
identifiability of the expropriated property, the legitimacy of its initial

ownership, and the unilateral nature of its removal'.[17] Of these requirements the first is decisive, for Blumenberg believes that it is impossible
to prove the identity and continuity of the substance of Christian
eschatology and the secular idea of progress. Whereas 'eschatology
speaks of an event breaking into history, an event that transcends and
is heterogeneous to it . . . the idea of progress extrapolates from a
structure present in every moment to a future that is immanent
in history'.[18] It is therefore improbable that 'theological eschatology,
with its idea of the "consummation" of history by its discontinuance,
could have provided the model for an idea of the forward movement of history according to which it was supposed . . . to gain stability
and reliability through its consummation or its approach to
consummation'.[19]

But if Christian eschatology did not provide the model, how did the
idea of progress originate? According to Blumenberg, the idea of
progress, entails 'a coordinative relation between the quantum of time
and the quality of achievement . . . in which the quantity of distance
in time becomes the chief premise of new possibilities'.[20] The concept
must therefore have evolved in a situation in which there was 'a
logical tie between time quantum and achievement quality'.[21] This
condition was met in the development of early modern astronomy in
which it was recognized that theoretical progress depended upon the
comparison of observations that could not, even in principle, be
undertaken in less than several lifetimes. Astronomy, Blumenberg
asserts, offered a 'breadth of the temporal horizon, that was absent
from the medieval consciousness even where apocalyptic expectations
or fears did not narrow it down to an immediate concern with
salvation'.[22]

However, Blumenberg argues that the idea of progress derived from
astronomy, with its 'regionally circumscribed and objectively limited
range', was later used by philosophers of history to answer questions
about the totality of history that had been posed within a Christian
framework. In this process, the idea of progress was 'removed from its
empirical foundations . . . and forced to perform a function that was
originally defined by a system that is alien to it'.[23] Yet, according to
Blumenberg, this development was not a secularization of earlier
Christian beliefs about history, for even in its over-extended form, the
idea of progress had no continuity of substance with the Christian
doctrines that had answered the same questions, only an identity of

function – a functional equivalence that Blumenberg terms a 'reoccupation' of the earlier position.

If Blumenberg's thesis is correct (and he is considered by some commentators to have 'dealt a death blow' to the secularization theory),[24] then a volume such as this, which combines the discussion of both sacred and secular theories of history, cannot be read as a gen- ealogy tracing the transformations of a single tradition, but only as an anthology of the answers offered to a single problem. These alternatives may not be mutually exclusive, but if (as in this case) a genealogical reading is invited, it is necessary to give some indication of why Blumenberg's objections might not be considered decisive.

                                      V

Lessing's *Education of the Human Race* serves as a good introduction to the problems inherent in Blumenberg's argument. In this brief work, Lessing gives an account of human progress that is secular rather than religious, teleological rather than eschatological. And in the preface to the nineteenth-century English translation, the translator uses examples of scientific progress to suggest the plausibility of Lessing's theory: 'Did the earth ever do other than go round the sun? yet how long is it since man found this out? . . . Are the spiritual truths of man's nature more easily discerned than the physical phenomena which surround him? Why should there not be development in these as well as in those?'[25] On this reading, Lessing's text would appear to be a perfect example of a secular teleology using a model of progress derived from astronomy.

However, Lessing's argument for moral progress is a direct extrapol- ation of the Christian idea of a progressive revelation: if that which was manifest in the Law came to fulfilment in Christ, may not that which was revealed in Christ yet be fulfilled in history? This argument is not derived, even by analogy, from the progress of science, for, as Lessing states, its sources are Christian, and are to be found in the New Testament and the Joachite tradition. Hence the rapturous declaration: 'It will assuredly come! the time of a new eternal Gospel, which is promised us in the Primer of the New Testament itself. . . . some enthusiasts of the thirteenth and fourteenth centuries had caught a glimpse of a beam of this new eternal Gospel. . . . Perhaps their "Three Ages of the World" were not so vain a fancy after all.'[26]

Lessing's *Education of the Human Race* provides an example of a theory whose form and roots were explicitly Christian subsequently being read in terms of the belief in scientific progress. It suggests that rather than being the paradigm for a secular teleology, scientific progress may be used as evidence for a theological model of teleology.

Blumenberg does not investigate this possibility, for he makes no serious attempt to differentiate between the varieties of Christian eschatology. His conclusion that there can have been no transformation of substance in the shift from Christian eschatology to secular teleology depends, in part, upon the exclusion of both Christian teleology and secular eschatology from the equation. Conveniently forgetting the entire Joachite tradition, or at least its high, teleologically orientated branch, Blumenberg (who does not distinguish between high and low variants of the same ideology) depicts eschatology as being narrowly and nervously concerned with the imminence of the Last Judgement. He thus fails to notice that, like astronomy, prophetic interpretation was founded upon a relationship between time and knowledge in which distance in time was the prerequisite of further understanding.

For prophetic interpreters it was almost axiomatic that the Bible had laid down a programme for the future which would be fulfilled, and so become more progressively more recognizable, over long periods of time. Richard More, the seventeenth-century Protestant translator of Joseph Mede's *Key of the Revelation*, was by no means unusual in referring to 'the obscuritie of this (as of all other Prophecies) untill the event should manifest them'.[27] The famous sixteenth-century Jesuit commentator Juan Maldonado spelt out the connection between the passage of time and the progress of knowledge in his remarks on Daniel 12.4 ('Many shall run to and fro, and knowledge shall be increased'). This text, he argued, revealed that knowledge would be increased as people, prompted by events, studied the prophecies to ascertain which had been fulfilled. But such knowledge was to be gained after the event and was thus wholly dependent on history: when Daniel wrote in the sixth century BCE, no one understood him; four hundred years later, after the persecution of Antiochus Epiphanes, people understood some of the things to which Daniel referred, although others, such as the prophecies relating to Antichrist, were still incomprehensible.[28]

Francis Bacon, a central figure in Blumenberg's secular genealogy of the idea of progress, made a comparably clear statement of the pro-

gressive and time-dependent nature of prophetic fulfilment and interpretation in *The Advancement of Learning*:

> [The] history of prophecy, consisteth of two relatives, the prophecy and
> the accomplishment; and therefore the nature of such a work ought to
> be, that every prophecy of the scripture be sorted with the event
> fulfilling the same, throughout the ages of the world . . . allowing
> nevertheless that latitude which is agreeable and familiar unto divine
> prophecies; being of the nature of their author, with whom a thousand
> years are but as one day, and therefore are not filled punctually at once,
> but have springing and germinant accomplishment throughout many
> ages.[29]

This passage is of particular importance because Bacon had already
provided an example of the fulfilment of prophecy a few lines earlier
– an example he used repeatedly in support of his belief that the
sciences could progress towards the *Instauratio Magna*, the great restoration of knowledge:

> And this proficience in navigation and discoveries may plant also an
> expectation of the further proficience and augmentation of all sciences;
> because it may seem that they are ordained by God to be coevals, that
> is, to meet in one age. For so the prophet Daniel speaking of the latter
> times foretelleth, *Plurimi petransibunt, et multiplex erit scientia* [Daniel
> 12.4]: as if the openness and through-passage of the world and the
> increase of knowledge were appointed to be in the same ages; as we see
> it already performed in great part.[30]

For Bacon, it would seem, the progress of science was a fulfilment of
prophecy, and belief in its continued progress an inference from the
partial to the complete fulfilment of prophecy. Read in the context of
his remarks about the nature of prophecy, Bacon's interpretation of
Daniel 12.4 suggests that, like Maldonado, he believed that knowledge
would continue to grow in fulfilment of prophecy because prophecy
itself was progressive in its fulfilment. He argued for the progress of
science not by extrapolation from that progress, but by coupling it with
the progressive knowledge derived from prophecy.

Blumenberg, who supposes that the idea of progress required
'the suppression of eschatological expectations or fears',[31] suggests
that Bacon was simply cloaking the newly broadened temporal

horizon of science in the restrictive vocabulary of apocalyptic. In his opinion, 'Bacon's idea of paradise is not eschatological' and his use of biblical prophecies simply a rhetorical device 'to make the accumulation of new discoveries and inventions appear trustworthy and promising'.[32] But there is evidence to indicate that the opposite was the case.

Both before and after Bacon gave his interpretation of Daniel 12.4, millenarian writers were using the same arguments in an explicitly religious context. Guillaume Postel, the eccentric sixteenth-century French polymath whom Bacon described as 'magnus peregrinator, et mathematicus',[33] and who saw himself as the *instaurator* of an imminent *restitutio omnium*, fed his hopes on exactly the same developments in knowledge and exploration:

> Today we can see clearly that, quite suddenly, Greek, Latin and Hebrew letters, along with all learning, divine and human, have made more progress in fifty years than in the previous thousand.... And we see another great change and marvel when we consider how, during the last ten years, through the efforts of sailors and merchants, the new world, which is greater than our own, has not only been discovered and conquered, but also converted to the Christian religion.[34]

Later, William Twisse, a Puritan divine, read Bacon's interpretation of Daniel 12.4 in the manuscript of *Valerius Terminus*, and effortlessly incorporated Bacon's reading of the text into a millennial vision of spiritual progress which foreshadows that of Lessing:

> If before the Law men had a light whereby they might finde the truth more clearly than we, then the former times were times of greater light and grace than the later; but this is contrary both to the generall judgment of the Christian world, and to universall experience. For as light naturally increaseth more and more untill it be perfect day, so it hath been with light spirituall.[35]

For both Bacon's predecessors and successors, developments in learning and navigation functioned as evidence for belief in the coming millennium. It is therefore difficult to accept Blumenberg's contention that Bacon is introducing a scientifically generated concept of progress. On the contrary, both Bacon (whom Blumenberg thinks of as establishing the idea of progress) and Lessing (whom Blumenberg sees as inflating the scientific idea to theological dimensions) would appear to be appropriating a well-defined and established Christian theology of progressive enlightenment through prophetic fulfilment in history.

VI

Although the secularization theorists may be right about the degree of continuity between religious and secular teleologies, Blumenberg's ideas have enriched the debate and can be redeployed by those who disagreee with his central argument. The organization of this volume is at odds with Blumenberg's thesis in so far as it invites a genealogical interpretation of the relationship between secular and religious theories of history, but it does not seek to restrict the discussion of ends to the model of secularization. In Blumenberg's work, discussion is first narrowed and then polarized into a disjunction between religious eschatology and scientific teleology. In this volume, the approach is the reverse. In addition to the focus on the connection between purpose and finality, and the continuity of that relation across the fracture of secularization, there is a concern with the diversity of ends and the multiple points of contact between them. And in this wider context, many of Blumenberg's insights are applicable.

Alongside the model of transformation through secularization it is helpful to employ two of the concepts that Blumenberg offers as alternatives to that idea: reoccupation and linguistic anachronism (which Blumenberg himself confusingly terms 'linguistic secularization'). The former is used by Blumenberg to account for the quasi-religious ambitions of supposedly secular philosophers of hisory, and embodies the notion of functional equivalence as an alternative to that of transformation of substance. The latter, with which Blumenberg seeks to explain the theological language of Bacon and other early advocates of progress, suggests that because the vocabulary appropriate to the expression of new ideas was often lacking, advanced thinkers frequently fell back on religious rhetoric. In consequence, 'The sphere of sacral language outlives that of the consecrated objects and is anxiously conserved and used as a cover precisely where philosophically, politically, and scientifically new thinking is being done.'[36]

Blumenberg's models of reoccupation and linguistic anachronism may not be able to explain the continuity between high-religious and secular teleologies – which, I have suggested, was substantial rather than just functional or rhetorical – but they are useful in interpreting the relationships that exist between and within some of the other categories of eschatological and teleological thought. For example, in relation to religious millenarianism, contemporary secular apocalyptic might be said to combine elements of transformation, reoccupation and anachronism. And the web of connections between punk, Situationism and medieval millenarianism might be explained in terms of Situationism's self-conscious linguistic anachronism, and punk's reoccupation, or perhaps transformation, of the Situationist position.

Amongst the contributions to this volume, it is possible to discern a variety of patterns. Edward Said's account of the creative pressures of living in the shadow of the end, makes the concept of 'late style' seem like a gentle reoccupation of the early medieval concern with imminent death and judgement described by Bernard McGinn. But the 'apocalyptic tone', discussed in Christopher Norris's essay, sounds more like an aggressive piece of linguistic anachronism. Other contributions are more difficult to categorize, and prompt a string of questions. Does Frank Kermode's description of 'waiting for the end' imply a functional or a rhetorical identity between religious and secular expectation? Is Krishan Kumar's 'debased millenarianism' the result of a transformation or a reoccupation of earlier positions? In what measure, according to Laurence Dickey, did Cieszkowski's theory of history combine the substantial and functional elements of its predecessors? How, in Elinor Shaffer's essay, does the transformation of biblical interpretation relate to the reoccupation of prophetic roles? Such questions are not confined to the secular sphere, or to the relationship between the religious and the secular. It is also fair to ask how the continuities between popular and scholarly millenarianism revealed in the essays of Marjorie Reeves and Richard Popkin are best understood. And is the political millenarianism of the Diggers and the liberation theologians a linguistic anachronism, a transformation of a purely spiritual concept, or, as Christopher Rowland implies, a continuation of early Christian concerns? Perhaps Judaeo-Christian apocalyptic itself is a reoccupation, or, as Norman Cohn would argue, a transformation, of Zoroastrian millenarianism?

The answers to these questions fall beyond the scope of this essay. But to address them it is useful to have a clearly differentiated awareness of the forms in which eschatological and teleological ideas are combined, the social and ideological contexts in which they are sustained, and the relationships by which they are connected.

NOTES

1 Francis Fukuyama, *The End of History and the Last Man* (London, 1992). The idea of a period of time left over at the end of history was first explored by Jerome, see Robert E. Lerner, 'Refreshment of the Saints: The Time after Antichrist as a Station for Earthly Progress in Medieval Thought', *Traditio*, 32 (1976), 97–144.

2 The benefits are described by Mircea Eliade in *The Myth of the Eternal Return* (Princeton, 1954).

3 Immanuel Kant, 'The Conflict of the Faculties', in *Kant: On History*, ed. L. W. Beck (New York, 1963), 81.

4 Richard Sorabji, *Time, Creation and the Continuum* (London, 1983), 190.

5 Augustine, *City of God*, XII, 13.

6 Kant suggests something along these lines in 'The Conflict of the Faculties'.

7 See Bernard McGinn, *The Calabrian Abbot* (New York, 1985), ch. 2.

8 See Marjorie Reeves, 'The Originality and Influence of Joachim of Fiore', *Traditio*, 36 (1980), 269–316.

9 For an overview, see Frank Manuel, *Shapes of Philosophical History* (London, 1965); two early explorations of the theme are Carl Becker, *The Heavenly City of the Eighteenth-Century Philosophers* (New Haven, 1932), and J. B. Bury, *The Idea of Progress* (London, 1932).

10 Paul Boyer, *When Time Shall Be No More: Prophecy Belief in Modern American Culture* (Cambridge, Mass., 1992).

11 Adam Parfrey, ed., *Apocalypse Culture*, rev. edn (Portland, Ore., 1990), jacket copy.

12 Greil Marcus, *Lipstick Traces: A Secret History of the Twentieth Century* (London, 1990).

13 See, for example, J. Wittreich and C. A. Patrides, eds, *The Apocalypse in English Renaissance Thought and Literature* (Manchester, 1984); and S. Friedländer, G. Holton, L. Marx and E. Skolnikoff, eds, *Visions of Apocalypse: End or Rebirth?* (New York, 1985). Contemporary concerns are explored in D. Kamper and C. Wulf, eds, *Looking Back on the End of the World* (New York, 1989).

14 For a useful review of the debate see Robert Wallace, 'Progress, Secularization, and Modernity: The Löwith–Blumenberg Debate', *New German Critique*, 22 (1981), 63–79.

15 E. L. Tuveson, *Millennium and Utopia* (Berkeley, 1949), pp. ix–x.

16 K. Löwith, *Meaning in History* (Chicago, 1949), 114.

17 Hans Blumenberg, *The Legitimacy of the Modern Age* (Cambridge, Mass., 1985), 23–4.

18 Ibid., 30.

19 Ibid., 30.

20 Hans Blumenberg, 'On a Lineage of the Idea of Progress', *Social Research*, 41 (1974), 6.

21 Ibid., 7.

22 Ibid., 18.

23 Blumenberg, *Legitimacy*, 49.

24 Martin Jay, *Fin-de-Siècle Socialism* (New York, 1988), 159.

25 Gotthold Ephraim Lessing, *The Education of the Human Race*, ed. and tr. F. W. Robertson (London, 1896), p. xiv.

26 Ibid., 70–2.

27 Joseph Mede, *The Key of the Revelation* (London, 1643), translator's introduction.

28 Juan Maldonado, *Commentarii in prophetas IIII* (Tournon, 1611), 653.

29 Francis Bacon, *The Advancement of Learning* (Oxford, 1974), 78.

30 Ibid.; see also Charles Webster, *The Great Instauration* (London, 1975), ch. 1.

31 Blumenberg, 'Lineage', 18.

32 Blumenberg, *Legitimacy*, 107.

33 Francis Bacon, *Works*, 7 vols (London, 1857–9), vol. 2, p. 147.

34 Guillaume Postel, *Histoire et considération de l'origine, loy, et coustume des Tartares, Persiens, Arabes, Turcs . . .* (Poitiers, 1560), 53–4, as translated in William Bouwsma, *Concordia mundi* (Cambridge, 1957), 271.

35 William Twisse, *The Doubting Conscience Resolved* (London, 1652), 93–4. On Twisse see also Webster, *The Great Instauration*, ch. 1, and Richard Popkin, *The Third Force in Seventeenth Century Thought* (Leiden, 1992), ch. 6.

36 Blumenberg, *Legitimacy*, 78.

PART I

2

How Time Acquired a Consummation

Norman Cohn

Unlike the beginning of the world, the end of the present world does not seem to have been of great interest to anyone until some time after 1500 BC. Much as they differed on other matters, Egyptians, Sumerians, Babylonians, Indo-Iranians and the rest were all agreed that the world had been established and set in order by the gods, and was still watched over by the gods, and would always remain more or less as it now was.

Not that the ordered world was undisturbed. There were chaotic forces, restless and threatening: every ancient world-view showed an awareness of the instability of things. Nevertheless, though it was constantly threatened, the ordered world would never be either destroyed or transformed.

So far as is known, the first person to break out of this static view of the world and to tell of a coming consummation, when the present, imperfect, unstable world will be replaced by a new, perfect and unthreatened world, was the Iranian prophet Zarathustra, commonly known by the Greek version of his name, Zoroaster.[1]

When did this happen? There are two opinions, which cannot be reconciled. According to a Zoroastrian tradition the prophet lived 258 years before Alexander, which would place him in the middle of the sixth century BC; and this has been accepted by some eminent scholars. However, the tradition in question has been shown to derive from a late calculation based on a purely Greek fiction.[2] For more than a hundred years linguistic and archaeological evidence has been accumulating in favour of the alternative view – which is, that Zoroaster lived in a far earlier period, some time between 1400 and 1000 BC, when the Iranians were still primarily pastoralists rather than agriculturalists.[3]

Zoroaster's own hymns, the *Gathas*, abound in references to the institutions, customs, technology and ways of thought of traditional pastoral society – whereas not a single simile is drawn from agriculture. In one place the prophet even prays to the supreme god for the gift of a camel, a stallion and ten mares. For that matter the very name Zarathustra probably meant either 'he who can manage camels' or 'he who has active camels'.[4]

As for the location of Zoroaster's activity, scholars disagree. Around 2000 BC the proto-Iranian tribes were living on the vast open steppes of southern Russia, but in the course of the second millennium they migrated southwards. Some scholars hold that Zoroaster's homeland was not far from the original homeland of the Iranians, somewhere south of the Urals, in what is now Khazakstan; while others hold that it lay somewhere on the route of their migrations southwards – either in the extreme east of present-day Iran or in western Afghanistan.

By the sixth century BC the religion founded by Zoroaster had penetrated into western Iran, and so effectively that it became the religion of the royal dynasty of the Achaemenians, who ruled over the first Iranian empire. And during the eight hundred years of the second and third Iranian empires – the Parthian and the Sasanian, from the second century BC to the seventh century AD – Zoroastrianism continued to function as a state religion. However, with the Muslim conquest of Iran in the seventh century the great days of Zoroastrianism began to draw to a close. Today there are only some 130,000 Zoroastrians in the world – 90,000 of them in the Indian subcontinent, whither their ancestors fled, many centuries ago, to escape from Muslim oppression. These are the Parsis.

The impact of Zoroastrianism is a very different matter. Though not generally recognized, it has been immense. For some centuries before Christ the basic Zoroastrian doctrines were widely disseminated. They had much influence amongst Jews and, even more, amongst the early Christians – and so, in the long run, upon the world-view of what was to become European civilization. This is particularly true of Zoroastrian notions about the consummation of time.

II

Zoroastrianism possesses sacred scriptures; they are known collectively as the *Avesta* – which probably meant something like 'Authoritative

Utterance'.[5] The extant *Avesta* is only a quarter of the original, and even that quarter was probably given written form only in the fifth or sixth century AD. Up to that time its preservation depended almost wholly on oral transmission, generation after generation, in priestly schools. However, though the time-gap between Zoroaster's proclamation and the sixth century AD is something like two thousand years, the transmission of that proclamation seems to have achieved astonishing accuracy.

Truncated though it is, the *Avesta* is still voluminous. It includes seventeen hymns composed by Zoroaster himself, the *Gathas*. The remainder of the *Avesta* is linguistically of later date, and is also less well preserved; nevertheless, present-day scholarship inclines to the view that it too contains much material that embodies the original teachings of Zoroaster. Then, apart from the *Avesta*, there are the Middle Persian books. These works underwent their final redaction only in the ninth and tenth centuries AD. However, they include both long passages of translation of lost parts of the *Avesta* and a summary of the whole of the original *Avesta*. Despite some obstacles, these various works have enabled scholars to reconstruct, with a reasonable degree of assurance, not only the teachings of Zoroaster himself and of the theologians who interpreted and elaborated upon those teachings, but also the world-view of the Iranian society into which the prophet was born.

Central to the traditional Iranian world-view was the notion of all-embracing order, which in the *Avesta* is called *asha*.[6] *Asha* cannot be translated by any single word in any modern language, but we know what it means. It was used to indicate the normal and right way for things to happen in the world. The order of nature, which regulates the alternation of day and night and the cycle of the seasons, and the order of human life, by which each individual goes from birth to death, were both included in *asha*; and so was the ritual order, which prescribed just how sacrifices were to be made to the gods. The moral order, by which human beings were supposed to regulate their conduct and their relations with one another, was also part of *asha*: he who behaved in accord with that principle would be just, upright, honest – and he would prosper. Speech that was in accord with *asha* was truthful speech; conversely, where *asha* prevailed there was no place for lying – or for liars. But indeed the realm of *asha* was universal: the movements of the sun, the moon, the stars were its visible expression. It was also the force that set in motion whatever conserved and increased life: thanks to *asha* the day broke, rivers flowed, nourishing plants grew tall, cows gave their milk.

Zoroaster took over the notion of *asha* but he also reinterpreted it. In the traditional Iranian world-view several gods were responsible for watching over and assisting the operation of *asha* in the world.[7] In Zoroaster's world-view the operation of *asha* was the particular concern of the god Ahura Mazda, 'Lord Wisdom'. Ahura Mazda may or may not have been known to Iranians before Zoroaster, but it was Zoroaster who gave him a position more exalted than any deity in the ancient world had ever occupied. For Zoroaster proclaimed that in the beginning Ahura Mazda, the wholly wise, just and good, had been the one and only divine being. Himself uncreated, Ahura Mazda was the first cause of everything in the universe that is good, whether divine or human, animate or inanimate, abstract or concrete – in short, of *asha* and everything that is in accord with *asha*.

Ahura Mazda's unique dignity as maker and guardian of the ordered world is the theme of one of the finest *Gathas*:

> This I ask Thee, tell me truly, Lord. Who in the beginning, at creation, was the father of Asha? Who established the course of sun and stars? Through whom does the moon wax, then wane? This and yet more, O Mazda, I seek to know.
> This I ask Thee, tell me truly, Lord. Who has upheld the earth from below, and the heavens from falling? Who sustains the waters and plants? Who harnessed swift steeds to winds and clouds?
> This I ask Thee, tell me truly, Lord. What craftsman created light and darkness? What craftsman created both sleep and activity? Through whom exist dawn, noon and eve, which remind the worshipper of his duty? . . . Who made the son respectful in heed to the father?[8]

It followed that Ahura Mazda was supremely deserving of worship – and in the Zoroastrian creed the religion is in fact called 'the worship of Mazda'.

But if in the beginning Ahura Mazda was the only divine being, that does not mean that he was the only being. Iranians had always recognized the existence of a principle that was the very negation of *asha* – a principle of falsehood or distortion, a force of disorder, incessantly at work in the world. They called it *druj*, meaning 'falseness', 'the Lie'. Zoroaster developed the concept further: Ahura Mazda had a mighty antagonist in Angra Mainyu, who was the spirit of destruction, of active evil.

In the *Gathas* the prophet has left a summary of this, his central revelation: 'Truly there are two primal spirits, twins renowned to be in conflict. In thought and word, in act they are two: the better and the bad'.[9] The words with which, also in the *Gathas*, Ahura Mazda repudiates his great opponent drive the point home: 'Neither our thoughts nor teachings nor wills, neither our choices nor words nor acts, nor our inner selves nor our souls agree'.[10]

In Zoroaster's thought the twin spirits embodied the forces that maintained the ordered world and the forces that strove to undermine it. Originally, superhuman and supernatural though they were, they had to make a choice between the two principles. Ahura Mazda, in accordance with his profoundly moral nature, chose to support *asha*, and Angra Mainyu, impelled by his moral perversity, chose to support *druj*.

So a struggle began whose vicissitudes constitute the past, present and future of the world. The setting of that struggle was the ordered world – indeed, the world existed for that very purpose. In creating it Ahura Mazda aimed to canalize the hostility and destructive fury of Angra Mainyu: it was a trap into which that monstrous being would fall and where he would wear himself out.

III

Human beings are deeply involved in the struggle between Ahura Mazda and Angra Mainyu. Just as, in the beginning, the two spirits chose to be respectively good and evil, so each individual must choose between the constructive and destructive values represented by the two spirits.

It seems that for Zoroaster this ethical dualism had a quite specific, concrete meaning: it was rooted in his own experience when, as a young man, he was both in a defenceless position himself and kept constantly aware of what was happening to other defenceless people. Although he was a fully qualified priest of the traditional religion, he must have started life as a poor man – and one who suffered greatly under his poverty, and the powerlessness that went with poverty. In the *Gathas* he appeals to Ahura Mazda for material succour: 'I know why I am powerless, Mazda; I possess few cattle and few men. I lament to thee.' 'Who is found as protector for my cattle, who for myself . . . ?' 'This I ask Thee, tell me truly, Lord, how shall I gain that reward, namely ten mares with a stallion and a camel?'[11]

However, that is not the heart of the matter. Underlying the interpretation that Zoroaster gives to the age-old concepts of *asha* and *druj* is an acute sense of a relatively peaceful social order threatened by aggression from outside. The most plausible explanation, it seems to me, is that advanced by the eminent Iranist Professor Mary Boyce. She argues that Zoroaster must have known two kinds of tribes. There were tribes which migrated steadily with their cattle, seeking nothing but good pastures where they could settle and prosper. And there were tribes which were true war-bands, ruthless, delighting in violence, eager to despoil and kill peaceable herdsmen. The prophet identified with the former, abominated the latter.[12]

There are in fact good grounds for thinking that the *Gathas* were composed while a society which had existed almost unchangingly for centuries, and which had never possessed very destructive weaponry, was coming into conflict with, and was being replaced by, a society of a new kind – more warlike and better equipped for war. It has been convincingly argued that originally the society from whom the Iranians were descended had no class of professional warriors: all adult males except priests were herdsmen.[13] Of course the tribes sometimes fought one another over disputed grazing grounds, but their campaigns can hardly have been more than skirmishes. But south of the Caucasus things were very different: there, chariot warfare and the professional warriors who alone could practise such warfare had existed since early in the second millennium.

By Zoroaster's time these innovations had spread to the steppes – and that changed everything. Chariots enabled chieftains and their bands of retainers to raid tribal settlements over wide areas, steal whole herds of cattle, kill human beings on a scale previously inconceivable. Life on the steppes changed utterly as it passed into a typical 'heroic age', turbulent, restless, with military prowess as its highest value and the seizing of booty as its highest aim.

Thus far Professor Boyce. Whether or not one accepts this explanation in every particular, the *Gathas* certainly do seem to reflect the tensions and miseries of a time when this new way of life was establishing itself. In these hymns the conscientious herdsman is presented as the righteous man *par excellence*, while the wicked man *par excellence* is the man who acquires fame and fortune by stealing cattle: 'Those wicked ones who appear in grandeur as lords and ladies, they too have ruined life, stealing the property of the [rightful] inheritor . . . Mazda declared ill things for them who with [their] habit of pleasure have ruined the life of the cow.'[14] These people 'with ill purpose increase with their tongues fury and cruelty, they the non-pastors among pastors'.[15] They were 'followers of the Lie', human allies of Angra Mainyu. Zoroaster permitted no mercy to them: they must be defeated and killed.[16]

Zoroaster's is the earliest known example of a particular kind of prophet – the kind commonly called 'millenarian' – and the experiences that determined the content of his teaching seem also to have been typical. Prophets who promise a total transformation of existence, a total perfecting of the world, often draw their original inspiration from the spectacle not simply of suffering but of one particular kind of suffering: that engendered by the destruction of an ancient way of life, with its familiar certainties and safeguards.[17] Zoroaster would seem to have been just such a prophet.

IV

The particular tensions in society that found expression in Zoroaster's ethical dualism passed, but the ethical dualism survived. It remained Ahura Mazda's intention that human beings should be his protagonists, upholding *asha*, fighting *druj*. In practice, this meant that every Zoroastrian was expected to do everything in his or her power to foster the well being and prosperity of the world, but also his or her own wellbeing and prosperity. To do so was itself an affirmation of the highest values, a fulfilment of the supreme religious duty.

Such an ideal was most unusual at that time. In other societies too people helped to sustain the order of the world, but they did so chiefly by contributing to the offerings that priests made to the gods. A Zoroastrian was more directly and constantly involved – and that is still true today. A Zoroastrian's obligations permeate the whole of life. Every Zoroastrian takes part, through the ordinary tasks of everyday life, in sustaining and strengthening the ordered world – indeed,

everyone is engaged in preparing the way for that final consummation
when the world will be made perfect.

Originally, this was a radically new perception of the world, of time
and of human responsibility. For other societies, and for Iranians
themselves before Zoroaster, the order of the world, though constantly
disturbed, was nevertheless essentially static: as things had been, they
remained. For Zoroaster and his followers, on the contrary, nothing
was static. Angra Mainyu's assault on *asha*, Ahura Mazda's defence of
asha, went on and on, yet they would not go on for ever. The world
was a battlefield, the battle was still in progress, but it would have an
end.

Time itself was in motion, it was moving forward. In Zoroastrian
theological writings a distinction is made between unlimited time, or
eternity, on the one hand, and 'limited' or 'bounded' time on the
other. The struggle between Ahura Mazda and Angra Mainyu is
contained within 'limited time'; its conclusion will mark the end of
'limited time' and the beginning of an eternity of bliss. For in the end
Angra Mainyu will be destroyed, *druj* will cease to operate, *asha* will
prevail totally and everywhere, the ordered world will be rid for ever
of the forces of chaos. Thus Ahura Mazda's intention will be ac-
complished, the divine plan will reach fulfilment.

Zoroaster seems to have modified traditional notions in another
respect: at the end of 'limited time' there was to be a universal bodily
resurrection.[18] The men who composed the Avestan material knew
well enough that such a prospect would seem incredible to many, and
they supplied a splendidly poetic response. 'From where,' they make
Zoroaster say, 'shall the body be reassembled which the wind has
blown away, and the water carried off? And how shall the resurrection
take place?' Ahura Mazda replies: 'When I created the earth which
bears all physical life . . . ; and when I created corn, that it might be
scattered in the earth and grow again, giving back increase . . . ; and
when I created the cloud, which bears water for the world and rains it
down when it chooses; and when I created the wind . . . which blows
when it pleases – then the creation of each of them was more difficult
for me than the raising of the dead. For . . . consider, if I made that
which is not, why cannot I make again that which was?'[19] Just as much
as his original creation, the resurrection of the dead was to be a
miraculous work of Ahura Mazda's, carried out as part of his plan for
the perfecting of all things.

The resurrection of the dead will be followed by a great assembly, embracing all who have ever lived. There every individual will be confronted with his good and evil deeds, and the saved will be distinguished from the damned as clearly as a white sheep from a black. Then the metal in hills and mountains will melt, the earth will be covered by a great stream of molten metal, and everyone will have to pass through the stream. To the righteous it will be like walking in warm milk; only the wicked will know that they are indeed in molten metal.[20] And the wicked will be destroyed. Zoroaster says as much in one of his hymns: 'That requital which Thou wilt assign to the two parties, O Mazda, by Thy bright blazing fire and molten metal, is a sign to be given among all living beings, to destroy the wicked man, to save the just.'[21] In fact the righteous will be not only saved but transformed: their bodies will become not only immortal but eternally young. Those who have reached maturity will remain for ever as if they were forty years old, the bodies of the young will remain fixed at fifteen.

The Middle Persian work known as the *Bundahishn* (meaning 'Creation')[22] tells how in every way the order intended by the supreme god will prevail against everything that would negate it. *Asha* will triumph totally over *druj*, and Angra Mainyu will be destroyed. The very appearance of the world will change. The earth will be flattened by the fiery flood, so that its surface will be a single level plain: the snow-covered mountains of Iran – first thrown up by Angra Mainyu – will be no more. In this perfect environment the surviving human beings will live in the most perfect harmony with one another. Husbands and wives and children, including of course the resurrected dead, will be reunited and will live together as they do in this present world – except that there will be no more begetting of children. All mankind will form a single community of devout Zoroastrians, all united in adoration of Ahura Mazda, and all at one in thought, word and deed.

The great transformation is called by words meaning 'the making wonderful'. It is a promise which, however remote its fulfilment, has always meant a great deal to Zoroastrians. Each year the coming state of bliss is prefigured in the New Year festival: held at the spring equinox, this is experienced as a rebirth of nature and of society and of individuals, a making new of the world.

The 'making wonderful' will indeed change everything. What lies ahead, at the end of time, is a state from which every imperfection will

have been eliminated; a world where everyone will live for ever in a
peace that nothing could disturb; an eternity when history will have
ceased and nothing more can happen; a changeless realm, over which
the supreme god will reign with an authority which will be unchal-
lenged for ever more.

V

When Zoroaster first foretold 'the making wonderful' he certainly
expected it to come about in the near future. The *Gathas* convey a
great sense of urgency: the prophet clearly believed that he had been
sent by Ahura Mazda at that particular moment to urge human beings
to align themselves with the right side at once, in the short time
remaining before the transformation of the world.

But Zoroaster died, his figure began to fade into the past, and still
the world was not transformed. The first generations of Zoroastrians
must have been as bitterly disappointed as the early Christians were to
be, a thousand years later. Subsequent generations consoled themselves
in ways that also recall the development of Christian belief. They
elaborated the notion of a future saviour in whom Zoroaster would be,
as it were, reincarnated, and who would complete his work.

The *Gathas* themselves gave a useful hint; for the prophet, when cast
down by the thought that he might not live to see 'the making
wonderful', had found consolation in imagining 'one greater than
good' who would come after him.[23] On the basis of this hint the
prodigious figure of the Saoshyant – meaning literally 'future benefac-
tor' – was constructed.[24]

The Saoshyant's birth will be miraculous. The prophet's seed, it is
said, is preserved in a lake in south-eastern Iran, where it is watched
over by 99,999 souls of the righteous dead. As 'limited time' draws to
its close a virgin will bathe in the lake, become pregnant with the
prophet's seed, and bear his son. That son is the Saoshyant, and he will
play the central role in every phase of the eschatological drama. He will
wield the 'victorious weapon' with which legendary heroes in the
Iranian past slew the monsters and ogres of their day. Grouped around
him will be certain 'deathless chieftains' – mighty warriors who once
led the Iranian peoples in war, and who ever since have been waiting
in remote places for the summons to the final battle. Together with

these comrades in arms, all of them 'thinking well, acting well, of good conscience', the Saoshyant will advance against Angra Mainyu and his allies, demonic and human.

That is not all. For fifty-seven years before 'the making wonderful' the Saoshyant will be resurrecting the dead and giving them back their bodies; he will also assemble the dead and the living for the fiery ordeal. According to some versions he will even take over from Ahura Mazda the task of bestowing immortality on the righteous. Finally, by gazing on the world he will make it immortal and incorruptible – thereby completing 'the making wonderful'.

The prophecy about the Saoshyant is very ancient – it certainly antedates the Achaemenian era, and may well date back almost to Zoroaster's time. But its appeal has proved perennial: it has helped generation after generation of Zoroastrians, through all the misfortunes that befell them, to keep alive their faith in the eventual perfecting of the world. Indeed, belief in the coming of the Saoshyant has flourished on misfortune. There is evidence to suggest that it was clung to most tenaciously at the very times when the Zoroastrian community suffered its greatest disasters. It was a vital factor in sustaining Zoroastrians in their faith when they were being persecuted by their Muslim rulers; and latterly it has flourished more among the oppressed Zoroastrians in Iran than among their more fortunate brethren, the Parsis of India.

VI

In the sixth century BC Zoroastrianism became the official religion of the first Iranian empire. At least from Darius the Great (522–486) onwards every Achaemenian monarch saw himself as Lord Wisdom's representative on earth.[25]

However, not everything in the religion of the *Gathas* was appropriate to a state religion. An institution endowed not only with great spiritual authority but also with great temporal power, possessed of temples, shrines and vast estates, served by a numerous priesthood, could hardly be impatient for a total transformation of the world. If Zoroastrianism was to function effectively as the dominant religion of a triumphant, firmly established empire, Zoroastrian eschatology had to be modifed. 'The making wonderful' had to be postponed, officially and definitively, to a remote future.

The necessary revision was achieved, not later than the first half of the fourth century BC, by certain scholar-priests. Perhaps inspired by the speculations of Babylonian astronomers, they divided 'limited time' into a number of equal periods. In one of the versions that have come down to us the totality of 'limited time' comprises 9,000 years, divided into three periods of 3,000 years each; in another, it comprises 12,000 years, divided into four periods. But in the original revision it was probably fixed at 6,000 years; and even in the 9,000- and 12,000-year versions, the last 6,000 years include everything that happens on this earth.

According to the *Bundahishn*, which expounds the full 12,000-year scheme, Ormazd (as Ahura Mazda is now called) ensures his final victory 3,000 years before the end, by causing Zoroaster to receive his revelation. The following 3,000 years is divided into three periods of a thousand years, each terminating with the appearance of a new saviour: the Saoshyant is triplicated. Each *Saoshyant* is born of Zoroaster's seed, and each has a redemptive task. By the end of each millennium, Zoroastrian teaching will have fallen into neglect; it is for each *saoshyant* in turn to give it new life – until the last-born brings about 'the making wonderful'.

In this scheme of world history the present moment had its place: it could only be some time before the appearance of the first *saoshyant*. But that meant that 'the making wonderful', which Zoroaster had expected to take place in his lifetime or shortly after it, and which, after his time, Zoroastrians had still awaited with impatience, lost all immediacy. Between the time when Zoroastrianism first became a state religion and the final transformation of the world there was set a comfortable interval of more than 2,000 years. Whatever their intentions may have been, and however purely philosophical their interests, the Zoroastrian priests had done something that had social and political implications: they had modified the prophet's original message in such a way that Achaemenian monarchs, and after them Parthian and Sasanian monarchs, could find in it an ideology perfectly suited to their needs.

VII

A puzzle remains. What, one wonders, could have led a man living around 1400 BC, in a predominantly pastoral society somewhere in central Asia, to decide that the troubled world he knew would shortly be utterly changed, transformed into a perfect world? I have a hypothesis to offer.

At the beginning of this essay I mentioned that in ancient societies the world, though essentially unchanging, was nevertheless felt to be constantly threatened by chaotic forces. In many societies this feeling was given expression in myths of the kind known to scholars as 'combat myths'.[26] Combat myths tell how, when the ordered world is about to be overwhelmed by chaotic forces, symbolized by a chaos-monster, and the old gods can only look on helplessly, a newcomer, a hero-god, steps forward, defeats the monster and saves the world. The hero-god becomes the new ruler of the universe – but the monster is not destroyed, and the hero-god has to go on fighting and defeating it again and again. The most celebrated example of a combat myth is no doubt the Babylonian myth of Marduk versus Tiamat; but there are others more relevant to our theme.

The Iranians were related to the Vedic Indians – indeed, until about 2000 BC the two constituted a single people, living on the steppes of southern Russia. From the great collection of Sanskrit hymns known as the *Rig Veda* we know that even after some five centuries of separation, the two peoples still had much in common.[27] Now, by far the most important god in the *Rig Veda* is the warrior and storm god Indra – and Indra's greatest achievement is his defeat of the arch-demon Vrtra.[28] Vrtra was imagined as a gigantic snake, and he represented primordial chaos. His name meant 'restrainer', 'blockage' – and indeed he held captive the cosmic waters, which in turn contained the sun. By slaying Vrtra and liberating the waters Indra enabled the ordered world to come into existence. Only, that was not the end. There were other demons to be dealt with, and Indra slew them too. Moreover, whatever their names, these demons were all Vrtra, and Indra's combats all had the same meaning. Nor can those combats ever end: over and over again the waters must be released, if the ordered world is not to sink back into chaos.

Naturally enough, the *Avesta* knows of no god comparable with this prodigious Indra. However, it does contain abundant evidence that before Zoroaster, combat myths were as familiar to the Iranians as they were to the Vedic Indians. I suggest that in Zoroaster's teaching the role of hero-god was taken over by Ahura Mazda. For Ahura Mazda not only watches over the order of the world – he also fights the forces of chaos, now embodied in Angra Mainyu.

But at this point one has to recognize what a vast gulf separates Zoroaster's teachings from the ancient combat myth. The aim of the war that Ahura Mazda fights is to remove every form of disorder from the world, wholly and for ever. So in the end Angra Mainyu is annihilated once and for all, along with all his host of demons and all his human allies. In place of repeated but incomplete victories we are promised a final and total one.

If I am right, Zoroaster was inspired by the ancient and potent combat myth to create a different and even more potent combat myth – which then became the world's first eschatological faith.

NOTES

1 On Zoroaster, and on Zoroastrianism in the ancient world: H. Lommel, *Die Religion Zarathustras nach dem Awesta dargestellt* (Tübingen, 1930), repr. 1971; R. C. Zaehner, *The Dawn and Twilight of Zoroastrianism* (London, 1961), repr. 1975; J. Duchesne-Guillemin, *La Religion de l'Iran ancien* (Paris 1962) (1.III of the series *Mana*; contains an excellent bibliography); B. Schlerath, ed., *Zarathustra, Wege der Forschung* (Darmstadt, 1970) (an anthology of essays covering the previous half-century); G. Gnoli, *Zoroaster's Time and Homeland* (Naples, 1980); id., *De Zoroastre à Mani* (Paris, 1985); M. Boyce, *A History of Zoroastrianism*, vols 1 and 2 (Leiden, 1975, 1981) (in the series *Handbuch der Orientalistik*, ed. B. Spuler); id., *Zoroastrians: Their Religious Beliefs and Practices* (London, 1979); id., *Zoroastrianism: Its Antiquity and Constant Vigour* (Costa Mesa, Calif., 1993). Parts of G. Widengren, *Die Religionen Irans* (Stuttgart, 1965), are also relevant.

   For a bibliography of the best translations of Zoroastrian writings see Boyce, *Zoroastrians*, 229–31. The quotations in the present paper are taken from Boyce, *Textual Sources for the Study of Zoroastrianism* (Manchester, 1984).

2 The sixth-century dating was still accepted by W. B. Henning, *Zoroaster, Politician or Witch-Doctor?* (Oxford, 1951), 35ff, and Zaehner, *Dawn and Twilight*, 33. For its erroneous basis see P. Kingsley, 'The Greek Origin of the Sixth-Century Dating of Zoroaster', in *Bulletin of the School of Oriental and African Studies*, 53 (1990), 245–64.

3 Cf. Boyce, 'Persian Religion of the Achemenid Age', in *The Cambridge History of Judaism* (Cambridge, 1984), 275–6; id., *History*, vol. 2, pp. 1–3; Gnoli, *Zoroaster's Time*, 159ff; H. E. Eduljee, 'The Date of Zoroaster', in *Journal of the K. R. Kama Institute*, 48 (Bombay, 1980), 103–60.

4   Yasna 44.18. The Yasna is that part of the *Avesta* which contains the texts recited during the act of worship (*yasna*); it consists of 72 numbered sections.

5   On the constitution of the Zoroastrian canon: H. S. Nyberg, *Die Religionen des Alten Irans*, tr. from the Swedish by H. H. Schaeder (Leipzig, 1938), ch. 8, esp. pp. 415–19.

6   Avestan *asha* is derived from Indo-Iranian *rita*, which is preserved in e.g. the *Rig Veda*. On *rita*: H. Lüders, *Varuna* (ed. L. Alsdorf) (Göttingen, 1959), vol. 2, esp. pp. 568–84 (the fullest account, though marred by an excessively narrow equating of *rita* with 'truth' only); Duchesne-Guillemin, *La Religion de l'Iran ancien*, 191–6 (includes a critique of Lüders); J. Gonda, *Die Religionen Indiens* (Stuttgart, 1960), vol. 1, pp. 77–9; Boyce, *History*, vol. 1, p. 27.

7   The nature of most of the old Iranian gods can be gathered from the hymns of praise, known as *yashts*, in the *Avesta*. The only complete English translation of the *yashts* is that by J. Darmesteter, *The Zend-Avesta*, part 2 (Oxford, 1883; repr. Delhi, 1965) which forms vol. 23 in the series *Sacred Books of the East*. It is out of date in many respects. A liberal selection of *yashts*, with valuable notes, is contained in W. W. Malandra, *An Introduction to Ancient Iranian Religion: Readings from the Avesta and the Achaemenid Inscriptions* (Minneapolis, 1983). For a good German translation of the complete set, also with valuable notes, see H. Lommel, *Die Yasts des Awesta* (Göttingen and Leipzig, 1927).

8   Yasna 44.3–5, 7.

9   Yasna 30.3.

10   Yasna 45.2.

11   Yasna 46.2; 50.1; 44.18.

12   Cf. Boyce, *History*, vol. 1, p. 252. Some scholars see the conflict as one between different social strata rather than between different kinds of society: see Kai Barr, 'Avest. *dragu, drigu*', in *Studia Orientalia Ioanni Pedersen dicata* (Copenhagen, 1953), 21–40; Bruce Lincoln, *Priests, Warriors and Cattle: A Study in the Ecology of Religion* (Berkeley, 1981), esp. chs 5 and 6; Gnoli, *Zoroaster's Time*, 185.

13   Cf. P. Friedrich, *Proto-Indo-European Syntax* (Butte, Mont., 1975), 44–6; Boyce, 'The Bipartite Society of the Ancient Iranians', in M. A. Dandamayev et al., eds, *Societies and Languages in the Ancient Near East: Studies in Honour of I. M. Diakonoff* (London, 1982), 33–7. The view propounded by Stig Wikander, *Der arische Männerbund* (Lund, 1938), and developed by Georges Dumezil in many of his works, that proto-Indo-Iranian and even proto-Indo-European society already possessed a class of professional warriors, can no longer be seriously maintained. It overlooks

the chronology of the Neolithic and Early Bronze Ages in the relevant area.

14 Yasna 32.11–12.

15 Yasna 49.4.

16 Cf. Yasna 46.4.

17 Cf. N. Cohn, *The Pursuit of the Millennium*, 3rd (revised) edn. (London, 1993), *passim*.

18 For Zoroastrian teaching concerning the afterlife see Lommel, *Die Religion Zarathustras*, 185–204; Zaehner, *Dawn and Twilight*, 55–7, 304–7; Boyce, *History*, vol. 1, pp. 109–17, 198, 236–41. For a detailed survey of Zoroastrian writings on the theme see Jal Dastur Cursetji Pavry, *The Zoroastrian Doctrine of a Future Life from Death to the Individual Judgment* (New York, 1926). For Zoroastrian teaching concerning the final state of the world see, in addition to the relevant passages in the general works listed under note 1 above: N. Söderblom, *La Vie future d'après le mazdéisme* (Paris, 1901); G. Widengren, 'Leitende Ideen und Quellen der iranischen Apokalyptik', in D. Hellholm, ed., *Apocalypticism in the Mediterranean World and the Near East*, Proceedings of the International Colloquium on Apocalypticism, Uppsala, 1979 (Tübingen, 1983), 77–162. Chapter 34 of the *Bundahishn* (see note 22 below) is especially relevant, and the present account of the great consummation is based on it.

19 *Bundahishn*, ch. 34: 4–5.

20 Cf. Yasna 44.15 and 51.9; Söderblom, *La Vie future*, 224; Boyce, *History*, vol. 1, pp. 242–4 (with footnotes giving references to fuller accounts in the *Bundahishn* and other Middle Persian books).

21 Yasna 51.9.

22 Text and translation: B. T. Anklesaria, *Zand-Ākāsīh, Iranian or Greater Bundahishn* (Bombay, 1964). Selected passages in translation are given in Boyce, *Textual Sources*.

23 Cf. Yasna 43.3.

24 The *Avesta* descibes the Saoshyant and his role in Yashts 13 and 19.

25 Cf. G. Gnoli, 'Politique religieuse et conception de la royauté sous les Achéménides', in *Acta Iranica*, 2 (1974), 118–90, esp. 162–9; K. Koch, 'Weltordnung und Reichsidee im alten Iran', in P. Frei and K. Koch, *Reichsidee und Reichsorganisation im Perserreich* (Göttingen, 1984).

26 On the combat myth in Antiquity see J. Fontenrose, *Python: A Study in Delphic Myth and its Origins* (Berkeley, 1959); M. Wakeman, *The Battle of God against the Monster* (Leiden, 1973); N. Forsyth, *The Old Enemy: Satan and the Combat Myth* (Princeton, 1987).

27 On the *Rig Veda* see J. Gonda, *Vedic Literature* (Wiesbaden, 1975). There is no complete and reliable English translation of the *Rig Veda*, but for a

remarkable translation of a selection of Vedic hymns see W. O. O'Flaherty, *The Rig Veda: An Anthology* (Harmondsworth, 1981). A complete and reliable translation into German is K. F. Geldner's *Der Rig-Veda*, 4 vols (Cambridge, Mass., 1951–7).

28   Cf. W. Norman Brown, 'The Creation Myth of the Rig Veda', in *Journal of the American Oriental Society*, 62 (1942), 85–98; id., 'The Mythology of India', in S. N. Kramer, ed., *Mythologies of the Ancient World* (New York, 1961), 281–6. The most relevant Rigvedic text is RV 1.32.

3

'Upon Whom the Ends of the Ages have Come': Apocalyptic and the Interpretation of the New Testament

Christopher Rowland

The first beast which Daniel saw . . . was like a lion . . . : this is kingly power which takes the sword and makes way to rule over others thereby . . . giving the earth to some, denying the earth to others.

The second beast was like a bear: and this is the power of the selfish laws . . . the power of prisons . . . confiscation of goods . . . hanging and burning . . .

The third beast was like a leopard . . . this is the thieving art of buying and selling the earth with her fruits one to another.

The fourth beast is the imaginary clergy-power, which indeed is Judas: and this is more terrible and dreadful than the rest.

. . . They are the curse and plague upon the creation . . . these reign in power while property rules as king . . . the creation will never be in quiet peace till these four beasts with all their heads and horns . . . do run into the sea again. . . . this work Christ will bring to pass, at his more glorious appearance . . . this makes way for Christ, the Universal love, to take the kingdom and the dominion of the whole earth.[1]

Even in a remarkably inventive and turbulent period for English religion the writings of Gerrard Winstanley stand out as a testimony both to the radical religious ideas of the seventeenth century and to the way in which apocalyptic ideas can be the lens through which human nature and society are viewed. From April 1649 to March 1650 Winstanley's career and writing were intimately bound up with a Digger commune situated at St George's Hill, Cobham, Surrey. As the term 'Digger' implies, the group of which Winstanley was a member was concerned to give practical effect to its convictions by digging the land. He was prompted by a revelation that he and his companions should dig the common land, thereby claiming what they regarded as their rightful inheritance as children of God. Their action provoked hostility from local landowners and complaints to the Council of State, and they were finally driven off the land in the spring of 1650.

Like many others of his generation who entertained hopes of a radical change in society, fired by apocalyptic images of upheaval, Winstanley experienced disappointment and disillusionment. 'The experience of defeat'[2] was to be the lot of many who looked forward with earnest expectation to a new order. That experience led some to political conservatism. For them a pragmatic approach to political power seemed more appropriate than the egalitarian dreams of those who earnestly expected the millennium. For others, concern for inner transformation enabled the radical hope to be channelled into a quest for sanctity of heart when the struggle for transformation of the wider world seemed futile. The longing for the fulfilment of the hope for a new world was internalized and individualized. Bringing it about became more a matter of the individual overcoming the passions of the flesh than working to ensure the end of the old order in the wider society. The quest for personal perfection compensated for the rather forlorn hope of seeing any dramatic change in the structure of things without some cataclysmic intervention from beyond.

But for a short period the possibility of radical change was in the air and the Diggers were among many who sensed that the Kairos had arrived. Central to the communal experiment of the Diggers was the belief that the earth was a common treasury. The ownership of land as private property conflicted with this fundamental right. Winstanley was concerned to expose the way in which the preoccupation with private property reflected a fundamental characteristic of humanity after the Fall of Adam. Private property was the curse of Adam, and opposed to God's will. Those who possessed land gained it by oppression, murder or theft. In this the rule of the Serpent manifested itself through 'a professional ministry, the kingly power, the judiciary and the buying and selling of the earth'. It is these that are referred to in the seventh chapter of the book of Daniel.

So the beasts and portents of the apocalypses refer not to some transcendent era but to the troubled times in which Winstanley lived. The struggle between the Dragon and Christ is linked to the pro-

motion of a common life freed from economic and institutional oppression. 'When the earth becomes a common treasury as it was in the
beginning, and the King of Righteousness comes to rule in everyone's
heart, then he kills the first Adam; for covetousness thereby is killed.'
The new heaven and earth is to be seen here and now, for 'royal
power is the old heaven and earth that must pass away'. The New
Jerusalem is not 'to be seen only hereafter'. So, he asserts, 'I know that
the glory of the Lord shall be seen and known within creation, and the
blessing shall spread within all nations'. Christ's second coming is the
establishment of a state of community, spread abroad in the creation.
God is not far above the heavens but is to be found in the lives and
experiences of ordinary men and women. God's kingdom will come
when there takes place 'the rising up of Christ in sons and daughters,
which is his second coming'.

Winstanley's use of the imagery of the book of Daniel to understand
the oppression of state power, reminds us of the importance of this
symbolism in the formation of radical Christian positions at other
periods in Church history. It is something deeply rooted in the primary
texts of Christianity, for in the gospels Jesus is reported as identifying
his ultimate triumph with the eternal rule of the heavenly Son of Man
which will take place after the destruction of the Beast, presumably
representing state power. The book of Revelation itself takes up the
theme of the Beast of Daniel and sees it at work in the exercise of
power by Rome in his own day; the time of the seer is regarded as a
critical moment in the life of humankind.

> And I saw a beast rising out of the sea, with ten horns and seven
> heads . . . and to it the dragon gave his power and his throne and great
> authority . . . Men worshipped the dragon, for he had given his author-
> ity to the beast . . . it was allowed to make war on the saints and
> conquer them. And authority was given it over every tribe and people
> and nation. (Rev. 13.1–7)

The purpose of this essay is to reflect on such usage and to consider
the fundamental importance of the apocalyptic tradition, derived as it
was from ancient Judaism, for Christian theology. In the earliest period
of Christianity, resort to the language and genre of apocalyptic enabled
the New Testament writers to have access to the significance of events
and persons *sub specie aeternitatis*. It buttressed the belief that fired the
first Christians in their diverse social settings that *they* were privileged

to be 'the ones on whom the ends of the ages had come' (1 Corinthians 10.11). The nature of that eschatological background has been the subject of fierce debate. While few would dispute the pre-occupation with the ultimate purposes of God in the New Testament, there is a significant difference of opinion between those who argue that the first Christians, in contrast to their Jewish contemporaries, expected the winding up of history and ultimately the appearance of a spiritual kingdom, and those who consider that the expectation was on the historical plane. Gershom Scholem neatly summarizes the difference of view when he contrasts the spiritual messianism of Christianity with the political messianism of Judaism.

A totally different concept of redemption determines the attitude to messianism in Judaism and Christianity. What appears to the one as a proud indication of its understanding and positive achievement of its message is most unequivocally belittled and disputed by the other. Judaism, in all its forms and manifestations, has always maintained a concept of redemption as an event which takes place publicly, on the stage of history and within the community. It is an occurrence which takes place in the visible world and which cannot be conceived apart from such a visible appearance. In contrast, Christianity conceives of redemption as an event in the spiritual and unseen realm, in the private world of each individual, and which effects an inner transformation which need not correspond to anything outside. Even the *civitas dei* of Augustine, which within the confines of Christian dogmatics and in the interest of the Church has made the most far-reaching attempt both to retain and to reinterpret the Jewish categories of redemption, is a community of the mysteriously redeemed within an unredeemed world. Events which for the one stood unconditionally at the end of history as its most distant aim, are for the other the true centre of the historical process, even if that process was henceforth peculiarly decked out as *Heilsgeschichte*. The Church was convinced that by perceiving redemption in this way it had overcome an external conception that was bound to the material world . . . the reinterpretation of the prophetic promises of the Bible to refer to a realm of inwardness, which seemed as remote as possible from any contents of the (Biblical) prophecies, always seemed to religious thinkers of Judaism to be an illegitimate anticipation of something which could at best be seen as the interior side of an event taking place in the external world, but could never be cut off from the event itself. What appeared to Christians as a deeper apprehension of the external realm appeared to the Jews as the liquidation and as a flight which sought to escape verification of the messianic claim within its most empirical categories by means of a non-existent pure inwardness.

The history of the messianic idea in Judaism has run its course inside the framework of this idea's never-relinquished demand for fulfilment of the original vision.[3]

Scholem is concerned with the contrast between Christian and Jewish messianism, but I want to suggest that this contrast exists in the messianic and eschatological doctrines of Christianity. Even if Scholem is right to suggest that Christianity has come to be identified with a spiritual messianism, there are important strands in the history of Christianity which bear witness to a political messianism akin to that which Scholem regards as characteristic of Judaism. In what follows, I want to suggest that both forms of messianism are endemic to Christianity, and that the rehabilitation of the complexity of the eschatological tradition forms a significant part of the story that can be told of modern as well as ancient theology.

The application of apocalyptic imagery to contemporary institutions and events in Winstanley's writing is one of countless examples from the Christian tradition. Antichrist is no remote supernatural figure, but stalks the earth confronting those with the insight to perceive the danger. This is exactly what we would expect when the solitary New Testament appearance of Antichrist refers not to supernatural figures but to the heretical and immoral opponents of the writer of 1 John. In this work, the language of eschatology is appropriated for the understanding of the contemporary world: 'Children it is the last hour and so you know that antichrist is coming, so now many antichrists have come . . . they went out from us . . . that it might be plain that they all are not of us' (1 John 2.18–20). Such an application is daring and potentially far more dangerous than the relegation of it to *de facto* irrelevance in a remote eschatological future. The present has become suffused with a critical character. It is a moment of utter significance within history and cannot be regarded with detached equanimity. A commitment is necessary, and action must follow from commitment to the cause. It is a moment pregnant with opportunity for fulfilling the destiny of humankind. Here indeed is the moment when heaven finally comes on earth.

The career of Winstanley contrasts with the perspective of so much of mainstream Christian tradition which has been greatly indebted to Augustine's *City of God*. A major exception to the Augustinian view has been the work of the medieval interpreter of the Apocalypse, Joachim of Fiore. In it eschatological events became imminent historical possibilities. Joachim's followers produced an eschatology which was to have a profound influence cn European thought in the centuries to come and linked eschatology to political change.

It is not sufficiently recognized that there are significant strands within the New Testament which invest present persons and events with a decisive role in the fulfilment of the Last Things. In various texts of the New Testament there are signs that the present becomes a moment of opportunity for transforming the imperfect into the perfect; history and eschatology become inextricably intertwined, and the elect stand on the brink of the millennium itself (not a term, it should be noted, used by New Testament writers themselves). Of course, the events of Jesus' life became hallowed as the irruption of the divine into history. In many of the stories told about him he is presented as proclaiming the present as decisive in God's purposes and himself as the messianic agent for change, but not as some dreamer awaiting the apocalyptic miracle wrought by God alone. It has been wrongly assumed that Jesus' and the early Christians' *eschatological* expectation was for an act of God brought in by God alone without any human agency – humankind, according to this view, being merely passive spectators of a vast divine drama with the cosmos as its stage. The foundation documents of Christianity suggest a different story. For many of their writers, history is illuminated by apocalypse; vision opens ultimate possibilities, and responsibilities which others could only dream of. Thereby they are equipped with insight hidden to others and privileged to enjoy a role in history denied even to the greatest figures of the past. 1 Peter 1.11 speaks for the outlook of many other New Testament documents in its emphasis on the privilege of the writer's time: 'It was revealed to the prophets that they were serving you in the things that have been announced to you . . . things into which angels long to look on.' But as we shall see in due course privilege is matched by the need for action.

In the book of Revelation history is illuminated by revelation and mystical insight. Revelation seems at first sight to stand apart from the rest of the New Testament, for it is the only full-length apocalypse. The Apocalypse has a reputation for preoccupation with the cataclysmic, the penultimate as well as the ultimate, extravagant symbolism and the fantastic retreat from reality. Its link with the end of the world has obscured other preoccupations perhaps more evident in contemporary

Jewish apocalypses. While one should not ignore the preoccupation with endings, its contents should not be reduced to the eschatological. Its world of thought may be illumined by a consideration of the related apocalyptic texts of Second Temple Judaism.

The apocalypses are the most significant group of writings in intertestamental literature.[4] These works, which purport to offer revelations of divine secrets, are similar in form and content to the New Testament apocalypse. The origin of this literary genre is much disputed, but it is clear that in their concern with the mysteries of God and his purposes the apocalypses have a close affinity with the prophetic literature. There is only one apocalypse included in the canon of the Old Testament, the book of Daniel. That should not be taken as an indication that the compilers of the canon had little interest in the apocalyptic tradition, for it is clear that there was a lively apocalyptic oral tradition in Judaism. Of this, the written apocalypses are probably the earliest evidence. The tradition has a long history. The discovery of fragments of the Enoch apocalypse at Qumran have pushed the date of this particular text back well before the second century BC, back, in other words, into that obscure period when the prophetic voice began to die out in Israel. The literary evidence of the apocalyptic outlook suggests that it continued to play a vital part within Jewish religion throughout the period of the Second Temple, and even in rabbinic circles persisted as an esoteric tradition which manifested itself in written form in the bizarre hekaloth tracts of early medieval Jewish mysticism and later on in the Kabbalah.[5]

While the apocalypses are the largest repository of the future hope among the Jewish texts now extant, we have not exhausted their significance once we have recognized the eschatological concerns of this literature. Other matters obtrude: for example, the vision of heaven, angelology, theodicy and astronomy. The fact that several apocalypses have turned up in the gnostic library from Nag Hammadi indicates that the relationship between apocalyptic and gnosticism needs to be reassessed, particularly in the light of the common concern of both the apocalypses and the gnostic texts with knowledge.[6]

In the discussion of apocalyptic in the last thirty years or so, there has been significant difference of opinion about its origins. Two accounts of its background call for some consideration, as they demonstrate the way in which assumptions are made about its character and place in the biblical tradition. On the one hand there are those who consider that apocalyptic is the successor to the prophetic movement, and particularly to the future of hope of the prophets. The concern with human history and the vindication of Israel's hopes is said to represent the formulation of the prophetic hope in the changed circumstances of another age. Those who take this line all stress the close links with prophecy, but also point out the subtle change which has taken place in the form of that hope in apocalyptic. H. H. Rowley's often-quoted contrast between the future hope in the prophets and in apocalyptic literature, sums up this approach: 'The prophets foretold the future that should arise out of the present, while the apocalyptists foretold the future that should break into the present'.[7]

This point of view has been very influential, because it has seemed to many that in the apocalyptic literature written around the beginning of the Christian era, the future hope has been placed on another plane. Its stress from first to last is on the supernatural and otherworldly, just as in Revelation 21 the seer looks forward to a new heaven and new earth with the old creation having passed away. But this view can be challenged on the basis of a detailed examination of the texts themselves. For one thing it is questionable whether the apocalypses do offer evidence of the 'otherworldly' eschatology which is so often regarded as characteristic of them. There has been much confusion in the discussion of apocalyptic, in particular its relationship to eschatology. In discussions of both subjects it can appear that the two are closely related and can be used virtually interchangeably. There is a widespread view which asserts that there existed in Judaism two types of future hope: a national eschatology found principally in the rabbinic texts, and otherworldly eschatology found principally in the apocalypses. The evidence from the apocalypses themselves, however, indicates that such a dichotomy cannot easily be substantiated. Apart from a handful of passages which are always cited as examples of otherworldly eschatology, the doctrine of the future hope as it is found in the apocalypses seems to be remarkably consistent with the expectation found in other Jewish sources.

On the other hand (somewhat surprisingly in view of the contents of the books concerned) it has been suggested that it is the Wisdom tradition of the Old Testament, with its interest in understanding the cosmos and the ways of the world, which was the real antecedent of apocalyptic, rather than the prophetic movement.[8] There are some points of contact between the apocalypses and the Wisdom books of the Hebrew Bible, particularly the fact that the former are concerned with knowledge, not only of the age to come but also of things in heaven and of the mysteries of human existence. We should note that the activities of certain wise men in antiquity were not at all dissimilar to the concerns of the writers of the apocalypses. Traces of this kind of wisdom, concerned as it is with the interpretation of dreams, oracles, astrology, and the ability to divine mysteries concerning future events, is to be found in the Old Testament, for example in the Joseph stories in Genesis. Most obviously it is present in the stories about Daniel, the Jewish seer who interprets the dreams of Nebuchadnezzar and is regarded as a superior sage to all those in the King's court. Dreams, visions and the like are all typical features of the apocalypses, and it is now recognized that this aspect of the Wisdom tradition may indeed provide an important contribution to our understanding of apocalyptic origins: 4 Ezra is preoccupied with theodicy and suffering and has several affinities with the book of Job, and the Enochic literature includes astrology and rudimentary geography.

We are best able to understand the disparate elements of the apocalypses if we see the underlying theme to be one which derives from the initial statement of the book of Revelation, 'The Revelation of Jesus Christ' (Rev. 1.1), rather than from the eschatological message which runs through much of the rest of the book. Revelation is not merely an eschatological tract satisfying the curiosity of those who wanted to know what would happen in the future. Though it contains much teaching about 'what must happen after this', its purpose is to reveal something hidden which will enable the readers to view their present situation from a completely different perspective. When seen in this light, the significance of many of the visions in the Apocalypse becomes clear: the Letters to the Churches offer an assessment of their churches' worth from a heavenly perspective; the vision of the divine throne room in Revelation 4 enables the churches to recognize the dominion of God; in Revelation 5, the death and exaltation of Christ is shown to mark the inauguration of the new age; and in chapters 13 and 17 the true identity of the Roman emperors and the City of Rome is divulged. Revelation is a text which seeks to summon to repentance and to give reassurance by showing – by means of direct revelation from God – that there is a heavenly dimension to existence, which could be, and was being, ignored by the churches of Asia Minor.

Revelation's purpose is to reveal that which is hidden in order to enable readers to understand their situation from the divine perspective. Like the apocalypses of Judaism it seeks to offer an understanding which bypasses human reason by being grounded in the direct disclosure through vision or audition. The apocalypse offers a basis for hope in a world where God's way seemed difficult to discern. It does this by unmasking the real significance of past, present and future. In addition, the book of Revelation is described as prophecy. This probably is in line with the conviction that appears to have been widespread in early Christianity that the spirit of God had returned, a sign that the last day had arrived (a point stressed by the author of the Acts of the Apostles when, in Acts 2.17, he describes the events of the Day of Pentecost as a sign of the Last Days).

Early Christianity emerged in a world where contact with the divine by dreams, visions, divination and other related forms of extraordinary insight was common.[9] Its emphasis on access to divine power, which it was believed would be typical of the Last Days, was an important element of its appeal. Paul, for example, made much of the dramatic, charismatic and experiential basis of his arguments. Access to privileged knowledge of the divine purposes was in certain cases linked to decisive action. So Paul took upon himself the role of divine agent to bring about the inclusion of the nations in the people of God in the Last Days.[10] Paul's sense of destiny is evident above all in his vocation as apostle to the Gentiles. In describing that vocation he speaks of it in terms derived from the divine vocations of the prophets of old (Gal. 1.15 alluding to Jer. 1.5 and Isa. 49.1). The mission to the Gentiles was intimately linked with the framework of an eschatological history in which Paul believed himself to be a crucial actor. As far as he was concerned, all of this came about through an apocalypse of Christ (Gal. 1.12). Arguably, something similar is true of the project which occupied the last years of his life: a collection of money for the relief of poverty in Jerusalem to be delivered there by him. It is a plausible hypothesis that this may have been understood as the fulfilment of the prophetic predictions about the pagans bringing their gifts to Zion in the Last Days. In the organization and execution of this unusual enterprise, Paul played a crucial role.

It is the conviction that he is the divine agent to whom God had revealed the Messiah which is at the heart of Paul's approach to the Scriptures. They are now read in the light of the conviction that the age of the Spirit has come. Christians in Corinth, for example, are told that passages in the Bible which seemed to be about Israel of old are in fact addressed directly to them: 'Now these things happened to them as a warning, but they were written down for our instruction, upon whom the end of the ages has come' (1 Cor. 10.11). So the present has become the moment to which all the Scriptures have been pointing, though their meaning can only be fully understood with that divinely inspired intuition which flows from acceptance of the Messiah. The present has become a time of fulfilment: 'Behold, now is the acceptable time; behold, now is the day of salvation' (2 Cor. 6.2). That being the case, new rules applied which would not have been appropriate for the old aeon. In Galatians, Paul appeals to the *experience* of his readers (Gal. 3.4) as the basis for a pattern of life which would turn its back on the age of humanity's adolescence before the Messiah came. In speaking of life within the messianic community, Paul uses language which indicates that those in that fellowship are not merely believers in the Messiah but are in some sense clothed with the Messiah's person (Gal. 3.27): they put on Christ like a garment. Paul himself when speaking of his own ministry speaks of the Messiah dwelling in him. There is thus a form of mystical solidarity between the apostle and those who respond to his message and the messiah himself, so that the divine is incarnated in the lives of his followers. Such ideas have become so much part of Christian doctrine that their startling quality can easily be missed. It would be no surprise if, when they heard all this, some of Paul's converts thought that they were already living in the glory of the messianic age, uncluttered by the shackles of human misery and thoroughly overwhelmed with the divine nature. Part of Paul's task in the first letter to the Corinthians may have been to disabuse them of such fantasies.

Even so, the divine presence of the eschaton is vividly present in the lives of the Christian communities. While Paul encouraged his readers to look forward to the revelation of the glory of Christ at his Parousia, this awesome event is regarded by Paul as being fulfilled in some sense in the presence of himself, the agent of the messiah, visiting and admonishing those embryonic communities. Paul is the embodiment of Christ whose person is to be imitated (1 Cor. 4.16). His coming, like that of his Lord, will be with power (4.19). Yet even in his absence, there will be no diminution in the extraordinary force of the apostolic persona as a result of the mysterious presence of Christ in him. When he arrives at a community he promises that his coming will bring divine blessing (Rom. 15.29). Like the Risen Christ of the

Apocalypse who stands in the midst of his churches (in Rev. 1.13ff) the apostle of Christ comes as a threat and a promise: a threat to those who have lost their first love or exclude the Messiah and his apostle; a promise of blessing at his coming for those who conquer.

The sense of privilege and destiny with which Paul's career is surrounded was shared by others in Paul's circle. It is most clearly expressed in the letter to the Ephesians, where not only the Apostle's but also the church's role as the bearer of the divine mysteries, is stressed (3.5ff). As Ephesians indicates, it was possible for a later generation to keep alive that understanding of the soteriological role of apostle and community. But that role is not confined to the apostolic circle alone. In Ephesians, there is portrayed the superhuman dimension of ecclesial existence. The role of the Church is portrayed not as some ordinary human group. Rather it is believed to have a supernatural mission to proclaim the gospel to the powers, in heaven and on earth. Life is shot through with apocalyptic insight and struggle. Ordinary events take on an extraordinary meaning, so that the struggle with the demonic is not just an eschatological affair but is met in routine human events. So the author speaks of wrestling with principalities and powers (6.12). The Holy War which in some contemporary Jewish texts was part of the Last Days, is for the writer of Ephesians an everpresent involvement. Those whose spiritual insight was so attuned might discern the conflict between the angels of light and darkness in the midst of humankind, thereby becoming witting or unwitting participants in the struggle.

But what happens when a decisive eschatological actor like Paul departs from the scene? This question has often exercised the minds of commentators on Christian origins. After all, once that sense of being part of a propitious moment disappears, the understanding of present activity as an integral part of the drama of the Last Days becomes more difficult to sustain. Imperceptibly the eschatological hope becomes merely an article of faith. Present activity ceases to be viewed as an indispensable intervention in history to usher in the Last Things. The departure of an important eschatological actor is the issue in the appendix to the Gospel of John, where a problem seems to have been posed by the death of the Beloved Disciple (21.23), indicating that there was an expectation current among the members of the community that this disciple would not die before the return of Jesus It would appear from these verses he has now died, so a question has been raised about the validity of the belief in the future coming of Jesus: 'The saying spread abroad among the brethren that this disciple was not to die; yet Jesus did not say to him that he was not to die, but, "If it is my will that he remain until I come, what is that to you?"' The sense of being part of a propitious moment, has been replaced by apparent confusion in the face of the removal of a figure who was expected to share all the climactic moments of the drama of history. So, the outlook of the community and its view of its future seem set to be deprived of their eschatological aura. The author of this chapter sets out to disabuse those who entertained hopes of the imminent return of Christ before the death of the Beloved Disciple. History has to go on without the enchantment of the eschatological glow of the apostolic era leading to the End. Many commentators on the New Testament have spoken of a crisis in early Christianity over the death of the key figures who, it was believed, would sit on thrones judging the twelve tribes of Israel (Matt. 19.28). There are enough hints in the New Testament to suggest that the apostolic era (for want of a better description) *was* imbued with an eschatological significance which was lost to subsequent generations, and as a result succeeding generations were to look back on that period as something of a golden age later to be tarnished by disputes and compromises.[11]

What I have outlined so far is an account of early Christianity's indebtedness to apocalyptic and eschatology which is part of the received wisdom of two centuries of historical scholarship. If that has been the major theme thus far, a 'subtext' of my narrative has been the way a concern for the future has dominated much of theology's scholarly endeavour on the New Testament. The recognition of the importance of apocalyptic for the understanding of Christianity, particularly the New Testament, has meant that Christian theologians have had to wrestle with the visionary and the eschatological as central features of their interpretative agenda. There has arisen a fascination with what seems so alien and repulsive to the modern mind. At one and the same time the strange world of the apocalypses, far removed from the demythologized world of the Enlightenment, has contributed a golden thread which runs through scholarship on early Christianity and, in part, ancient Judaism also.

There were several reasons for the rediscovery of the significance of eschatological beliefs in the second half of the nineteenth century. An apocalypse like 4 Ezra was part of the Vulgate. The exploration of Abyssinia led to the discovery of Jewish apocalyptic works like 1

Enoch, which for centuries had been part of the Old Testament canon of the Ethiopic church. Awareness of these Jewish texts gradually infiltrated the world of scholarship because their contents resonated dramatically with the New Testament. The Apocalypse of Enoch,[12] for example, now extant in full only in Ethiopic (though fragments have been found among the Dead Sea Scrolls), contains ideas similar to those of Daniel, Revelation, and the gospels, and confirms that the world of Jesus and the first Christians was very much that of the Jewish apocalypses.

I have already quoted that great scholar of the kabbalistic and messianic tradition of Judaism, Gershom Scholem, in particular his contrast of the political messianism of Judaism and the spiritual messianism of Christianity. This is a view which commands widespread assent in modern scholarship on early Christianity. A distinction between history and eschatology is frequently made, with some making a clear hiatus between the mundane realities and the transcendent glory of the Eschaton. Typical of this, and important for its influence on New Testament interpretation, is the view of Johannes Weiss in a book written 100 years ago.[13] Weiss summarized Jesus' message as an imminent expectation of the coming of a transcendent divine sovereignty which would sweep away the mundane politics of ordinary history by its cataclysmic splendour. When Weiss spoke of Jesus' *eschatological* expectation, he was in no doubt that the kingdom of God which Jesus expected was not only otherworldly, but would be brought in by God alone without any human agency. So for him the eschatological character of the gospel necessarily means that the early Christians denied both a fulfilment of their hopes in history, and the need for human agency in their fulfilment.

Such ideas made perhaps their most dramatic impact on the study of the New Testament in the work of Albert Schweitzer. Schweitzer reviewed the various attempts to pierce through the pages of the New Testament to the historical Jesus over the previous hundred years.[14] He himself proposed that Jesus' mission could only be understood if one took seriously the eschatological convictions found in Jewish apocalypses. In his view, Jesus expected an imminent irruption of the divine into human history to end history. Faced with the non-appearance of the eschatological cataclysm which he expected within weeks of sending out emissaries to summon and warn of the imminent catastrophe, Jesus eventually set out for Jerusalem to take upon himself the tribulations which conventional wisdom about messianism said must precede the coming of God's Kingdom. In the hope that his suffering would soak up the tribulations of the Last Days, Jesus moves to his death, only to be shattered by the wheel of history as it turns and crushes him. In the face of imminent catastrophe political reform was futile. What was necessary was devotion to preparation for the eschaton which was about to overtake the world. In Schweitzer's view, the early church dealt with this disappointed hope in Paul's Christ mysticism, the identification of the messianic age in the lives of believers and Church. Much of what has been written since Schweitzer's work has been an attempt to come to terms with the impact of the eschatological ideas brought to the fore in such a dramatic way by such exegetical pioneers. Yet, for Schweitzer, despite its problematic character, eschatology was the means whereby Jesus' message could continue to speak to every generation precisely because its strangeness meant that it could never be transformed to the compromises of history:

> Men feared that to admit the claims of eschatology would abolish the significance of his words for our time; and hence there was a feverish eagerness to discover in them any elements that might be considered not eschatologically conditioned. . . .
> But in reality that which is eternal in the words of Jesus is due to the very fact that they are based on an eschatological world-view, and confirm the expression of a mind for which the contemporary world with its historical and social circumstances no longer had any existence. They are appropriate, therefore, to any world, for in every world they raise the man who dares to meet their challenge, and does not turn and twist them into meaninglessness, above his world and his time, making him inwardly free, so that he is fitted to be, in his own world and in his own time, a simple channel of the power of Jesus.[15]

The influence of eschatology was not only felt within the narrow confines of biblical scholarship, for the eschatological emphasis found in the work of Weiss and Schweitzer was to spill over in dramatic form into the theology of the immediate post- (First World) War scene in the commentary of Karl Barth on the Epistle to the Romans.[16] This extraordinary work was written as a direct counter blast to the integration of mainstream German theology into German culture, exemplified by the theological establishment's support of the First World War. Eschatology offered a stark alternative to the world of destruction and devastation of 1919, and to the compromises which had contributed to it. It was a situation that provoked acute pessimism about humanity's resources to build a better world. Barth asserted that knowledge of God could come only through God's own revelation, which humanity had either to accept or reject. Like the apocalypses of old, which seemed to offer some explanation of human existence and God's purposes through a revelation, Barth stressed the subordination of the human intellect to the revelation of God. He repudiated human attempts to comprehend God. Instead he stressed the centrality of revelation as the only basis for understanding anything about God.

Contemporary with Barth and equally committed to the eschatological inheritance of the Jewish tradition, but with a very different assessment of it, is Ernst Bloch. He rehabilitated the perspectives of Joachim of Fiore and Gerrard Winstanley and recognized the significance of utopian elements in a variety of cultures. He was himself committed to the rehabilitation of that millenarian, apocalyptic inheritance on the fringes of orthodox Christianity. His mammoth book, *The Principle of Hope*, explores the ways in which that longing for a future age of perfection has coloured the whole range of culture in both East and West.[17] It is as the philosopher of Utopia that Bloch will be remembered. In speaking of the New Jerusalem Bloch links God and humankind closely in a new age firmly embedded in human history. Now the tabernacling of God is with humanity; heaven is on earth; God's throne is not hidden behind the vault of heaven. The heavens are rent and the throne of God is in the midst of those who are privileged to see God and share the divine character. Bloch considers that utopia is not something far off in the future, but is at the heart of human experience; it is already at hand in an anticipatory and fragmentary way.

Despite its kaleidoscopic quality, the work of Ernst Bloch often provides suggestive insights into the character of Christian doctrine and its mutation into an ideology. For example, he contrasts two christological models, one of which argues for the vindication of the down-trodden, while the other served to support imperial oppression and hierarchicism.[18] The first is the central apocalyptic symbol of the gospels, the Son of Man, who comes on the clouds of heaven to establish justice for the poor and outcast. The second is the Lord Christ who is enthroned in heaven in a glorious state similar to the imperial oppressors of the poor. He contrasts the expectation of the Son of Man as liberator and vindicator, who would come to transform the lot of the lowly, with the figure of the Kyrios, buttress of authorities. He shows how the former expectation has moved to the margins of the Christian tradition, ostracized by the exponents of the dominant ideology who forged an alliance between Church and state. Gradually, he argues, the Son of Man belief has been displaced by the divine Kyrios, a title which, as he puts it, 'admirably suited the purposes of those in the imperial court who would reduce the Christian community to a sort of military service of their cultic hero'. This is a process which is evident from the pages of the New Testament itself, where the title 'Son of Man' rapidly fell into disuse.

Bloch's own work, echoed in a more attenuated form in the later writing of Walter Benjamin[19] and even Theodor Adorno, all of whom were close friends of Gershom Scholem,[20] reminds us of neglected aspects of the eschatological tradition and its political potential. In the light of Bloch's work it is not surprising that Christians and some Marxists influenced by this utopian tradition have been united in a common quest for change and a new social order based on peace and justice in this world. Modern political theology owes a great debt to Bloch's fascination with Christian millenarianism and his insight into its potential. The Tübingen professor Juergen Moltmann is particularly indebted to him. Moltmann's *Theology of Hope* has itself contributed to the development of a political theology in Europe in the post-war period. It has echoes in turn, in the influential political theology of Latin America, liberation theology, where the language of utopianism has sometimes been used as a way of speaking of the relationship between the future Kingdom and present movements for social change in Church and State, particularly among the down-trodden at the base of Latin American society. In their refusal to divide history and eschatology, the present from the future, liberation theologians have inherited that alternative political eschatology championed by Bloch.

My concern has been to offer a reminder of the importance of the visions of hope for changing the world manifest in some movements for radical change in Christian history. I have suggested that these should be viewed not as some kind of aberration, but as an authentic outworking of central themes in the biblical tradition. It is true that there is no compelling evidence to link early Christians with the revolutions in Judaea in 66 or 132 AD. Indeed, in the New Testament utopian fantasy is reduced to a minimum. Nevertheless, at the heart of the record of its self-understanding in the New Testament, Christianity chose in Jesus and Paul to recall instances of individuals with an understanding of the ultimate significance of their historical actions. Christian theology has been in part an attempt to articulate that basic datum in theological intricacy and practical exemplification. It has asserted the fact and the hope of heaven on earth, and yet has had to deal with the problem of (as Scholem puts it) the verification of its messianic claim. To assert that there is a fundamental ambiguity at the heart of Christianity is to pinpoint the problem which arises from Christianity's indebtedness to apocalyptic. In the New Testament we have documents which are saturated with hope and the conviction that an insight of ultimate significance has been vouchsafed which relativizes all other claims. Yet life on the brink of the millennium is psychologically and politically impossible to sustain. The New Testament, rooted as it is in apocalypse and eschatology, also breathes the spirit of accommodation, domestication and stability. The fiery enthusiasm of Paul sits uneasily with the staid and sober ethic which is so evident in his epistles. Herein lies one of the enigmas of Christianity.

Christianity found ways of enabling those who aspired to perfection to go on living in the midst of imperfection. In the New Testament we find the conviction that the veil into heaven has been breached and the institutions of this world and the next defeated. And yet, alongside this there is evidence that those powers are ordered by God and all still seems to be left as before. From the earliest stage of its genesis early Christians had to wrestle with this conundrum, and they did so by using their apocalyptic inheritance as the basis for explaining how the beyond could manifest itself amidst the obscurities of the present. Matthew 25.31ff offers an interpretation of the eschaton which abruptly interrupts the preoccupation with the eschatological future. The eschatological judge decides between the righteous and unrighteous, not on the basis of theological rectitude, but of service to the needy. Ordinary acts of charity are given the aura of eschatological significance.

The fragmentary story of Gerrard Winstanley with which we started is symptomatic of the explosive impermanence of a certain type of apocalyptic. He bursts briefly across the sky like some comet but then disappears without trace, remembered only by pamphlets reflecting his eccentric activity and remarkable theology. Whether he wrote after the dissolution of the Digger commune remains unknown. The apocalyptic zeal which brooked no obstacle was dissipated. While his ideas may have contributed to the radical ferment of later generations, the effectiveness of his work and theology, like that of other radicals, was lost or suppressed. They were not a complete departure from the fundamentals of Christian eschatological doctrine, for in many respects they were all too close for the comfort of doctrinal exponents who sought an altogether more stable environment.

To read apocalypses is to be overwhelmed – and perhaps alienated – by what seems unsavoury and at times profoundly unhealthy. And yet apocalyptic has expressed a critical response to the injustices of the world, frequently on behalf of the powerless, and opened eyes closed to realities which have become accepted as the norm. Its role in Christianity has proved remarkably pervasive. Winstanley is a witness to a significant strand of Christian tradition in which the intensity of the visionary hovers on the brink of fanaticism. Deep within the beliefs of those like Winstanley lies a millennial dream of the rediscovery of an evangelical piety which will transform humanity. Yet the point of it all is not fantasy but a form of life based on service and simplicity. The millennial dream is a fragment of religion which has never entirely perished in the welter of the fantastic and barbarous, for despite its awesome manifestations, it has continued to kindle a flame of humanity and hope.

NOTES

1 G. Winstanley, 'Fire in the Bush', in *Winstanley: The Law of Freedom and Other Writings* (Cambridge, 1973). Various themes in this essay are explored in C. Rowland, *Radical Christianity* (Oxford, 1988).

2 Christopher Hill's book, *The Experience of Defeat* (London, 1985) catalogues the effort to come to terms with disappointment in writings by late seventeenth-century authors as diverse as Milton and Bunyan. Hill has returned to the theme of radical biblical interpretation in *The English Bible* (London, 1992).

3 G. Scholem, *The Messianic Idea in Israel* (London, 1971), 1–2. For a comparison between Jewish and Christian messianism see W. D. Davies' essay, 'From Schweitzer to Scholem: Reflections on Sabbatai Sevi', in *Jewish and Pauline Studies* (London, 1984), which picks up on themes in Scholem's *Sabbatai Sevi* (London, 1973).

4 A survey of Jewish and Christian apocalypticism may be found in C. Rowland, *The Open Heaven* (London, 1982).

5 See G. Scholem, *Major Trends in Jewish Mysticism* (London, 1955), and I. Gruenwald, *Apocalyptic and Merkavah Mysticism* (Leiden, 1978).

6 F. Fallon, *The Enthronement of Sabaoth* (Leiden, 1978).

7 *The Relevance of Apocalyptic* (London, 1947). A much earlier date for the origin of apocalyptic in the prophetic tradition has been offered by P. Hanson, *The Dawn of Apocalyptic* (Philadelphia, 1974). The Enoch material from Qumran also indicates that the origins of apocalyptic are to be dated much earlier than the second century BC: see J. T. Milik, *The Books of Enoch* (Oxford, 1976) and M. Barker, *The Older Testament* (London, 1987).

8 An influential exponent of this view has been G. von Rad, *Old Testament Theology* (Edinburgh, 1962).

9 E. R. Dodds, *Pagan and Christian in an Age of Anxiety* (Cambridge, 1965) and R. Lane Fox, *Pagans and Christians* (Harmondsworth, 1986).

10 On the eschatological significance of Paul's vocation see J. Munck, *Paul and the Salvation of Mankind* (London, 1959).

11 See further C. Rowland, *Christian Origins* (London, 1985), 285ff.

12 See J. T. Milik, *The Books of Enoch* (Oxford, 1976).

13 J. Weiss, *Jesus' Proclamation of the Kingdom of God*, trs. R. H. Hiers and D. L. Holland (London, 1971). For a more extended historical survey see *Die Idee des Reiches Gottes in der Theologie* (Giessen, 1901). On Weiss, see F. Lannert, *Die Wiederentdeckung der neutestamentlichen Eschatologie durch Johannes Weiss* (Tübingen, 1989).

14 *The Quest of the Historical Jesus*, tr. W. Montgomery (London, 1931).

15 Ibid., 400.

16 K. Barth, *The Epistle to the Romans*, tr. E. Hoskyns (London, 1933).

17 Three vols, trs. N. Plaice, S. Plaice and P. Knight (Oxford, 1986). For an introduction to Bloch's thought see W. Hudson, *The Marxist Philosophy of Ernst Bloch* (London, 1982).

18 In *Atheism in Christianity* (London, 1972).

19 Particularly evident in 'Theses on the Philosophy of History', in *Illuminations* (London, 1970).

20 D. Biale, *Gershom Scholem: Kabbalah and Counter-History* (Cambridge, Mass., 1982).

4

The End of the World and the Beginning of Christendom

Bernard McGinn

An inscription from a late seventh-century crypt near Poitiers puts my theme in a nutshell: "Alpha and Omega. The Beginning and the End. For all things become every day worse and worse, for the end is drawing near."[1] The conviction that increasing misery of life was a sign that the end was near and accompanying fear of the impending return of Christ as universal judge of living and dead was widespread in the centuries between 400 and the beginning of the new millennium after the passage of the year 1000. Over sixty years ago, in a book that has been seen as one of the earliest manifestos of the contemporary movement toward European unity, Christopher Dawson assessed the significance of these six centuries in the history of European civilization as "the most creative age of all, since it created not this or that manifestation of culture, but the very culture itself – the root and ground of all the subsequent cultural achievements."[2] My purpose here is not to argue for or against Dawson's evaluation, but to pursue a paradox that he and others have not examined – how the formation of a distinctive Western European culture was the product of leaders whose hopes were not centered on building a new society but on the expectation of the end of all human effort in the Last Judgment. I shall argue that the "First Europe," as it has been called,[3] was created not in spite of these apocalyptic beliefs, but rather very much because of them; that is to say, an apocalyptic mentality, though one of a distinctive nature, was foundational to the ages which saw the emergence of Christendom.

Between the first appearances of the term *christianitas* around the year 400 AD, when it was employed largely in the sense of the correct practice of the Christian religion, and its widespread use in Latin and in the nascent European vernaculars of the ninth century and after to identify the territory in which the Christian religion was rightly observed (the sense of the Old English *cristendome*), decisive changes restructured the entire ancient Roman *oikumene*.[4] The fabric of Roman government was destroyed; the urban character of ancient society severely crippled, even eradicated, in many areas. New peoples, primarily Germanic and Celtic in the West, rose to importance. And, above all, a new form of sacral society, medieval Christendom, was created. As one of the greatest historians of late antiquity and the early Middle Ages, Henri Marrou, put it: "The notion of Christendom established a synthesis between the two processes of christianization and civilization."[5]

Medieval Christendom, of course, was never what people today like to call a historical "reality" – medieval society was politically fragmented, violent and fractious even by twentieth-century standards, and perhaps not even "really" Christian as some modern historians like to argue. But the ideal, or the myth, of Christendom as a unified world order exercised a powerful role in medieval culture. The historian who disregards it merely because it was never fully achieved displays a rather limited conception of human motivation. As Ernst Kantorowicz recognized in a brief essay that appeared fifty years ago, this order was an a priori of medieval political thought, and one that always must be seen in the light of Christian belief about the end. In his words, "the medieval Myth of World Unity has a predominantly messianic or eschatological character. Against this background the myth stands out and becomes almost reality."[6]

The Christians of the centuries that saw the creation of Christendom were heirs to the apocalyptic beliefs of their predecessors, though they have often been seen as either neglecting them by abandoning expectations of an immediate return of Jesus, or else as adding little to the inherited tradition in any creative way. This seems to me to be a misleading evaluation of the complex role that apocalypticism played in the transition from the ancient world to the First Europe. In order to show why, I shall give a brief and necessarily superficial sketch of early Christian apocalypticism as a prelude to a slightly less superficial look at how apocalypticism contributed to what Dawson called the making of Europe.

By apocalypticism I mean a particular view about the nature and purpose of history, one that first became evident in the literary genre of the mediated revelations, or apocalypses, of Second Temple Judaism, but that was by no means restricted to this type of literature either in Judaism or in Christianity.[7] The apocalyptic view of history is structured according to a divinely-predetermined pattern of crisis, judgment, and vindication. God's control over history, conceived of as a foreordained and unified stucture, is more evident to believers the worse things are imagined to be. A sense of the present as a time of crisis made evident by the proliferation of evils, both natural and moral, nourished conviction that a coming divine judgment would mark the definitive vindication of the just and punishment of the wicked. For the apocalypticist the whole of history is a book in which God's plan can be read, at least in general, and often even in close detail.

Belief in the imminence of the Last Judgment has often been seen as the distinguishing mark of apocalypticism. This is true, but we must remember that imminence comes in many forms. From its origins, apocalypticism allowed both for predictive and non-predictive, or what we might call psychological imminence, in which life is lived under the shadow of the end. In Jewish apocalypticism the Old Testament book of Daniel contains the mysterious prophecy of the seventy weeks that involves a precise calculation of the coming end (Dan. 9), while the later apocalypse called 4 Esdras inveighs against attempts at such calculations (4 Esd. 4.51–2). In the New Testament, the presence of the Danielic figure of 1,260 days in John's Apocalypse (see 11.3 and 12.6), as well as the identification of the seven heads of the Beast with seven Roman rulers (Apoc. 13), hint at predictive imminence, while in the Apocalyptic Discourse of the Synoptic Gospels Jesus warns against attempts to predict the day or the hour of his return (see Matt. 24.36, Mark 14.32). What I have called psychological imminence is the conviction that the final drama of history is already underway and that current decisions and actions are to be made in the light of the approaching end, even when we cannot determine how near or far off it may be. This form of imminence tends to condense past actions and future hopes into attitudes and decisions to be realized in the present moment. I think it is the voice that speaks in the seventh-century quotation with which I began – "all things become every day worse and worse, for the end is drawing near."

The earliest believers in Jesus of Nazareth as Messiah interpreted his life, death, and their hopes for his return in the light of contemporary Jewish apocalypticism. It is not incorrect to see apocalypticism as the mother of all Christian theology,[8] as long as we do not restrict this nurturing to a single form of apocalyptic belief, or exclude the influence of other religious motifs in the formation of first-century Christianity. The hypothesis that Christianity underwent a fundamental change in the second century as archaic apocalyptic expectations of the imminent return of Christ yielded to belief in the Savior's ongoing presence in the church, is at best a half-truth.[9] A certain cooling down of predictive imminence was only a part of a more complicated development in which apocalyptic hopes for judgment and reward were rarely abandoned, but often spiritualized or reformulated, and at times even recreated to meet new needs. An example can be found in the writings of the early third-century Roman presbyter Hippolytus, who greatly contributed to the development of the Antichrist legend by devoting the earliest treatise to the final apocalyptic foe, but who also redated the time of the end by calculating that Christ came not at the conclusion of the sixth and last millennium of history, i.e., immediately before the end, but in the middle of it, that is, in the year of the world (*anno mundi*) 5500.[10]

During the fourth century, as the Roman Empire became Christian, a wide variety of reactions to apocalypticism become evident among the major Christian leaders and thinkers. These diverse attitudes were important for the subsequent role of apocalypticism on at least two key issues: the respectability of predictive views of the end; and belief in the coming earthly reign of Christ and the saints, the Christian millenarianism that appears in the twentieth chapter of John's Apocalypse and in many other early Christian documents.

The North African Christian rhetorician Lactantius, a functionary at the court of Constantine, is a good representative of continuing belief in the coming earthly messianic kingdom, as well as in a modified form of predictive apocalypticism.[11] Even at the end of the fourth century predictive apocalypticism was alive and well, as the witness of Martin of Tours (d. 397), who believed that Antichrist had already been born, and the writings of the North African bishop Quintus Julius Hilarianus show.[12] But the late fourth century and early fifth century also saw a strong reaction against apocalypticism in the Latin West, spearheaded by two major intellectual leaders, Augustine of Hippo and Jerome. The great translator's opposition was grounded in his reaction against "Judaizing," that is, literalist interpretations of the biblical promises about the messianic kingdom; but he also popularized Eusebius's revision of the Hippolytan dating of Christ's coming to *anno mundi* 5228, a time scheme which put the end off until roughly 800 AD. The bishop of Hippo's opposition to apocalypticism was more far-reaching, involving not only an exegetical reaction against predictive imminence and a literal millenarian kingdom, but also an attack upon the theological foundations of apocalypticism itself. Augustine, of course, did not reject scriptural teaching about the events of the end (see *City of God* 20.30), but he insisted that apocalyptic predictions applied only to the future and provided no clues for the meaning of contemporary events. He maintained a strict agnosticism toward all attempts to determine the time of the end. While his theology of history is certainly eschatological in that the temporal process is given shape and meaning by its telos in the Last Judgment that will separate the sheep from the goats, Augustine immanentized eschatology by moving the meaning of history within the soul – the world ages and their goal are the model for the true meaning of history, the moral development of the believer.[13]

Augustine's powerful attack on millenarianism and expectations of the end had a major impact in the early-medieval centuries – no one was to rebut his arguments, in direct fashion at least, until Joachim of Fiore at the end of the twelfth century. The dominant role of Augustinianism in early-medieval thought has been one of the reasons why many historians have neglected the part played by apocalyptic beliefs in the formation of Christendom. It is clear that literal hopes for a thousand-year earthly reign of Christ after his return are not found in the early Middle Ages. Most of the major thinkers, lay and clerical, of the centuries between 400 and 1000 also avoid any predictions of the date of the end. Once again, my point is not to deny the importance of Augustine's anti-apocalypticism, but rather to insist that the story is a more complicated one than a simple triumph of the bishop of Hippo's theology of history would allow. Augustine was too eminent to attack, but he often seems to have been disregarded.

Even among the bishop's early followers we find evidence that it was possible to neglect his teaching about refusing to see present crises as signs of the imminence of the end, as the example of Bishop Quodvultdeus of mid-fifth-century Carthage shows.[14] Early medieval sources, both in the West and in the Byzantine East, contain a number of references to the approaching end of a clearly predictive character. For example, the late-sixth-century *Paschal List of Campania* records that in the years 493 and 496 some "arrogant fools" (*ignari praesumptores*) and "crazies" (*deliri*) announced the coming of Antichrist as a preparation for what would have been the six-thousandth and last year of the world in the Hippolytan dating.[15] At the end of the eighth century, the Spanish monk Beatus of Liébana believed that there were only fourteen years left in the sixth millennium, though he added the proviso that the times could be shortened or lengthened as God saw fit.[16] A continuing line of revisions of both the Hippolytan dating of the ages of the world (AM I) and Jerome's revision of this (AM II) hints that the chronographers at least found it difficult to abandon the early Christian structure of history originally based upon apocalyptic calculation.[17] But the importance of apocalypticism in the period between 400 and 1000 lies less in these continuations of older Christian hopes and fears than in the new creations of the time, creations that were important factors in the ideology of nascent Christendom.

The general reaction against predictive imminence spearheaded by Augustine seems to have facilitated a situation within which non-predictive, or psychological, imminence underwent developments that were to become central to most medieval Christian views of the end. Prominent among these shifts (though by no means exhaustive of them) was an emphasis on the threat of the Last Judgment as a spur to missionary activity and moral reform. Precisely because the time of the end could not be calculated but was still felt as impending, it might be used as a powerful argument for efforts to spread the gospel and to insure its proper observance – an argument that was not subject to the disconfirmations that predictive apocalypticism has always, at least thus far, entailed. In art and literature, as well as in theology, the centuries of the making of Christendom were obsessed with the theme of the coming judgment, though rarely with precise predictions for its coming. Although fear of judgment had been found in Christian texts from the beginning,[18] I would suggest that early-medieval rejection of predictiveness may paradoxically have allowed end-time anxiety a more pervasive, if necessarily somewhat diffuse, power.

It is true that when general fear of judgment was cut free from precise calculations of the time of the end, it often seems to have lost any note of the imminence that characterizes apocalypticism in the proper sense. Many early medieval references to the Last Judgment seem to be literary topoi rather than expressions of personal motivation of an apocalyptic character. But each case must be investigated on its own merits, and even as a topos, appeal to the Last Judgment reveals something about the mentality that strove to create a more adequate religious ordering of society during these centuries.

A similar logic, it could be argued, also helps explain another aspect of early Christian apocalypticism's contribution to medieval culture, the numerous visions of heaven and hell that were primarily designed to effect moral conversion, first in the recipient and then in the audience addressed by the account. These texts, most popular between the sixth and the twelfth centuries,[19] were the descendants of a visionary trajectory that can be traced through those Jewish and early Christian apocalypses that recount an otherworldly journey of a seer or important biblical figure, such as the well-known *Visio Pauli*.[20] The details of the medieval visions, however, as well as their lack of any interest in the coming end of history, argue that we are dealing with a new, non-apocalyptic genre, though one that shares the moralizing shift evident in the new attitude towards the Last Judgment.

Alongside the emphasis on the coming judgment as a motive for missionization and moral reformism, the other major development in apocalyptic traditions in the period between 400 and roughly 1000 was the growth of imperial legends concerning the Last Roman Emperor. These new apocalyptic scenarios had two important functions in facilitating the emergence of Christendom as an ideal of world order – first, they gave the Christian Roman Empire a continuing role in the divine plan despite its decline and seeming collapse; and second, they helped preserve the optimistic element in Christian apocalyptic hopes by shifting attention away from the condemned millennial kingdom that was to last for a thousand years *after* Christ's return to a *pre-millennial* reign of the Last Emperor.

The examples that I will use to illustrate the role of apocalypticism in the early medieval period must necessarily be selective, but I hope they will provide at least a taste of the case that a more extensive treatment might establish. I will concentrate on attitudes toward the

Last Judgment, concluding with a few remarks on the Last Emperor legends. The evidence will be drawn from art and literature, as well as from more narrowly theological sources.

The fifth-century Gallic bishop Orientius was not the first Latin Christian poet to deal with the Last Judgment, but when we compare the depictions found in his *Commonitorium* with those in the poems of Commodian (probably third century) we can note a significant difference.[21] Commodian's accounts, like that found later in Lactantius,[22] occupy a less dominant place in the whole narrative of the last events because they function as part of a complex apocalyptic scenario in which there are actually two judgments, one before and one after the millennial kingdom.[23] Orientius's poem, written about 430 AD in the light of the barbarian raids on Gaul (*uno fumauit Gallia tota rogo*, "All Gaul smoked as a single funeral pyre" is its most famous line [2.184]), is basically a moral treatise without any detailed scenario of the events leading to the end. Its purpose is to denounce vices and encourage morality through constant meditation on what later became the traditional four last things – death, judgment, heaven, and hell. While Orientius believes that the end is near, in typically Augustinian fashion, he refuses to put a date on it.[24] His account of the Last Judgment is based on Matthew's description of the division of the sheep from the goats (see Matt. 25.31–46), but is notable for the imaginative additions it makes to the biblical narrative, especially its almost sadistic fascination with the coming punishments of the damned (ll. 275–312), the dramatic way in which it pictures the glorious countenances of the just (ll. 340–6), and its powerful presentation of the universality of the judgment (ll. 355–67). Let me quote from this last part:

> Every forefather with quickened step will pass rapidly along,
> Leading his children and his stock.
> Every ancestral stock will be conducted in a dense line
> With the progenitor amidst his descendants. . . .
> Whoever has been born from the beginning of the world
> To the last day that will be its end,
> Souls just and unjust from every land,
> Will be brought to a single place by the command from the East.
> Yet no soul among so many thousands will proceed from there
> Which has not been numbered by its Lord.[25]

In Orientius's poem we meet, for the first time, the carefully articulated scene of judgment which stares down at us from scores of later medieval cathedral facades.

The impact of this sense of the imminence of the Last Judgment for missionary action in the barbarian West can be seen from an important passage in St Patrick's *Confession*. In the middle of his defense of his mission, written a few decades after Orientius's poem, Patrick cites Acts 2.17 about the last days and Matthew 24.14 about preaching the Gospel to all nations before the end of the world to ratify his career – "So we have seen it, and so it has been fulfilled: behold we are witnesses that the Gospel has been preached as far as those places beyond which no one lives."[26] Patrician commentators have been so busy defending the Apostle of the Irish against millenarianism,[27] noting that he makes no prediction about the end of the world, that they have missed the obvious – Patrick's sense of impending, if not predictable, judgment was a key element in his belief in the importance of his mission. All peoples must be brought into the realm of Christian belief so they can play their part in the great drama of the coming end.

This same sense of the foreboding judgment is found in a number of texts that reflect the ideals and actions of those preachers who sought to Christianize both the *rustici*, the semi-Christian rural folk of the decaying Roman world, as well as in the missionaries to the pagan Germans of the north. Martin of Braga in his sermon "On the Castigation of the Rustics" of *c*.572, a text later used by the Anglo-Saxon missionaries to Germany, provided a brief model catechism that stressed Christ's judgment at the end of the world as a motive for Christian behavior.[28] Gregory the Great, writing to the newly converted Ethelbert of Kent in 601, shows how much his own non-predictive sense of the end was a factor in his fostering the English mission:

We also wish Your Majesty to know, as we have learned from the words of Almighty God in holy Scripture, that the end of the present age is already drawing near and that the unending kingdom of the saints is approaching. . . . All these things are not to come in our own days, but they will all follow upon our times. . . . These signs of the end of the world are sent ahead so that we may have a concern for our souls. Awaiting the hour of death, by our good actions may we be found ready for the Judge who is to come.[29]

While I would not want to claim that this sense of the end was the only motivation in the long and complex series of initiatives that resulted in the baptism of the First Europe, and while references to the end made by some missionaries, like Boniface, often seem to be mere polite notices of an element in the Creed,[30] the examples of Patrick, Gregory, and others indicate that what I have called non-predictive apocalypticism played its part in the conversion process.

The theme of impending judgment also surfaces in telling examples from the everyday life of Christians in these centuries. One day Caesarius of Arles noted some of the congregation leaving the church after the gospel reading. He rushed to the doors to bar the way, shouting: "What are you doing, my sons? . . . Stay here! Listen to the sermon for the good of your souls and listen carefully! You will not be able to do this on Judgment Day!" However powerful the fear of judgment may have been, his biographer informs us that after this Caesarius prudently ordered the doors to be closed after the readings.[31]

We can gain some understanding of the widespread role of fear of Doomsday by a glance at three typical figures of nascent Christendom: Columba, Gregory the Great, and Bede. None of these founders of Christendom can be termed an apocalypticist in the sense of someone who predicted the time of the end, but all of them lived "in the shadow of the Second Coming."[32]

Both Celtic mythology, and to a greater extent the ancient German myths, contained accounts of the end of the world;[33] but the role that the Last Judgment played in early Irish Christianity was based more on biblical and apocryphal texts than on native traditions.[34] Its earliest witness is the wild and wonderful poem known as the *Altus Prosator*, which most authorities ascribe to St Columba, the founder of Iona and missionary to the Picts. There seems little reason to doubt this ascription, which makes the poem one of the oldest in the Irish tradition.[35] As the product of the "latest and noblest of Ireland's prophets," the *Altus Prosator* acquired a quasi-canonical status as is shown by the extensive introductions and glosses that accompany it in the manuscript tradition.[36]

Written in a rugged ecclesiastical Latin of rhyming couplets, and using the Old Latin biblical text, Columba's epic consists of twenty-three stanzas arranged in alphabetic order. The first four stanzas (A–D) treat of what is prior to our world: the Trinity, the creation of the angels, and the fall of Lucifer and the other wicked angels. Creation, its praise of God, and the fall of humanity are described in stanzas five through eight (E–H). The third part of the poem, consisting of stanzas nine through thirteen (I, K, L, M, N) contains cosmological speculation about the tides, the nature of hell, the waters above the earth, and the like, topics that were also of interest to many of the ancient apocalypses of the otherworldly-journey type.[37] The following three stanzas give what I take to be an abbreviated account of the history of salvation,[38] while the final and longest part of the poem, stanzas R through Z, present the Last Judgment. The R stanza begins with famous lines based on Zephaniah 1.16:

> Regis regum rectissimi prope est dies domini
> dies irae et vindictae tenebrarum et nebulae
> diesque mirabilium tonitruorum fortium
> dies quoque angustiae meroris ac tristitiae
> in quo cessabit mulierum amor ac desiderium
> hominumque contentio mundi huius et cupido.

In the translation of Bernard and Atkinson:

> The day of the Lord, the Kings of Kings most righteous, is at hand:
> a day of wrath and vengeance, of darkness and cloud;
> a day of wondrous mighty thunderings,
> a day of trouble also, of grief and sadness,
> in which shall cease the love and desire of women
> and the strife of men and the lust of this world.

The Judgment stanzas deal with the expected topics: the unrolling of the "books of conscience" (S), the trump of the general resurrection (T), Christ's descent and the final conflagration (X), the celestial liturgy of Apocalypse 4 (Y), and heaven and hell (Z). Stanza U is obscure, but has a possible connection with the revised apocalypticism of the early Middle Ages. It describes three stars, probably Orion and Venus in its two guises as the morning and evening star, as types of Christ because, although their courses are partly hidden, they cannot fail to reach their appointed goal. This suggests that though the coming Judge is now concealed from sight, his return is as certain as the movement of the heavens.[39] Columba's poem is not only the finest Latin evocation of Doomsday before the famous

Dies Irae, but is also illustrative of the new sense of judgment typical of nascent Christendom.

Later Irish descriptions of the Last Judgment, especially in the Irish apocryphal literature, show how much the new peoples of Christendom were fascinated by this decisive aspect of the biblical view of history. This was especially true during the tenth and the eleventh centuries, when Latin apocrypha were translated into Irish and inspired a rich development of texts in the native language. The work generally known as *The Fifteen Signs of Doomsday* was one of the most popular medieval accounts of the end, known in some 120 versions in a wide variety of languages.[40] William W. Heist has shown how the many later forms of this text depend upon the tenth-century Irish version found in the *Saltair na Rann*, or *Psalter of Quatrains*, which in turn is based upon the seven signs of judgment found in the *Apocalypse of Thomas*, a work surviving in two Latin versions of no later than the fifth century.[41] The origin of this apocalypse is unknown.[42] Even if it is not a product of the special form of interest in the Last Judgment that marks the centuries after 400, its dissemination and influence during this period is significant.[43]

According to one version of the legend of the *Altus Prosator*, it was written for Gregory the Great in return for gifts he had sent to the Apostle of Scotland. While this story is scarcely to be believed, it is not hard to think that the pope would have appreciated the poem, if not for its strange Latinity, at least for how closely it matched his own thoughts about the coming judgment. Gregory has long been noted among students of medieval apocalyptic thought for his combination of a vivid sense of the terror of his times as a sign of the end along with a resolute resistence to apocalyptic calculations and an equally Augustinian immanentizing of apocalyptic images and events. The latter is most evident in the pope's treatment of Antichrist. Gregory does not deny that there is a coming final human enemy to appear shortly before the end, but his major concern is to show how the spirit of Antichrist, the force of deception, hypocrisy, and false religion, has invaded the church and grows ever greater as the end draws near.[44]

Gregory's letters and sermons are filled with groans and sighs about the horrors of his day as signs of the approaching end. But the purpose of this lugubrious rhetoric is always the same: not prediction, but moral reform. "Let us despise with all our being this present – or rather extinct – world. At least let worldly desires end with the end of the world; let us imitate what deeds of good men we can," as one of his *Homilies on Ezekiel* puts it.[45] The pope's writings do not contain many actual descriptions of the Last Judgment,[46] but we need not take it as a mere topos when his biographer John the Deacon avers: "In all his sayings and works Gregory pondered upon the imminent final day of coming retribution, and the more he noted the end of the world to press more closely as its devastations mounted, the more carefully he considered the affairs of all."[47]

This judgment, indeed, provides the hint that allows us to put together Gregory's pessimism about the future with his considerable efforts in every sphere of Christian society. Without attempting a full review of the great pope's eschatology, we can agree with Jacques Fontaine's statement, "It is more *because* he [Gregory] strongly believed in the nearing end of this world that he realized with greater intensity the urgency of effective preaching, of more active charity, and of a preaching of the Gospel that extended beyond the shores of the Mediterranean as far as Britain conquered by the Angles."[48] It is not necessary to side with historians like Walter Ullmann,[49] who argued that Gregory consciously turned away from the old Roman world of the Byzantine Empire to embrace the new barbarian West, to see in the activities of his papacy, and especially in his writings, which can be described as the main moral textbooks of the next five centuries, a key factor in the birth of medieval Christendom. Gregory himself, however, was not concerned with building a new society on earth, but in preparing those left alive before the Second Coming for their true *patria*, heaven. The key to understanding his myriad activities, as J. N. Hillgarth has noted, is to be found in his central conviction "that an immortal soul is the only thing that man possesses and that the whole of life has to be lived in the light of the approaching Judgement."[50]

Most of the clerical leaders of the Latin West in the following centuries were Gregorians, that is, monastics whose basic attitudes were deeply influenced by the great pope's writings. Venerable Bede, the premier Anglo-Saxon scholar of the early Middle Ages, is typical. Like Gregory, Bede adhered to the Augustinian program of refusing to engage in speculation about the time of the end. His *Commentary on the Apocalypse* was one of the major representatives of the moralized reading of the last book of the Bible that Augustine had popularized, an interpretation which repudiated any literal understanding of the thousand-year kingdom of chapter 20.[51] But, as Henry Mayr-Harting once put it, "Bede worked with a tearing sense of hurry."[52] His prodigious output in so many different fields of knowledge was marked by the same sense of urgency about the end of time that one sees in Gregory.[53] So much remained to be done to establish a true Christian society before the judgment, which could come at any time, that Bede's cell seems to have been more a beehive of activity than a haven of monastic *otium*.

The Northumbrian scholar's teaching about the Last Judgment was expressed both in prose and in poetry. He concluded his popular treatise *De temporum ratione*, the *Explanation of Time*, with a survey of the last things, including both a discussion of Augustine's views on the dating of the judgment in chapter 68 and a succinct account of the event itself in chapter 70.[54] Somewhere between 716 and 731, at the request of his friend Bishop Acca, he composed a poem *De die iudicii*, a more personal witness to the role that meditation on coming judgment played in his life and in the mentality of early-medieval culture. In his *Ecclesiastical History* 4.24, Bede had noted that the poet Caedmon had made many songs "on the terrors of the Last Judgement, the horrible pains of Hell, and the joys of the kingdom of heaven. . . . by which he sought to turn his hearers from delight in wickedness, and to inspire them to love and do good."[55] The *De die iudicii* is such a poem of apocalyptic repentence, but one addressed primarily to himself. It begins with Bede seated in a typically medieval garden, when a powerful wind suddenly descends and disturbs his soul:

> And so, I remembered the sins I had committed,
> And the stains of life, the hateful time of death,
> And the great day of judgment with fearful testing,
> And the strict Judge's perpetual anger toward the guilty.[56]

Bede's account of judgment, heaven, and hell may not have been very original, or even inspired poetry, but its moralizing message exactly fitted the times.

Bede's mention of Caedmon's *carmina* on Doomsday, and the fact that his own poem was translated into Old English in the tenth century as *Be Domes Daege*, or what is called today *Judgment Day II*, remind us of the rich trove of poetry related to the theme of Judgment Day among the Germanic peoples of the early Middle Ages. The three major Old English "Doomsday" poems,[57] and the Old High German

Muspilli of *c.* 850, with its picture of the titanic struggle between Antichrist and Elijah in which the latter's blood ignites the world conflagration, shows that in the vernacular at least, ancient Germanic myths of the end mingled with Christian beliefs, both biblical and apocryphal, in the creation of Christendom's portrayal of the Last Judgment, a picture that was meant to be always kept in mind even if its time could not be calculated.

Early-medieval figurative representations of the Last Judgment, I believe, can also be seen in this light. Christian apocalyptic iconography is a rich, and richly debated, subject. Scenes from the Johannine Apocalypse, especially those relating to the heavenly liturgy of chapters 4 and 5, proliferated in Christian art from the end of the fourth century.[58] Other images were meant to signify Christ as coming Judge. Many scholars argue that the *etimasia*, or empty throne, that appears often in mosaics of the fifth and sixth centuries, symbolizes Christ's return as arbiter of living and dead, whether this is seen as a proximate event or not.[59] In the impressive early sixth-century apse mosaic of SS Cosma e Damiano in the Roman Forum, the golden-tuniced Christ who looms against a backdrop of heavenly clouds certainly evokes the awe found in the late antique accounts of the Parousia, such as that found in Lactantius.[60] But this is primarily a presentation of Christ as Judge, an *adventus domini*, not a portrayal of the Last Judgment itself as the ultimate separation of good from evil.[61] An early depiction of the Last Judgment as such, one which dates from the same period in the beginning of the sixth century, is the rendition of the separation of the sheep from the goats found in a well-known panel from the nave of Sant' Apollinare Nuovo in Ravenna.[62] Like much Christian catacomb art, this scene, with its deliberate simplicity, serves more as a symbolic trigger than as an actual representation – it reminds the onlooker of an item of belief. Such late antique examples show that Christian art was still working its way toward more synoptic and impressive depictions of the Doomsday that would fit the role that it had come to play in contemporary piety.

In Latin Christendom, at least, the earliest surviving attempts to portray the full impact of the awesome Last Judgment, scenes which in some cases combine both the Parousia and the Judgment, are to be found in the barbarian art of the Celts and Germans.[63] Naturally, it is possible that these may depend in part on lost portrayals produced in Late Antiquity, such as those that probably lie behind the Last Judgment pictures from the tenth-century Beatus manuscripts.[64] This new iconography of nascent Christendom was much dependent on the Little Apocalypse of Matthew and its parallels for its overall structure, and it seems tied, at least in part, to the role of the cross as the sign *par excellence* of the end.

Since the second century, at least, the sign of the returning Son of Man mentioned in Matthew 24.30 had been interpreted as the cross (see, e.g., Apocalypse of Peter 1.8–11). After the discovery of the True Cross by the Empress Helena in the fourth century, the great relic of salvation was decorated with gold and gems and enshrined in the complex of buildings on the site of Christ's Crucifixion and Resurrection built by her son, Constantine. Subsequently, Theodosius II erected a golden cross on the site of Calvary, and this monument and the other embellished crosses (*crux gemmata*) that appear in Late Antique art were essentially emblems of Christ's victory over death and reminders of his coming *adventus*.

The motif of the cross, both as enshrined in the physical relic of the True Cross in Jerusalem, and in its various symbolic manifestations, was crucial to the Christian life and piety. The image of the cross not only recalled the saving events of Christ's earthly life, but also announced his return as Judge. From this perspective, just as any centrally planned church structure can be seen as sharing in the sacrality of the circular Anastasis, the Church of the Resurrection,[65] the proliferation of monumental crosses in Western art from the late seventh century (they were also found in the East, especially in Armenia) can be thought of as forms of re-presentation of the power of the True Cross, including its eschatological significance. The popularity of such monumental imagery can also be connected with a sense of renewed eschatological awareness triggered by the attack of the forces of evil on Jerusalem, the apocalyptic city, and its chief relic, the Cross.

In 614 the Zoroastrian Persians captured Jerusalem and carried off the True Cross. The Cross was soon regained under the Emperor Heraclius and fortunately brought to the imperial capitol at Constantinople before Jerusalem was taken by the Arabs in 638. The Holy City was to remain under non-Christian domination for over five centuries, with the Cross exiled from its true home. This background helps explain the growing role of the cross as eschatological sign in early medieval art. For example, Emile Mâle interpreted the jewelled cross that the Jerusalem-born Pope Theodore ordered for the mosaic in the chapel of Saints Primus and Felician in Rome's own circular church, Santo Stefano Rotondo (*c.* 645), as a special re-presenting of Jerusalem and its chief relic in the West during a time of trouble and confusion.[66] More recently, other scholars have argued that the famous High Crosses of early-medieval Ireland can be interpreted in the same light.[67]

The earliest Irish crosses, such as those of Ahenny dating to perhaps the early eighth century, have an interlace decoration that appears to be a stone imitation of the decoration of surviving examples of the *crux gemmata*. Incised crosses on stone pillars, some of which may even be earlier, as in the case of Fahan Mura Cross Slab (seventh century?), are well-represented in western Ireland.[68] During the course of the eighth century, Irish artists began to include portrayals of both the Crucifixion and the Parousia in their manuscripts, as shown by a Gospel Book now found in St Gall, which has the crucified Christ facing Christ the Returning Judge.[69] A ninth-century Irish Gospel Book from Bobbio, now in Turin, perhaps originally from the same scriptorium in Ireland, has a more evolved view, one that is closer to the impressive monumental versions found on ninth- and tenth-century Irish crosses. Here a scene of the Ascension is immediately followed by one of the returning Christ who stands in the center as a giant figure bearing the cross, his sign of triumph. In the upper right corner a diminutive angel blows a trumpet, while above and below Christ are eight small fullstanding figures and no less than eighty-six half-figures.[70] This proliferation of the representatives of "all the tribes of the earth" seems to hint at the universality of the judgment that is about to begin.

In the Irish High Crosses a classic pattern emerged, as can be seen from the famous Cross of Muiredach (d. 922) at Monasterboice in County Louth. This has the Crucifixion on one side (in this case the west face) and the Judgment on the other.[71] The fusion of the Second Coming and Last Judgment is evident in the rich iconography. As in the Bobbio Gospel, Christ stands in the center bearing both the cross and a sprouting bough, the symbol of resurrection. Above his head is the dove of the Holy Spirit; to the right a seated figure plays on a pipe, while to the left another seated figure (David?) plays a harp. Behind the harper are the ranks of the elect led by an angelic trumpeter and someone holding what must be the book of life. On the other side the damned are pushed away by devils bearing a pitchfork and another book. Below, St Michael weighs a soul while transfixing a prone demon with a tau-cross.

Exactly how far back this impressive iconography goes is difficult to say. Possibly ninth-century examples are the South Cross at Kells and the Cross from Arboe in Tyrone.[72] Other well-known examples of judgment scenes from the period *c.* 900–1000 include the Cross at Durrow, the Cross of the Scriptures from Clonmacnoise, and the West Cross at Monasterboice. The High Crosses are the most impressive monuments of early Irish Christianity, focal points for the religious experience of the entire community. What did these earliest portrayals of the Last Judgment in monumental art mean to their audience? Taking the clue from the writings of Columba, Gregory and Bede, I would argue that they were intended to transfer the Last Judgment from the future into the present, that is, to present in visual fashion what I have called the psychological imminence of the end.[73]

The same centuries also saw the beginnings of Last Judgment iconography in the Germanic areas of Christendom. The earliest example seems to be a Merovingian sarcophagus of the seventh century from Jouarre whose presentation of Matthew 25 features not the symbolic sheep and goats but two lines of *orantes* figures stretching out to the right and left sides of the enthroned Christ, with angels blowing trumpets to complete the scene.[74] The differences between this and the Irish examples, especially the absence of the cross, indicates the variety of iconographic traditions concerning the Last Judgment at work in early Christendom. The enigmatic Ruthwell Cross, from a Northumbrian cultural milieu and probably dating to about 730 AD, though quite different from the Irish Crosses, contains both a portrayal of Christ as World Ruler based on Apocalypse 5 and a scene of Christ as Judge with the inscription, "Jesus Christ, Judge of Righteousness; the beasts and the dragons recognized the Savior of the World in the desert."[75] The Stuttgart Psalter, probably made in northern France about 820, includes a scene of Christ separating the sheep from the goats in imitation of late antique sources (fo. 6v), as well as a number of more original attempts to portray his role as Judge weighing the merits of all humankind (e.g., fo. 9v, illustrating Ps. 9.9, "et ipse iudicat orbem in iustitia, iudicat populos in aequitatibus"). The contemporary Utrecht Psalter also included several depictions of the Last Judgment (e.g., fo. 5r, also illustrating Ps. 9.5–9). Shortly after 800, the west interior wall of the church of St Johann at Mustair in Switzerland was decorated with a partly-destroyed mural of Doomsday emphasizing the majesty and universality of the event. Something of the way in which these, and doubtless other images now lost, sought to fuse the appearance of the Son of Man and his apocalyptic sign with the dread of the universal judgment he would bring can be found in the early ninth-century verses from St Gall intended for the decoration of a lost church:

> Lo the trumpets blare forth which dissolve death's rule,
> The Cross gleams in the heavens; cloud and fire go before.
> Here the exalted saints sit down with Christ the Judge
> To justify the devout and to damn the wicked to hell.[76]

There is no space here to try to provide even a summary account of the rich iconography of the Last Judgment through the eleventh century. Particularly impressive depictions were produced by the Reichenau school shortly after 1000, such as those found in the Bamberg Apocalypse (fo. 53r), the Pericope Book of Henry II (fo. 202r), and the Lectionary of Bernulph (fo. 41v). Beat Brenk has given a detailed account of these and many other early-medieval scenes of Doomsday, and has also discussed the relation between Eastern and Western portrayals. All of this evidence, both literary and pictorial, suggests that after the Augustinian attack on predictive apocalypticism the traditional pessimistic pole of early Christian apocalypticism, once centered on calculating the time of Christ's return, had been transmuted to a form of what I have called psychological imminence based on a sense of living in awareness of the dread Day of Judgment.

An analogous shift in early-medieval apocalyptic eschatology also seems evident in the case of the optimistic pole of early-Christian apocalyptic hopes: the belief in the earthly reward of the righteous. The evidence here is less extensive, but still impressive. Fear of judgment was omnipresent and can be easily illustrated from theology, art, and literature; hope for a better time to come, either the reign of the Last World Emperor, or a forty-five-day respite for repentance after Antichrist's defeat,[77] was novel and perhaps partly suspect. But these hopes were among the most original creations of early-medieval apocalypticism and it seems no accident that it was only after the demise of expectations of a thousand-year earthly reign of Christ and the saints that the first pre-millennial Christian convictions that something better was in store for true believers beyond the dismal present become evident.

Politically speaking, that is, insofar as revised optimistic apocalypticism played a role in the formation of Christendom, the imperial legends concerning the Last Roman Emperor had considerable significance. While much about the evolution of this new form of apocalypticism remains obscure, it is not hard to give a brief overview.[78] The earliest surviving account of the Last Roman Emperor as an apocalyptic figure is found in the *Revelations of the Pseudo-Methodius* which were written in present-day Iraq by a Syriac supporter of the Byzantine *basileus* about 692.[79] The historical context was the rise of Islam, especially the conquest of Jerusalem and the Holy Land, an event for which there was no place in the inherited Christian scenario of the end.[80] Building upon a wealth of legends, old and new, about imperial savior figures (there may have been an earlier appearance of an apocalyptic Christian emperor in a lost early Latin translation of the text known as the *Tiburtine Sibyl*), the anonymous author of these revelations created a comprehensive apocalyptic explanation for the rise of 'Islam and the contemporary troubles of Rome. This example of the a posteriori function of apocalypticism, by which I mean the expansion of the apocalyptic scenario to include transcendentalized versions of recent events, was to remain powerful political propaganda for a millennium.[81] The Pseudo-Methodian *Revelations* were soon translated into Greek, then into Latin in the early eighth century (they eventually appeared in many vernacular versions in both the East and the West). The text was printed early and often, and as late as 1683 excerpts were published on broadsheets to encourage the troops of the Holy Roman Emperor Leopold I in the defense of Vienna against the Turks.

The *Revelations* begin with the expulsion of Adam and Eve from Paradise and proceed with an account of world history over its 7,000 years' duration, giving special attention to the figure of Alexander the Great from whose stock the Byzantine emperors are seen as descending.[82] The seventh millennium witnesses the destruction of the Persian Empire and the rise of the "sons of Ishmael," that is, the Arabs, who wreak destruction on the sinful Christians – typical apocalyptic *vaticinia ex eventu*, or prophecies after the event. Then the *Revelations* pass to true prophecy:

Then suddenly there will be awakened perdition and calamity as those
of a woman in travail, and a king of the Greeks will go forth against
them [i.e., the Ishmaelites] in great wrath, and he will be roused against
them like a man who shakes off his wine [Ps. 77.65], and who plots
against them as if they were dead men.

This Byzantine emperor and his sons defeat the Ishmaelites, inflicting
on them a yoke a hundred times harder than what they had put on the
Christians. "And there will be peace on earth the like of which had
never existed, because it is the last peace of the perfection of the
world."[83] During this messianic period the enclosed nations of Gog and
Magog will come forth, only to be defeated by angelic intervention.
Then the Last Emperor will reign in Jerusalem until the appearance of
the Antichrist, when he will ascend Golgotha and set his diadem on
the top of the Holy Cross, thus signifying the handing over of the
empire to God. An important role is given to the True Cross: "And
immediately the Holy Cross will be raised to heaven, and the King of
the Greeks will give up his soul to his Creator. And immediately every
leader and every authority and all powers will cease."[84] The *Revelations*
close with a brief account of Antichrist's career and his destruction
when Christ comes in judgment.

The Byzantine East remained the creative source for the legend of
the Last World Emperor between *c.* 700 and 1000, but the popularity
of the legend in the West is witnessed by the number of surviving
manuscripts of the Latin versions of the Pseudo-Methodius and later of
the mid-tenth-century *Letter on the Antichrist* written by the monk
Adso, which incorporates the earliest surviving version of the legend
where a Western heir to Roman claims is the hero.[85] From the
perspective of the role of apocalypticism in the making of Christendom, I would suggest that the figure of the Last Emperor functioned
in two ways. First, it kept alive a connection between the Christian
Roman Empire of Constantine and the new Europe that recognized
that this empire was no longer a living reality, whatever claims some
had made to have inherited its mantle. The significance of Rome in
God's plan was saved by projecting it into the future. Second, the Last
Emperor as a surrogate for Christ in his victory over the forces of evil
opposing the Christian world-order became the vehicle for the terres-
trial optimism that had been a part of Christian apocalypticism from its
origins. If belief in the thousand-year kingdom of Apocalypse 20 had
been excluded from official Christian teaching by the spiritualizing

exegesis of the Fathers, it crept back in through the murky world of pseudonymous and apocryphal texts and commentaries. This is another demonstration of my claim that the centuries between 400 and 1000 witnessed not the death of apocalypticism, but its transformation.

These long-dead views of the end of the world inspired impressive works of poetry and art. Fervent belief in them was an important part of the motivation of the leaders of the First Europe, both clerical and lay. In their apocalyptic specificity, of course, the conception of the dread Doomsday and the universal reign of peace of the Last Emperor are strange to us today, relics – if impressive ones – of beliefs that have been either discarded or reinterpreted by modern science and modern theology. But belief in some kind of coming day, be it of judgment on pervasive evil or of peace beyond imagination, still fuels creative imagination. Let me close with some words of the modern Austrian poet and novelist Ingeborg Bachmann from an interview shortly before her death in 1973:

> I don't believe in materialism, this consumer society, this capitalism, this monstrosity that goes on here. . . . I really do believe in something, and I call it "a day will come." And one day it will come. Well, it probably won't come, because they've always destroyed it for us, for so many thousands of years they've always destroyed it. It won't come and yet I believe in it. For if I can't believe in it, then I can't go on writing either.[86]

NOTES

1   From the Crypt of the Abbot Mellebaudis. See E. Le Blant, ed., *Nouveau recueil des inscriptions chrétiennes de la Gaule*, Collection de documents inédits sur l'histoire de France (Paris, 1892), no. 248 (p. 260). I am using the translation of J. N. Hillgarth, *Christianity and Paganism, 350–750* (Philadelphia, 1986), 16.

2   Christopher Dawson, *The Making of Europe: An Introduction to the History of European Unity 400–1000 A.D.* (London, 1932), p. xv. On Dawson as a prophet of European unity, see the Rt Hon Lord Rawlinson of Ewell, "Europe; the Greater Unity. Christopher Dawson Centennial Lecture," *The Downside Review*, 10 (1991), 52–63.

3   See C. Delisle Burns, *The First Europe* (London, 1948).

4   On the development of *christianitas* and the related vernacular terms, see Denys Hay, *Europe: The Emergence of an Idea* (New York, 1966), ch. 2;

and John van Engen, "The Christian Middle Ages as an Historiographical Problem," *American Historical Review*, 91 (1986), 539–41.

5   Henri Irenée Marrou, "La place du haut moyen âge dans l'histoire du christianisme," *Il passaggio dall'antichità al medioevo in Occidento* (Spoleto, 1962), 629.

6   Ernst H. Kantorowicz, "The Problem of Medieval World Unity," first published in the *Annual Report of the American Historical Association for 1942*, III (1944), 31–7; reprinted in his *Selected Studies* (Locust Valley, 1965), 76–81 (quote from 78).

7   What follows is based on several earlier treatments of mine designed to describe the essential features of apocalypticism, beginning with my *Visions of the End: Apocalyptic Traditions in the Middle Ages* (New York, 1979), "Introduction," 1–36; see also, "Early Apocalypticism: The On-going Debate," in *The Apocalypse in English Renaissance Thought and Literature*, eds C. A. Patrides and Joseph Wittreich (Manchester, 1984), 2–39; and "John's Apocalypse and the Apocalyptic Mentality," *The Apocalypse in the Middle Ages*, eds Richard K. Emmerson and Bernard McGinn (Ithaca, 1992), 3–19.

8   This famous phrase was first used by Ernst Käsemann in his 1960 essay translated as "The Beginnings of Christian Theology," *Apocalypticism: Journal for Theology and Church*, vol. 6, ed. R. W. Funk (New York, 1961), 40.

9   This view is associated with the "consistent-eschatological" interpretation of early Christian history made popular by Albert Schweitzer and Martin Werner.

10   This form of apocalyptic time-structure and its revisions were to remain central to Western chronography down to 1000 AD. See Richard Landes, " 'Lest the Millennium be Fulfilled': Apocalyptic Expectations and the Pattern of Western Chronography 100–800 CE," *The Use and Abuse of Eschatology in the Middle Ages*, eds Werner Verbeke, Daniel Verhelst, and Andries Welkenhuysen (Leuven, 1988), 137–211 (especially 144–9 and 161–5). Landes refers to the Hippolytan dating as AM I.

11   The seventh book of Lactantius's *Divine Institutes*, composed about 313, adopted the modified predictive apocalypticism first worked out by Hippolytus. Hence, Lactantius claimed that the end was less than two hundred years off, though he also says that "the current situation indicates that the collapse and ruin of everything will soon take place" (*Institutes* 7.25). For the thousand-year reign of Christ and the saints, see *Institutes* 7.23–4. For a translation and commentary on book 7, see Bernard McGinn, editor and translator, *Apocalyptic Spirituality* (New York, 1979), 17–80.

12   For these texts and other contemporary witnesses to predictive immi-

nence, see my *Visions of the End*, 51–5.

13 For remarks on this, see B. McGinn, "Influence and Importance in Evaluating Joachim of Fiore," *Il profetismo gioachimita tra Quattrocento e Cinquecento* (Genoa, 1991), 23–5.

14 Quodvultdeus's *Book of the Promises and Predictions of God* of *c*. 450 saw in the triumph of Germanic Arians a sign of the approach of the end.

15 See Fabio Troncarelli, "Il consolato dell'Anticristo," *Studi Medievali*, 3a serie, 30 (1989), 567–92.

16 For these texts of Beatus, see *Visions of the End*, 77–9. Beatus's *Commentary on the Apocalypse* is generally cautious, but his enemy Elipandus of Toledo accused him of publically preaching the imminence of Antichrist.

17 For the history of this aspect of early medieval apocalypticism, see Landes, " 'Lest the Millennium be Fulfilled'."

18 In the first century of Christian writing, that is, *c*. 50–150 AD, virtually every document, in and outside the New Testament, contains a reference to the coming judgment. In the Apostolic Fathers, for example, see Didache 16, 2 Clement 16–18, Shepherd of Hermas Vis. 4, 1 Clement 23, and weakly in Ignatius, Eph. 11.1.

19 For a survey, see Peter Dinzelbacher, *Vision und Visionsliteratur im Mittelalter* (Stuttgart, 1981), especially chs V, IX–XII, and XVII. Dinzelbacher distinguishes these Type I visions from the more personal and mystical Type II visions that begin in the twelfth century and that are more common in the later Middle Ages.

20 For a survey of the genre of Jewish and early Christian apocalypses emphasizing the distinction between those containing an otherworldly journey and those that do not, see *Apocalypse: Morphology of a Genre*, ed. John J. Collins (Missoula, 1979). On the development of the tradition, see Martha Himmelfarb, *Tours of Hell: An Apocalyptic Form in Jewish and Christian Literature* (Philadelphia, 1983).

21 Commodianus, *Instructiones* lib. II, iiii "De die iudicii," a 12-line account (*Corpus Scriptorum Ecclesiasticorum Latinorum* 15:64–5); and *Carmen apologeticum*, lines 999–1060. On the apocalypticism of Commodian, see Jean Daniélou, *The Origins of Latin Christianity* (London, 1977), 99–123.

22 Lactantius, *Divine Institutes* 7.19–20.

23 This seems to be rooted in the double judgment found in John's Apocalypse, where the first battle and judgment on the dragon is described in Apoc. 19.11–20.3, and the second and final judgment is recounted in 20.7–15.

24 See Orentius, *Commonitorium* 2.163–4: "lassa senescentem respectant omnia finem / et iam postremo uoluitur hora die." I quote from the edition to be found in the dissertation of Sister Mildred Dolores Tobin, *Orientii Commonitorium: A Commentary With An Introduction And*

Translation (Washington, 1945).

25   Orientius, *Commonitorium* 2.355–68 (with omissions):

> atque omnis raptim celeratis gressibus ibit
>   deducens subolem prosapiamque pater.
> cunctaque contento ducetur linea tractu,
>   cum fuerit medius progenitor genitis. . . .
> sed fuit a primi genitum quod tempore mundi
>   usque diem mundo qui modo finis erit,
> omnibus e terris animas iustasque reasque
>   uno constituet iussio prima loco.
> nec tamen ulla illinc tanta inter millia perget,
>   quae non sit domino dinumerata suo.

The actual description of the judgment scene occupies only lines 347–93, but I would argue that the proleptically described punishments of the wicked (ll. 275–319) and joys of the saved (ll. 320–46) should be seen as parts of the Last Judgment scenario. In the above translation I have adopted M. Tobin's version, but with several significant changes, notably in taking *iussio prima* in a poetic sense as a "command from the East," which fits traditional Christian apocalyptic beliefs better.

26   *Saint Patrick: Confession et Lettre à Coroticus*, ed. R. P. C. Hanson (Paris, 1978. SC 249), *Confessio* 34: "quod ita ergo vidimus itaque suppletum est: ecce testes sumus quia evangelium praedicatum est usque ubi nemo ultra est." For other references to the last times in Patrick, see *Confession* 40 and *Letter* 11.

27   See e.g., *The Works of St. Patrick*, tr. and annotated by Ludwig Bieler (London, 1953), 87 n. 81; and Noel Dermot O'Donoghue, *Aristocracy of Soul* (Wilmington, Va., 1987), 75–8.

28   Martin of Braga, *De castigatione rusticorum*, ed. C. W. Barlow, *Martini episcopi Bracarensis Opera Omnia* (New Haven, 1950), 183–203. For a translation, see Hillgarth, *Christianity and Paganism*, 57–64.

29   Gregory, *Registrum* XI.37 in P. Ewald and L. Hartmann, *Gregorii I Papae Registrum Epistolarum* (MGH. Epist. Sel. I) 2.309–10. The translation is from *Visions of the End*, 64.

30   See, e.g., Boniface, *Sermones* 1 and 5 (PL 89.845B and 854C–55A).

31   *Vita S. Caesarii Arelatensis a discipulis scripta* I.27, in *S. Caesarii Arelatensis Opera Omnia*, ed. Gervase Morin (Maredsous, 1942) 2.306; tr. of J. N. Hillgarth in *Christianity and Paganism*, 37. Caesarius also preached on the Last Judgment; see his Homilia XIV in PL 67.1075–7D.

32   I adopt the phrase from Timothy Weber's book about American millenarian thought, *Living in the Shadow of the Second Coming: American*

Premillennialism 1875–1982 (Chicago, 1987).

33   See H. R. Ellis Davidson, *Myths and Symbols in Pagan Europe: Early Scandinavian and Celtic Religions* (Syracuse, 1988), 188–95.

34   The role of the apocrypha in Ireland has been studied by D. N. Dumville, "Biblical Apocrypha and the Early Irish: A Preliminary Investigation," *Proceedings of the Royal Irish Academy*, vol. 73, Section c, no. 8 (1973), 299–338; Martin McNamara, *The Apocrypha in the Irish Church* (Dublin, 1975, repr. 1984); and Maire Herbert and Martin McNamara, eds, *Irish Biblical Apocrypha* (Edinburgh, 1989). For investigations of early Irish views of the end, see St John D. Seymour, "The Eschatology of the Early Irish Church," *Zeitschrift für celtische Philologie*, 14 (1923), 179–211; and Brian Grogan, "Eschatological Teaching of the Early Irish Church," *Biblical Studies: The Medieval Irish Contribution*, ed. Martin McNamara (Dublin, 1976), 46–58.

35   I will use the edition of J. H. Bernard and R. Atkinson, *The Irish Liber Hymnorum*, 2 vols (London, 1898), 1:62–83 for the text (based on 7 mss.), and 2:142–69 for a translation and commentary. B. J. Muir, "Two Latin Hymns by Colum Cille (St Columba)," *Revue du moyen âge latin*, 39 (1983), 205–16, provides the most recent discussion and the text from an eighth witness.

36   The phrase about Columba as prophet appears in one of the Irish prefaces (1.66). Dumville, "Biblical Apocrypha," 332–3, suggests that the early Irish view of *canoin* signified not just the biblical canon but any "text of special authority" which was subject to glossing.

37   A number of scholars, such as Bernard and Atkinson (*Liber Hymnorum* 2.143) and Dumville ("Biblical Apocrypha," 319) have noted affinities between the *Altus Prosator* and the well-known apocalypse 1 Enoch that survives in its entirety only in Ethiopic. These include: (1) the interest in fate of the ancient giants in ll. 58–9 – cf. 1 En. 6–14; (2) the binding of the devils lest they terrify humans in ll. 41–3 – cf. 1 En. 10.12 and 18.16; (3) the cosmological speculations of stanzas nine through thirteen – cf. 1 En. 17–18, 54, 60, etc.; (4) the concern with the motions of the stars of stanza 19 – cf. 1 En. 78; and (5) the judgment account of stanzas 16–22 – cf. 1 En. 100–8. Most of these parallels are too broad to prove real dependence, but the issue deserves further examination. A Latin fragment of 1 En. 106.1–18 that survives in a ninth-century Breton ms. (London, BM Royal 5.E.13, fos 79v–80r), edited by M. R. James in *Apocrypha Anecdota* (Cambridge, 1893), 146–50, shows that some contact would not have been impossible.

38   The basic point of stanzas O, P and Q seems to be to show that the Old Testament was a divine dispensation, but not a saving one until Christ's coming. Stanza O insists that Christ alone, as the Lamb of Apoc. 5, can

unroll the sealed book of history, "fulfilling the prophetic announcements of his coming" (*explens sui presagmina aduentus prophetalia*, l. 85). Stanzas P and Q deal with the Tree of Life and Moses ascending Sinai, both of which can be seen as types of Christ's saving activity. It is interesting to note that the ninth-century Irish scholar, John Scottus Eriugena, also interpreted the Tree of Life as signifying Christ.

39   Here is stanza U from the *Liber Hymnorum* 1.79:

> Uagatur ex climactere Orion celi cardine
> derelicto Uirgilio astrorum splendidissimo
> per metas tithis ignoti orientalis circuli
> girans certis ambagibus redit priscis reditibus
> oriens post biennium uesperugo in uesperum
> sumpta in proplesmatibus tropicis intellectibus.

This interpretation develops that suggested by Bernard and Atkinson in 2.165–6.

40   The fundamental study remains that of William W. Heist, *The Fifteen Signs of Doomsday* (East Lansing, 1952). Heist lists 96 versions he consulted in his Appendix A and includes notices of another 24 versions in Appendix B. On the Irish versions, see McNamara, *Apocrypha in the Irish Church*, nos 104 through 104J.

41   The text and a translation of *The Fifteen Signs*, consisting of verses 8017–393 of the *Saltair na Rann* can be found in Heist, 2–21; another translation of verses 8017–336 is no. 29 in *Irish Biblical Apocrypha*. Most authorities date the *Saltair* to the end of the tenth century, but another view holds for a date of *c.* 850–900.

42   The oldest ms. of the probably original shorter version dates to the fifth century. For an edition, see R. Bihlmeyer, "Un texte non interpolé de l'Apocalypse de Thomas," *Revue Benedictine* 28 (1911), 270–82. Both versions are translated in M. R. James, *The Apocryphal New Testament* (Oxford, 1969), 555–62.

43   The seven signs – one for each day of the final week – both announce the end but also forestall it, at least temporarily, since they are of such an extravagant character that they are clearly not yet present.

44   On Gregory's view of Antichrist, see my *Antichrist: Two Thousand Years of the Human Fascination with Evil* (San Francisco, 1994), 80–2.

45   *Sancti Gregorii Magni. Homiliae in Hiezechielem Prophetam* 2.6.24 (*Corpus Christianorum* 142:313): "despiciamus ergo ex toto animo hoc praesens saeculum vel exstinctum; finiamus mundi desideria saltem cum fine mundi; imitemur bonorum facta quae possumus." For some other typical passages, see *Registrum* 3.29, 3.61, and 10.15; *Mor. in Job* 34.1.1;

Dialogi 3.38; etc.

46 Accounts can be found in such texts as *Moralia in Job* 9.63.95–66.106 (PL 75:910–18); and 33.20.37 (PL 76:697D–98C).

47 See PL 75:214B; the translation is from *Visions of the End*, 299, section 5, n. 2.

48 Jacques Fontaine, "L'expérience spirituelle chez Grégoire le Grand," *Revue d'histoire de la spiritualité*, 52 (1976), 152.

49 Walter Ullmann, *A Short History of the Papacy in the Middle Ages* (London, 1972), 57.

50 J. N. Hillgarth, "Eschatological and Political Concepts in the Seventh Century," *Le septième siècle: Changements et continuités. The Seventh Century: Change and Continuity*, eds Jacques Fontaine and J. N. Hillgarth (London, 1992), 220.

51 Bede's *Commentary* can be found in PL 93:129–206. On Bede's role in early medieval Apocalypse exegesis, see E. Ann Matter, "The Apocalypse in Early Medieval Exegesis," *The Apocalypse in the Middle Ages*, 39–50.

52 Henry Mayr-Harting, *The Coming of Christianity to England* (New York, 1972), 217, whose comparison between Bede and Gregory on their shared sense of the coming end gives good support to my argument (see 217–18).

53 For an introduction to Bede's writings, see George Hardin Brown, *Bede the Venerable* (Boston, 1987).

54 *De temporum ratione* 68 and 70 in *Corpus Christianorum* 123B:537–8, 539–42.

55 I am using the translation of Leo Sherley-Price, *Bede: A History of the English Church and People* (Baltimore, 1962), 247.

56 See the edition of the poem in *Corpus Christianorum* 122:439–44, of which these are lines 6–9:

> Vtpote commemorans scelerum commissa meorum,
> Et maculas vitae, mortisque inamabile tempus,
> Iudiciique diem horrendo examine magnum,
> Perpetuamque reis districti judicis iram . . .

For studies of the poem, its sources and influence, see Leslie Whitbread, "A Study of Bede's *Versus de die iudicii*," *Philological Quarterly*, 23 (1944), 193–221; and "The Sources and Literary Qualities of Bede's Doomsday Verses," *Zeitschrift für deutsches Altertum und deutsche Literatur*, 95 (1966), 258–66.

57 For a survey, see Graham D. Caie, *The Judgment Day Theme in Old English Poetry* (Copenhagen, 1976).

58 For an overview, see Dale Kinney, "The Apocalypse in Early Christian Monumental Decoration," *The Apocalypse in the Middle Ages*, 200–16.

59 On the *etimasia*, and parousiac themes in general, see Geir Hellemo, *Adventus Christi: Eschatological Thought in 4th-Century Apses and Catecheses* (Leiden, 1989).

60 On the mosaic of SS Cosma e Damiano, which dates to the pontificate of Pope Felix IV (526–30), see Ernst Kitzinger, *Byzantine Art in the Making* (London, 1977), 92–4.

61 There is certainly a distinction between the Second Coming, or Parousia, characterized by the angels blowing trumpets and the appearance of the Son of Man in the clouds with his sign (usually understood as the cross), as described in Matt. 24.29–31, and the Last Judgment itself which has the Judge seated on the throne of glory and separating the just from the unjust (Matt. 25.31–46; Apoc. 20.11–15). In later portrayals, however, these two events were often conflated.

62 The panels of Sant' Apollinare date from the time of the Ostrogothic ruler Theodoric who died in 526. For an analysis, see Kitzinger, *Byzantine Art in the Making*, 63–4. Paulinus of Nola (Letter 32.17) describes a lost apse mosaic in Fondi of *c.* 400 which showed Christ dividing the sheep from the goats, and there is also a Christian sarcophagus of *c.* 300 in the Metropolitan Museum in New York showing this division. These early renditions may have a more ethical than eschatological significance, as Theodore Klauser argues concerning the Metropolitan sarcophagus in *Jahrbuch für Antike und Christentum*, 10 (1967), 245.

63 Two useful surveys of medieval iconography of Parousia and Last Judgment are Beat Brenk, *Tradition und Neuerung in der christlichen Kunst des ersten Jahrtausands: Studien zur Geschichte des Weltgerichtsbild* (Vienna, 1966); and Yves Christe, *La vision de Matthieu (Matth. XXIV–XXV): Origines et développement d'une image de la Seconde Parousie* (Paris, 1973).

64 See, for example, the judgment from fos 219v–220r of the Pierpont Morgan Beatus as illustrated in *A Spanish Apocalypse: The Morgan Beatus Manuscript*, Introduction and Commentaries by John Williams; Codicological Analysis by Barbara A. Shailor (New York, 1991). Bede, in his *Historia Abbatum* 6, records that among the scenes of the Apocalypse that Benedict Biscop brought back from Rome to decorate his church at Jarrow was one of the Last Judgment – *extremi discrimen examinis, quasi coram oculis habentes*. These may well be distant ancestors to the Last Judgment pages to be found in the illustrated Beatus mss.

65 See Richard Krautheimer, "Introduction to an 'Iconography of Medieval Architecture'," originally written in 1942, and reprinted in his *Studies in*

Early Christian, Medieval, and Renaissance Art (New York, 1969), 115–50.

66 Emile Mâle, *The Early Churches of Rome* (London, 1960), 70–5. On the architectural relation between Santo Stefano and the Anastasis, see Krautheimer's 1935 paper, "Santo Stefano Rotondo in Rome and the Rotonda of the Holy Sepulchre in Jerusalem," *Studies*, 69–106.

67 See especially Hilary Richardson, "The Concept of the High Cross," *Irland und Europa: Ireland and Europe*, eds Proinseas Ni Chathain and Michael Richter (Stuttgart, 1983), 128–32. For more on the High Crosses, consult Nancy Edwards, "The Origins of the Free-standing Stone Cross in Ireland: Imitation or Innovation?" *The Bulletin of the Board of Celtic Studies*, 32 (1985), 393–410. The standard older account of the High Crosses remains Françoise Henry, *Irish Art during the Viking Invasions (800–1200 A.D.)* (Ithaca, 1967), ch. 5.

68 On these slabs and their dating, see Nancy Edwards, *The Archaeology of Early Medieval Ireland* (Philadelphia, 1990), 161–3; and R. B. K. Stevenson, "Notes on the Sculptures of Fahan Mura and Carndonagh, Co. Donegal," *Journal of the Royal Society for the Antiquities of Ireland*, 115 (1985), 92–5. Carndonagh, which includes the figure of Christ, was long thought to be early, but now has been redated to the ninth or tenth centuries.

69 This is clearly an illustration of the Second Coming based on Matt. 25.29–31, in which Christ appears in the heavens bearing the cross and flanked by angels blowing trumpets. Below the twelve apostles representing "all the tribes of the earth" (25.30) gaze upward in awe awaiting judgment. On this illustration, see B. Brenk, *Tradition und Neuerung*, 68–9; Y. Christe, *Vision de Matthieu*, 53–4; and J. J. G. Alexander, *Insular Manuscripts: 6th to the 9th Centuries* (London, 1978), 66–7.

70 Turin, Biblioteca Nazionale Cod. O.IV.20, f. 2a. There are descriptions in Brenk, *Tradition und Neuerung*, 69; Christe, *Vision de Matthieu*, 54; Alexander, *Insular Manuscripts*, 80–1; and especially F. Henry, *Irish Art*, 95–9.

71 For a discussion of these representations of the Last Judgment, see especially Henry, *Irish Art*, 162–75.

72 On this cross, see Robin Flower, "Irish High Crosses," *Journal of the Warburg and Courtauld Institutes*, 17 (1954), 94–5.

73 Aaron Gurevitch in his essay "The West Portal of the Church of St Lazare in Autun: The Paradoxes of the Medieval Mind," *Historical Anthropology of the Middle Ages* (Chicago, 1992), puts it well in describing the effect that the twelfth-century Autun Last Judgment was meant to convey – "imagination, moved by hope and fear, transferred the Last Judgment from the future into the present time" (p. 96). Unfortunately, Gurevitch explains this in terms of a split between the theoretical

thought of theologians and the popular mind incapable of understanding temporal progression. Whatever the differences between learned and popular approaches may have been in the early-medieval period, my argument is that the presentiality of judgment is found in the theologians too.

74 Brenk, *Tradition und Neuerung*, 43–7.

75 The Latin text is: "Iesus Christus Iudex Aequitatis. Bestiae et dracones cognoverunt in deserto Salvatorem Mundi." Much has been written about this famous object. See especially the papers in *The Ruthwell Cross*, ed. Brendan Cassiday (Princeton, 1992). For the identification of these scenes, I am following Paul Meyvaert's essay in this collection entitled "A New Perspective on the Ruthwell Cross: Ecclesia and Vita Monastica," 95–166, especially 135–8. On the relation to the Irish Crosses, see Eamonn Ó Carragain, "The Ruthwell Cross and Irish High Crosses: Some Points of Comparison and Contrast," in *Ireland and Insular Art: A.D. 500–1200*, ed. Michael Ryan (Dublin, 1987), 118–23.

76 *Carmina Sangallensia* VII:

> Ecce tubae crepitant quae mortis jura resignant,
> Crux micat in caelis, nubes praecedit et ignis.
> Hic resident summi Christo cum judice sancti
> Justificare pios, baratro damnare malignos.

As found in J. von Schlosser, *Schriftquellen zur Geschichte der karolingischen Kunst* (Vienna, 1896), no. 931, on p. 331. On these *tituli*, see Christe, *Vision de Matthieu*, 12 and 38.

77 The history of this motif has been investigated by Robert E. Lerner, "Refreshment of the Saints: The Time after Antichrist as a Station for Earthly Progress in Medieval Thought," *Traditio*, 32 (1976), 97–144.

78 The last attempt at a general review of the imperial legends, Frans Kampers' *Kaiserprophetien und Kaisersagen im Mittelalter* (Munich, 1895), is now much outdated. Paul J. Alexander contributed much to the study of the Eastern origins and development of the legends, though some of his conclusions have not survived scholarly scrutiny. Of special importance are his "Byzantium and the Migration of Literary Works and Motifs: The Legend of the Last Roman Emperor," *Mediaevalia et Humanistica*, n.s. 2 (1971), 47–82; and *The Byzantine Apocalyptic Tradition* (Berkeley, 1985). A number of selections from the relevant texts and discussions can be found in my *Visions of the End*, especially sections 1, 7, 10, 15, 16, 20, 30, 31, and 33. See also my *Antichrist*, ch. 4.

79 There is still no critical edition of the whole Syriac text, but a translation from one ms. can be found in Alexander, *Byzantine Apocalyptic Tradition*,

36–51. On the dating, I follow G. J. Reinink, "Pseudo-Methodius und die Legende vom Römischen Endkaiser," *Use and Abuse of Eschatology in the Middle Ages*, 82–111.

80 On the relation between the Pseudo-Methodius and Christian attitudes toward Jerusalem and the Holy Land, see Robert L. Wilken, *The Land Called Holy: Palestine in Christian History and Thought* (New Haven, 1992), ch. 12.

81 On the a posteriori function of apocalypticism, see *Visions of the End*, 28–36.

82 Alexander the Great had already acquired a function in Christian views of the end through the legend of his enclosure of the twenty-two unclean nations behind brass gates until the time of their coming forth before the end of the world; see *Visions of the End*, section 3, for a brief introduction, and especially the detailed study of Andrew Runni Anderson, *Alexander's Gate, Gog and Magog, and the Enclosed Nations* (Cambridge, Mass., 1932).

83 These passages are from the Syriac text, using Alexander's translation in *Byzantine Apocalyptic Tradition*, 48–9. For a translation of the Latin version, see *Visions of the End*, 75.

84 Alexander tr., 50. The reason for this, as the text itself explains slightly earlier, is so that the Cross will be present in heaven with Christ at the time of his return.

85 For a translation and study of Adso's *Letter*, see *Apocalyptic Spirituality*, 81–96.

86 Ingeborg Bachmann, *Wir mussen wahre Satze finden: Gespräche und Interviews* (Munich, 1983). I am using the translation of Gabriele Annan from her review of Bachmann's work entitled "From the Eternal War," *New York Review of Books* (March 5, 1992), 12.

5

Pattern and Purpose in History in the Later Medieval and Renaissance Periods

Marjorie Reeves

In the early thirteenth century the ground-plan of history and the expectations concerning future time built upon it were still largely conceived in Augustinian terms of Seven Ages analogous to the Seven Days of Creation, culminating in a Sabbath Age.[1] Augustine had placed this Seventh Age outside the time process, affirming that the climax of history had already taken place in the Incarnation and that what remained of the time process was simply a period of watchfulness, repentance and soul-garnering, lived under the shadow of impending Judgement. There was no room for further revelation or for any idea of 'progress' within history: the blessed Sabbath was the rest of the saints beyond time. But already in 1200 a new perspective was beginning to interact fruitfully with this inherited and inherently pessimistic pattern in the imaginations of many thinkers. The Abbot Joachim of Fiore, who died in 1202, had expounded his vision of a progressive Trinitarian pattern in history – 'given' to him by the *spiritualis intellectus* – in a number of works which were already circulating in Western Europe.[2] His threefold pattern acted as a catalyst for aspirations, already moving in the eleventh and twelfth centuries, towards a more positive expectation of the Church's achievement in the Last Age. This scheme, with its development through the stages (*status*) of Law and Grace to a future Age of Illumination in the Spirit, was in essence non-Augustinian, since it gave a purpose to the time process itself in a progressive movement towards a further spiritual climax within history.

But the Abbot, like his contemporaries, accepted the traditional concept of Seven Ages and lived in the shadow of the Last Things,
believing that the appearance of the worst Antichrist was imminent.
The Church's pilgrimage through the wilderness towards the splendid
Promised Land of the *Ecclesia Spiritualis* was marked by tribulation
milestones and multiple Antichrists, reaching a climax in the manifestation of a double Antichrist at the end of the Sixth Age (symbolized
in the crossing of Jordan). Again, while breaking with Augustinian
tradition by bringing the Seventh, Sabbath Age, into history, he accepted the imperfection of all earthly achievement and expected a
deterioration in the Seventh Age or Third *Status*, which would be
closed by a final Antichrist, leading immediately to the Last Judgement.
The Seventh Age must always be distinguished from the Eighth of
eternal blessedness. Thus the view of historical purpose offered by
Joachim at the beginning of the thirteenth century was characterized
by a blend of the traditional pessimistic pattern with a new, more
positive expectation of transition to an age of human fructification
preceding End-time. However, throughout the period under review,
what may be roughly termed the Augustinian and the Joachimist views
of Last Things existed side by side, in opposition or in interaction.

In the first half of the thirteenth century the popular reputation of
Joachim in general stressed his role as a prophet of Antichrist, while the
full implications of his Trinitarian doctrine were not yet perceived. But
recently Dr Fiona Robb has pointed us to evidence that already by
1203 the Abbot's Trinitarian expositions were being studied in the
highest ecclesiastical circles:[3] a letter of Pope Innocent III to Jean des
Bellesmains, former Archbishop of Lyons, specifically draws on the
writings and *figurae* of Joachim. The channel of communication was
probably Ranier of Ponza, a disciple of Joachim who had close links
with the Pope. This Papal letter, while showing an astonishing affinity
with Joachim's approach to the mystery of the Trinity, only touches in
one phrase the concept of progressive revelation which stems from
Joachim's doctrine. But Dr Robb directs us to another letter of 1203
by Ranier to Arnald-Amaury, the General of the Cistercian Order, in
which he uses the whole range of Joachim's historical typology and
number symbolism, including the pattern of threes, to point to the
prophetic role of St Bernard and the Cistercian Order in relation to the
Age of the Spirit. Interpreters of Innocent III's policies now see him as
forward-looking in his handling of change and new initiatives in the

Church, especially in the formation of new types of religious order. It may be that he was open to the influence of Joachim's prophecies concerning 'new spiritual men' to lead the Church into the Third *Status*. Ranier's letter certainly points to the key role of the religious in this latest age: 'God spoke through Moses and Aaron in the order of laity, through Peter and Paul in the order of clergy, and in these latest days he has spoken through the order of monks.'[4]

'In these latest days': phrases such as this recur in thirteenth-century writings, signalling the general sense of crisis in an age which felt itself to be on the threshold of End-time.[5] The theme struck home particularly in the new religious orders where fervent members believed they had been called to a special vocation in the latest age. This could take the orthodox form of a new urgency to renew the apostolic life and fulfil the Gospel prophecy that the whole world must be converted before the End. Thus the Franciscan missionary drive was largely fuelled by the assumption of this prophetic role. As early as 1216 Jacques de Vitry observed that 'in the twilight of this world' God had sent the Friars Minor to renew the apostolic life before the advent of Antichrist.[6] Their mission carried them to the fringes of Europe and beyond, whence they sent back rumours of the forces of Gog and Magog massing behind the legendary Gate of Alexander in the Caucasus. There was a widely current belief that when 'the Roman Empire' failed any longer to hold back the barbarian menace, then the final tribulation would engulf Christendom. Roger Bacon responded to these rumours by urging the Church to pay attention to the warnings of the prophets and the signs of the times.[7] In the mid-century William of St Amour, Master in the University of Paris, declared that 'we are now close to the perils of the latest times before the coming of Antichrist'.[8]

But this pessimistic scenario was shot through with gleams from the Joachimist vision of the Age of the Spirit, that is, the fulfilment of the Trinitarian pattern within history which Joachim had placed between the greatest tribulation of the Church and the winding up of the *saeculum*. His prophecies of the new spiritual men to lead into this Third *Status* and the *ordo monachorum* or *contemplativoum* which would embody the quintessence of its new life, offered a positive and thrilling role to those members of religious orders who looked for a break-through into a new life. Among Fransciscans the explicit parallel drawn between Christ's advent and that of Francis seems to imply a

Trinitarian pattern: as the Second *Status* came to fruition in the Incarnation, so the appearance of Francis heralds transition to the third. This interpretation is reinforced by the high authority accorded to Francis's Rule and Testament, elevated to a position as inviolable as the Scriptures. Only one Friar Minor apparently carried these claims to the logical and dangerous extreme of claiming that the authority of the church of the Second *Status* had now passed to the leaders of the *Ecclesia Spiritualis* and that of the Scriptures had been superseded by the Eternal Evangel, i.e. the works of Joachim.[9] The scandal created by Gerard of Borgo San Donnino in Paris in 1254/5 effectively silenced the extreme Joachites, but the essential element in the Joachimist programme of crucial and positive roles to be played in the Last Age by human agencies touched many imaginations and formed an effective counterpoise to negative expectations of direct supernatural intervention. Thus St Bonaventure, while obliged to discipline the extreme Joachites, caught the vision of a further stage of spiritual illumination, a seraphic state to which St Francis had attained and to which his Order aspired.[10] The scholastic Petrus Ioannis Olivi interpreted the conflicts of his own day in apocalyptic terms of the 'carnal' against the 'true' church of the age to come.[11] At the other end of the spectrum the Apostolic Brethren claimed the role of the new spiritual men,[12] while inquisitorial records show Olivi's humbler followers witnessing to their expectation of the Third *Status* and their own role in defending the flame of spiritual illumination.[13]

In Provence and Catalonia groups of Franciscan tertiaries and others, loosely termed Beguins, clung to their belief that they held the key to the Last Age.[14] Similarly, in Italy, Fraticelli were scattered throughout Tuscany and Umbria, eventually seeking refuge in the Kingdom of the Two Sicilies. Driven out of the Church by persecution, they developed a concept of the 'saving remnant': in the imminent onslaught of Antichrist the larger part of the Church would apostatize and be destroyed; only the faithful remnant would enter the blessed third age beyond. They saw themselves as gathered in the frail bark of the true church, the Noah's Ark of the Last Age, piloted to safety by St Francis, Olivi and Joachim through the 'deluge' of false Christians and Antichrists.[15]

Side by side with this new expectation inspired by the vision of the *Ecclesia Spiritualis* in the Last Age, the traditional negative reaction to the certain advent of Antichrist and Last Judgement remains strong.

Every representation of the Last Judgement in churches kept this
scenario alive in the imagination. In 1260 the Flagellant movement
which swept through Italy, thence spreading to France and Germany,
encapsulated in a particular crisis this mood of terror.[16] Here there is an
anomaly. The year 1260 was particularly associated in Joachimist nu-
merology with the transition from the Second to the Third *Status*. Yet
the actions of the Flagellants seem to express only terrified penitence in
expectation of an imminent End and the many chronicle accounts of
the movement show no Joachimist traits. The voice of the Flagellants
is heard rather in the great *Dies Irae* hymn which takes final shape in
this period:

> Day of anger, day of terror,
> All shall crumble into ashes
> Witness David with the Sybil.
> What a tremor shall assail them
> When the judge shall come to judgement,
> Shattering all at once asunder.
> Sounds the Trump with awful note
> Through the tombs of deathly region . . .[17]

In general, there seems always to be a certain ambivalence between
expectation of the Age of the Spirit and certainty of catastrophic Last
Things. Even for Joachim the Trinitarian pattern stands in relationship
with the seven tribulations of a double-seven pattern in which the
Church must suffer as Israel once did.

It was precisely such waves of hysterical religious emotion that the
Church sought to curb. Although living in the shadow of Domesday
induced a salutary penitence in the faithful, they were forbidden to
seek by calculations and 'signs' to determine the advent of Antichrist or
the Day of Judgement. Christ's injunction: 'It is not for you to know
the times and the seasons which the Father hath put in his own power'
(Acts 1.7) was the key text used to stifle all such speculation. At the
end of the thirteenth century a heated academic debate arose at Paris
and Oxford on the legitimacy of speculating on the approach of Last
Things. This was sparked off by Arnold of Villanova's tract *De Tempore
Adventus Antichristi*[18] in which he produced a number of academic
arguments in defence of such calculations. Henry of Harclay, Chancel-
lor of Oxford University, led the opposition in a weighty *Quaestio:
Utrum Astrologi vel Quicumque Calculatores possint probare Secundum*

Adventum Christi [Whether it is possible for astrologers or any other calculators to determine the time of Christ's Second Coming].[19] In 1310 Nicholas of Lyra wrote a *Quodlibet: Utrum possimus scire an Antichristus sit natus vel non natus adhuc* [Whether it is possible for us to know that Antichrist is already born or not yet born].[20] Perhaps the Dominican John Quidort (John of Paris) represents the position of many in his *Tractatus de Antichristo*, beginning conventionally with 'It is not for you to know . . .', but gathering prophecies and calculations which pointed to the conclusion that the world was nearing its end.[21]

Arnold's clash with the scholastics pin-points the contrast between academic debate and passionate involvement in the expectation of Last Things. He grew increasingly radical, becoming the focus in Catalonia for groups of 'Beguins' and tertiaries who expected revolutionary change. From his house he published tracts for the times in Catalan and collected prophecies in his library.[22] His message for the faithful was to be vigilant and watchful, guarding the treasure of the future while waiting for the imminent crisis. This attitude is still apparent in a mid-fourteenth-century tract produced by a Catalonian group, entitled *Summula seu breviloquium super concordia Novi et Veteris Testamenti* [Summary or précis of the concord of the New and Old Testaments].[23] This updates Joachim's pattern of the generations of history, prophesying immediate and violent political tribulations and multiple Antichrists. Existing authorities, secular and ecclesiastical, will be finally overthrown and the period of blessedness will be reached under a new Zorobabel who will unite the crown and the crook. Significantly, the essence of the new age is expressed as highest evangelical poverty rather than as further spiritual illumination.

It was possibly in Arnold's circle or in a connected group in Provence that the famous *Vaticinia de summis pontificibus* [Prophecies concerning the supreme pontiffs] first appeared.[24] Whatever their provenance – and the current debate remains unresolved – they embody an early fourteenth-century expectation that a worldly papacy would be transformed in the Last Age by a succession of Angelic Popes (or a single one). These prophecies derive from a Byzantine model, the so-called 'Oracles of Leo the Wise', a series of fifteen enigmatic prophecies of emperors, each consisting of a symbolic *figura*, a caption and a short text. The transition from a violent political regime to a new life blessed by angels occurs about two-thirds of the way through the series. The latest scholar to work on the Leo Oracles, Dr Vereecken, does not believe they were originally set in the context of Last Things, but as appropriated by their Western adaptors, who substituted popes for emperors, they became essentially a part of the drama of End-time.[25] This drama calls for a radical break in the papal succession. The electors are summoned by a divine voice to seek the hermit among the rocks as the next pope. In the Last Age the ideals of poverty and contemplation must be enthroned. But in this prophetic sequence the visionaries found a way of uniting traditional authority with radical change: it is still the chair of St Peter to which the Angelic Pope is summoned and the historic authority of the Latin Church remains unbroken to the end of the times.

There can be no doubt that, in one way or another, the Angelic Pope figure occupied an important place on the stage of End-time throughout the fourteenth, fifteenth and first half of the sixteenth centuries. As a counterpoise to the ubiquitous Antichrist figure, it embodied the hope of an era of positive achievement within history before time ran out. In the mid-fourteenth century a second series of fifteen Pope Prophecies was produced, probably in a Florentine milieu. This features a traditional climax in the advent of Antichrist, but it is significant that when the first sequence of fifteen ran out with Urban VI, the two series were put together with the later series placed first, so that the Antichrist symbol fell harmlessly in the middle and the full series of thirty still reached its climax in the Angelic figures. This was the prophetic text which achieved such popularity in the Renaissance period. A second eschatological figure, that of a Last World Emperor, with a history going back to seventh-century Syria,[26] stems in the first instance from the older, negative pattern of history. A great emperor will arise who will conquer many lands, hold back the barbarians and provide a temporary era of peace and prosperity. But at the rumour of Antichrist's appearance he will surrender his office and his spirit to God, for only divine intervention can win the final conflict with evil. In the later Middle Ages, however, this classic account of the final collapse of earthly authority becomes tinged with the colours of a positive Joachimist role in the Last Age. Some pro-Hohenstaufen propaganda takes on this colour. It is impossible to say how far Frederick II really arrogated to himself a messianic role, but the deliberate parallel he makes between Bethlehem and his own birth-place, Jesi, adapting the words of the prophet Micah to himself, certainly carries the overtones of a new saviour in the third age.[27] Again, Pierre Dubois, in his propaganda for Philip IV's proposed crusade, uses the image of a Second Charlemagne.[28] At this very moment a small prophetic text, known as the *Liber de Flore* and associated with the Pope Prophecies, envisages a blessed partnership between an Angelic Pope and a French Emperor in the work of bringing the whole world into one sheepfold under one shepherd.[29] Whether regarded merely as a useful propaganda tool or as embodying a serious and final purpose, the assumption of an eschatological role was a powerful instrument.

The course of events in the last decades of the fourteenth century and the early fifteenth century lent themselves most aptly to interpretations heralding the final cosmic conflict between good and evil. It is possible that the very length of the Great Schism, due to the obstinacy with which contending popes stuck to their roles, owed its bitterness to the eschatological backdrop against which the drama was played out. In the Joachimist programme the great tribulation at the end of the sixth age featuring the concept of a double Antichrist – false pope and wicked tyrant – had already been developed. In 1378 an unknown Calabrian Joachite, Telesphorus of Cosenza, produced a prophetic scenario which gained wide attention because of its contemporary relevance.[30] A Satanic agent would arise masquerading as the emperor and would elect for himself a false pope. In the ensuing conflict the true, Angelic Pope and his faithful servant, the French king, would be finally victorious after great tribulations. Then, in a blessed partnership, they would initiate the Sabbath Age of peace and harmony.

Associated with Telesphorus's *libellus* was a Second Charlemagne prophecy which sketched a triumphant programme for a great French king culminating in his coronation as emperor by an angel.[31] But the period of the Schism also called forth disillusioned and pessimistic responses. Henry of Langenstein, Vice-Chancellor of the University of Vienna, was initially captured by the Joachimist programme and in 1390, in an Ascension Day sermon before the whole university, accorded high praise to Joachim for his methods of predicting Last Things. There is, however, a note of defence against critics in his championship, and two years later he had made a complete volte-face, launching a violent attack against Telesphorus of Cosenza, Joachim and all such recent prophets.[32] The bitterness of this tract conveys a mood of extreme disillusionment: the world is ageing, the Church is declining from its meridian, charity is failing, the prophets of *renovatio* have deceived us. Similarly, in the fifteenth century Jacobus de Paradiso in a tract, *De Septem Statibus Ecclesie* . . . [Concerning the Seven Ages of the Church], declares that it is impossible for the Church to be reformed by human agents: 'I believe therefore that the world will go on declining into evil ways, down to the depths of wickedness, until the Son of Perdition appears.'[33]

If theological debate in academic circles turned largely on the legitimacy of seeking to predict the events of End-time, it was in ardent circles of devout religious people that the debate concerning expected roles in the last drama continued unabated in the last part of the period we are considering. In 1378 a circulating prophecy in Florence gives evidence of a Fraticelli group still active in Tuscany. Here the Roman Church is utterly condemned as the New Babylon, but a '*papa santo incoronato dagli angioli*' [a holy pope crowned by the angels] is shortly to be expected.[34] Much more orthodox, yet still concerned with the prophetic future were the discussions in the circle at Santo Spirito, the Augustinian convent at Florence. Here the letters of the Vallombrosan hermit, Giovanni delle Celle, disclose a sense of urgency in reading the signs of the times. Giovanni anxiously studies the Beast which is the final *figura* in the second series of Pope Prophecies: 'This beast is Antichrist, and truly someone has said to me that it should be another pope: hence on this matter one of two things must be true: either the book that I saw is corrupt or someone has added his own interpretation; and so the outcome remains to be seen.'[35] Manuscript sources in Florence show that an undercurrent of expectation concerning Antichrist and *renovatio mundi* under an Angelic Pope continued in the fifteenth century, providing fertile ground for Savonarola's message. In 1399 a widespread movement of penitent groups known as *Bianchi* swept through northern Italy, calling forth emotional outbursts focused on the final drama to be played out in Rome, where a new pope would appear *c.*1400 and there would be peace and mercy in all the world.[36]

In the fifteenth century Venice became a centre for prophetic expectations – perhaps because of the famous legend associating Joachim with mosaics in San Marco.[37] Here *c.*1454 Domenico Mauroceno compiled a book of prophetic excerpts and requested a Dominican, Fr Rusticianus, to select, abbreviate and arrange this material. Its core was the *libellus* of Telesphorus and the surviving copy was one made by a certain Andreas at St Cyprian's monastery from an exemplar at S. Georgio Maggiore. So interest in Telesphorus's programme of schism and *renovatio* under Angelic Pope and French Emperor was widespread in Venice, no doubt partly because the compiler managed to introduce a special role for the Venetian fleet in support of the 'good' forces when the cosmic battle between schismatic and true popes and emperors is fought out. Mauroceno's concern with prophecy was known outside Venice. Writing to him in 1495 from Florence, Pietro Delphino, General of the Camaldosi, reports a visit of the scholar, Zenobius Accaiuoli, bringing him prophecies which included one on the Angelic Pope. So now Delphino asks Mauroceno to send him a copy of the *papalista* (i.e. the Pope Prophecies) which is in his possession.[38] It was a manuscript close to the St Cyprian copy which was used in 1516 by an Augustinian hermit, Silvestro Meuccio, for the first of a series of Joachimist publications from Venice which included Joachim's three main works.[39] There is earlier evidence in this Order of an interest in Joachim's prophecy of new spiritual men, but now the great role of the expected reforming hermit order is openly claimed for the Augustinians.[40] Silvestro's prefaces to these editions show us a devout group studying the prophecies, seeking to read the signs of the times and waiting for the certain crisis. Even their humanist General, Egidio of Viterbo, revealed his concern with apocalyptic expectation by urging Silvestro to publish Joachim's *Expositio in Apocalypsim*.[41]

The political dimension of prophecy in the fifteenth and sixteenth centuries raises interesting, but often insoluble, problems of motivation. Did rulers and politicians ever seriously set their ambitions and strategies within the context of End-time or did they simply regard the heightened images of prophecy as useful for rhetorical and diplomatic purposes? Did these images actually influence political reactions or responses? In the mid-fifteenth century a significant little episode points up these questions. By this time, we recall, there were on the prophetic stage two types of ruler: the wicked chastiser and the 'good' ruler who would restore the Church and inaugurate the blessed age. For the Italian/French school of prophecy the expected wicked chastiser would be a Frederick III. So when in 1453 the actual Frederick III appeared in Rome to be crowned many asked if he was that terrible tyrant and did not know whether to run away or stay. Aeneas Silvius Piccolomini tells us that Pope Nicholas V himself was in two minds:

'he was both frightened and hopeful; on the one hand he feared to relinquish his power, on the other he coveted the glory of crowning Caesar.'[42] Entertaining him, the Pope reportedly taxed Frederick directly with his evil prophetic role, to which Frederick replied: 'My intention towards the Church of God is good and right; if God wishes to ordain otherwise concerning me or through me, in Him lies the power, who alone knows all things, to arrange matters according to his righteous will.'[43]

The element of fatalism in Frederick's answer appears again in the next great prophetic crisis in Italy. In the Florence of Savonarola there was a strange mingling of prophetic currents.[44] The friar himself drew on biblical and orthodox medieval sources for his proclamation of imminent chastisement for Florence, Rome and Italy. But he also drew on the Joachimist vision of the blessed age to follow. Here medieval concepts of the Sabbath Age and Third *Status* become fused with the cyclical pattern of the returning Golden Age belonging to the classical tradition. On the eve of the upheaval in Florence, the Platonists were looking for the *plenitudo temporum*, yet were assailed by fears of Antichrist. In 1492 Marsilio Ficino proclaimed in a famous letter the arrival of the Golden Age as manifested in the burgeoning arts, the flowering of humane letters and the invention of printing.[45] Yet when Savonarola sounded forth the solemn knell of imminent woe, members of the Platonic Academy became his penitents, the *piagnone*. These included Pico della Mirandola and Giovanni Nesi, who in 1496 published the *Oracolo de novo saeculo* in which catastrophe and renewal are juxtaposed in a strange mixture of Neoplatonism, occult mysteries and medieval prophecy.[46] His vision is of a Florentine New Jerusalem which fuses the Joachimist Age of the Spirit with the classical Age of Gold.

The conjunction of Savonarola's prediction of approaching chastisement with the advent of Charles VIII's invading army struck a note of fatalistic terror in Florentine hearts. Charles VIII himself probably believed in his eschatological role, having been primed with Second Charlemagne prophecies in which the destruction of Florence and Rome formed part of the expected programme.[47] Florence opened its gates to the French king in the hope that cooperation with the prophetic agent would avert disaster. In the history of Charles's ill-fated expedition we meet the type of situation that recurs in the following years. On the one hand, few politicians are strong-minded enough to snap their fingers at the prophets: they half believe that the programme to be carried out by divinely appointed agents is inevitable. On the other hand, they set busily to work – as the Papacy did in the case of Charles VIII – to defeat that programme by all possible subtleties of diplomacy and manœuvres of armies. The prophets, of course, were always defeated, but the politicians could never wholly dismiss them.

Certainly in the Renaissance Italy of the early sixteenth century the prophetic figures of End-time were stalking the land. While the pessimistic note was struck by wild hermits who ran through the cities announcing the advent of Antichrist,[48] optimism was rekindled by a strange text known as the *Apocalypsis Nova*, brought to light under mysterious circumstances, which declared that the future Angelic Pope was already present, though undetected, in Rome.[49] This book, attributed to the Blessed Amadeus de Silva, is in the form of conversations with an angelic being in which the messages concerning the expected pope form part of a series of curious theological disquisitions. But it was this prophetic announcement that stirred up such widespread interest and popularized the *Apocalypsis Nova*. How far did it create aspirants to this role and influence their purposes? A notable but enigmatic case is that of Cardinal Carvajal, who was one of the chief actors involved in bringing the book to light.[50] He has generally been interpreted by historians as an ambitious, worldly ecclesiastic who failed in his main aim of becoming pope. On this view his promotion of the schismatic Council of Pisa (1511–12) is seen as a step towards the achievement of his ambition. But his concern with prophecy and the 'signs' of End-time in the contemporary world had already found detailed expression in a lengthy homily of 1508 and at least one contemporary affirmed that he believed himself called to the Angelic role, while he retained for his own use the original copy of the *Apocalypsis Nova*. There is further evidence of his championship of reform in the Church and his protection of religious groups with a prophetic orientation. The collapse of the desperate Pisan manœuvre brought him low and his final hope of the tiara was dashed when Adrian VI was elected in 1522. Yet, even so, in a speech of welcome to Adrian, he still turned to prophecy, calling on the new pope to take up the prophetic role and inaugurate the age of reform. Carvajal comes across as an actor against the backcloth of End-time, 'driven by prophetic visions that often seemed to assign to himself a major role in

their fulfilment'.[51] Associated with Carvajal in summoning the Council
of Pisa was Cardinal Guillaume Briçonnet. Clearly, French support for
the schismatic council was in part politically driven but, again, a
mixture of motives emerges, for the Briçonnet family was well known
for its involvement in the circles of the French *préreforme*. Guillaume's
brother Denis belonged to the religious coterie, the *Eterna Sapienza*,
which centred round the Milanese nun, Archangela Panigarola.[52] Possibly already before the Council of Pisa, Denis Briçonnet was ac-
quainted with the *Apocalypsis Nova* and certainly by *c.*1514 the Angelic
Pope had become one of the main themes of prophetic expectation in
the *Eterna Sapienza* society.

The intertwining of prophecy and politics is manifest throughout
Leo X's pontificate. Did the pope himself give any credence to the
expected Angelical? It has been suggested that at one stage he did cast
himself in this role and it was probably claimed for him by more
than one contemporary. But to a Medici pope, scheming to keep the
papal succession in his own family, the power of the prophets was a
menace, a destabilizing influence to be suppressed. A portrait of the
saintly Cardinal Sauli by Sebastiano del Piombo, dated 1516, has
recently been interpreted as conveying by various symbols the message
that he was destined to be the future Angelic Pope.[53] But in 1517
Sauli was inexplicably accused of being involved in a conspiracy against
Leo X. He was imprisoned and died shortly after his release. The
suggestion – hinted at by a contemporary – is that Leo felt threatened
because he heard that the prophecy was being applied to Sauli.
Professor Jungić, who has advanced this interpretation, further
links Raphael's famous portrait of Leo X (dated 1517–18) with the
Sauli portrait and hazards the guess that Raphael, in appropriating
symbols from Piombo, is presenting Leo himself as a possible Angelic
Pope.[54]

The prophets certainly caused much trouble to the politicians in the
early sixteenth century. The memory of Savonarola was still strong
among his disciples: the first half of his prophetic programme (chastisement) had been fulfilled but the second part (*renovatio mundi*) was still
expected. This sparked off several disturbances by claimants to
the Angelic role. In a visit to Florence in 1516 Leo X attempted to
stifle these radical elements by getting a formal condemnation of
Savonarola's doctrine on a provincial council.[55] Instead, he drew a
surprising defence of the friar's essential doctrine from several respected

theologians, including Contarini. The prophetic and eschatological expectations of the age might be menacing but they could not be dismissed. Leo's further attempts to suppress the prophets led to the appointment of a commission in the Fifth Lateran Council to formulate guidelines for the control of apocalyptic preachers and prophets. Learned ecclesiastics in the Council were certainly anxious to check popular forms of seeking to predict the future by divination, astrology, dreams, personal revelation and so forth. Yet, as Professor Minnich has written, 'The twelve homilists who addressed the Lateran Council often wrapped themselves in the mantle of a prophet. They claimed that the Church was in its last age . . . and that God would punish Christendom if the Council failed to bring about a reformation . . . On the horizon, however, was dawning a new age. Let the Council purify the Church and usher in the glorious End-times.'[56] Minnich analyses the outlook of key members involved in drawing up the decree *Supernae majestatis praesidio* (1516) to regulate preaching, showing how seriously they took the function of prophecy in these last days.[57] The decree, while singling out abuses for condemnation and imposing limits on apocalyptic preachers, confirmed the true role of the prophet. 'Thus Renaissance prophecy, with its abuses condemned and its preachers controlled, but with its legitimacy formally acknowledged, passed into the legislation of the universal Church on the very eve of the Reformation.'[58]

The most striking example of a highly placed Renaissance churchman whose outlook was governed by eschatological expectation was Cardinal Egidio of Viterbo, General of the Augustinian hermits, humanist scholar, member of the commission on prophecy, yet famous for his apocalyptic preaching. In his vision of the future the two currents of classical myth and medieval prophecy mingled. He responded enthusiastically to the idea of a returning Golden Age, yet his sermons constantly gave solemn warning of the approaching Last Things. The two fundamentally incompatible patterns of history – cyclical and linear – are strangely held together here. The juxtaposition of the two is vividly illustrated in a celebratory sermon delivered at St Peter's before Julius II in 1506. It was inspired by news of Portuguese conquests in the Far East. Apostrophizing the Pope, Egidio exclaims: 'We have spoken of the golden age . . . Therefore now act, most blessed father. See how God calls you by so many voices, so many prophecies, so many deeds well done.' Then he makes a striking connection between the famous Virgilian oracle 'Iam redit et virgo, redeunt Saturnia regna' [Now the Virgin returns, the reign of Saturn returns] and Old Testament prophecy. To read correctly the great contemporary happenings one must above all turn to the sacred text: *Scrutamini scripturas.*[59]

Strands from classical mythology, neo-Platonism, Hebrew cabbalism and biblical prophecy are woven together in Egidio's vast *Historia Viginti Saeculorum*, finished in 1519,[60] which has been described as the 'storia assoluta della umanite sub specie aeternitatis'. It is striking that here he breaks away from both classical and medieval patterns of history to shape his own double pattern of ten ages before and ten after the Incarnation, based on the cabbalist mounting scale to ten, the perfect number. But the tension between the optimistic and pessimistic outlooks, between interpreting history as mounting to a climax or declining from pristine perfection is once again evident here, for Egidio also uses the descending scale of ages symbolized by metals which he derived from both the Book of Daniel and Hesiod. Nevertheless, the concords between pre- and post-Incarnational history reveal a progressive movement towards a final apotheosis of the Church in the tenth (or twentieth) age. In a fascinating way Egidio uses a double pattern of 'signs' from classical legend and history (including Etruria) and from Old Testament *figurae*, to trace the gradual fulfilment of God's design. Psalm 19 prophesies the opening out of divine purpose in the ninth (or nineteenth) age: verse four, 'Their sound has gone forth to all the earth', wonderfully points to the newly discovered lands, east and west, while Julius II is likened to the giant of verse five who rejoices to run the course, since he has promoted the glory of Rome in so many ways. So Egidio moves to his expected climax of history in the tenth or twentieth age. All the signs point to Leo X as the first pontiff of the dawning Golden Age. He bears the sacred number and the mystical name of Leo; the family name Medici signifies the curer of wounds and the laurel associated with his grandfather Lorenzo the Magnificent symbolizes the glories of the age. All the aspects of the new age are now coming together: a new understanding of the Scriptures and a new blossoming of rhetoric, poetry and the arts; new reform of the Church in doctrine and morals; the opening up of new worlds before amazed eyes. Christians are now called to achieve the conversion of all humanity and to bring all peoples into one sheepfold before the End. The inner harmony of all knowledge and the outer unity of all races are coming together: *plenitudo temporum, plenitudo gentium, plenitudo doctrinae.* The irony of such a prophecy in the year 1519 needs no underlining.

At first sight it seems impossible to connect this ecstatic vision with the *realpolitik* of sixteenth-century Europe. Yet prophecies formed part of the diplomatic currency in circulation here also. The Second Charlemagne walks again. When the Emperor Maximilian I married Mary of Burgundy, French and German prophetic traditions were brought together and their conjunction was hailed in the *Prognosticatio* of Johann Lichtenberger and various pamphlets.[61] It came to fruition in Maximilian's grandson, Charles. Prophecies even invaded the Imperial election chamber in 1519, but already in 1517 Charles's imperial chancellor-to-be, Gattinara, was exhorting Charles, by then King of Spain, to take up his destined role as victor over the Saracens and inaugurator of the final world *monarchia christianorum.*[62] In the heady moment of the Imperial election not only Gattinara but others in Charles's entourage were gripped by 'the elation of prophetic, providential mythology associated with the Emperor of the Last Days . . . The currency of such thinking is strikingly evident in high places at this time.'[63] It is impossible to know how far Charles himself was influenced by this prophetic image but the actual shaping of events in the contest for control of Italy between Charles V and Francis I of France was interpreted by contemporaries on the two levels of political reality and prophetic meaning. This emerges clearly in the aftermath of the imperial victory at Pavia in 1525. Gattinara himself had by this time shed the language of eschatology but he still pressed upon Charles a larger-than-life role in urging him to reform the Church, extirpate heresy and recover Jerusalem. In 1526 Valdés, a secretary in the imperial chancellery, speaking for Gattinara in a report on the results of Pavia, identified the Spaniards as the elect people of God and interpreted the victory as releasing Charles to recover the empire of Constantinople, to retake the Holy Sepulchre at Jerusalem and to fulfil the Saviour's words 'Fiet unum ovile et unus pastor' [There shall be one sheepfold and one shepherd].[64] At the same moment a Franciscan in Rome, Pietro Galatino, was 'reading' the prophetic future in Joachimist terms: Charles and Francis would be reconciled, Charles would lead a united force triumphantly against the last great menacing army of Turks and the 'Pastore Angelico' would inaugurate the reign of the Spirit in an age of new spiritual understanding and universal preaching. The immediacy with which this programme is expected is astonishing: 'iam, iam in januis esse creditur' [now, now it is believed to be on the threshhold].[65]

But there was always the possibility that the forces of evil would prove too much for the prophets of a Golden Age. Even Egidio ended his history on a sober note. After the prophetic euphoria of 1525 the scene darkens rapidly and Italy becomes rife with dire predictions, rumours of portents and dreadful monstrosities, menacing preachers of Antichrist. According to André Chastel, between 1520 and 1530 fifty-six known authors were concerned with prophecy and astrology and 133 pamphlets on such themes were published in Italy.[66] Thus it is not surprising that the immediate political realities which led to the Sack of Rome in 1527 became engulfed, as it were, in a huge apocalyptic image of disaster. 'Some kind of underlying determinism seemed to control this sequence of fortuitous events.'[67] Writing from Rome in the midst of the terrible happenings, Cardinal Gonzaga declared: 'our Father in heaven wants to scourge Christianity', and later: 'All this did not happen by chance but through divine justice. For there were more than ample warnings.'[68] But afterwards with astonishing rapidity the old prophetic pattern of *renovatio* to follow chastisement was resurrected. The harlot Rome had indeed fallen, fulfilling the fate of New Babylon in the Apocalypse, but Rome the New Jerusalem would rise again. Even Clement VII's escape from the Castel San Angelo is now interpreted as a miracle. In the following confused period the hard realities of the political struggle are again masked by the resurrection of those apparently enduring medieval images of World Emperor and Angelic Pope. In the early 1530s the old oracles are revived in a new cluster of prophetic publications.

It was in 1530 that Clement wrote urgently to Egidio of Viterbo asking him to seek the meaning of these cataclysmic events. Egidio responded with his final work *Scechina* (1532), that is, 'the habitation of God with men'.[69] Although concerned largely with the new mystical understanding of the Scriptures through the cabbala, there is also a strong dimension of political prophecy in the work, which is dedicated to Charles V. If the warnings of the divine voice are not heeded further scourges will fall on Rome, but on the other side of the coin Charles's role is still to be the new Moses leading the human race to liberty, the new Caesar to conquer the barbarians, the new David to gather all peoples into one sheepfold. Emperor and Pope are called into the old holy alliance of prophecy. 'Now is the propitious time of which the prophets speak; now you, the new prince, are called to celebrate "the Kalends" and to renew the earth's orb.'[70]

Apart from one surprising work from a Viennese professor as late as 1547,[71] Egidio's *Scechina* is, in many respects, the last great statement of a powerful medieval tradition. There were certainly scattered echoes in the following centuries, but in many ways expectations of the Last Age take other forms or are marginalized. A drama of tribulation and renovation played out by larger than life, yet human, characters in the last act of history could only perhaps spring from the imagination of a medieval Christendom.

NOTES

1   See R. Lerner, 'The Medieval Return to the Thousand-Year Sabbath', in *The Apocalypse in the Middle Ages*, eds R. Emmerson and B. McGinn (Ithaca and London, 1992), 51–77.

2   B. McGinn, *The Calabrian Abbot: Joachim of Fiore in the History of Western Thought* (New York and London, 1985); E. R. Daniel, 'Joachim of Fiore: Patterns of History in the Apocalypse', in *The Apocalypse in the Middle Ages*, 72–88. For recent bibliography on Joachim of Fiore, see M. Reeves, *The Influence of Prophecy in the Later Middle Ages*, new edn (Notre Dame, 1993). The pagination of this edn is the same as the original 1969 edn.

3   See Fiona Robb, 'Did Innocent III Personally Condemn Joachim of Fiore?' *Florensia*, anno vii (1993), 81–9. I am most grateful to her for permission to cite her evidence briefly.

4   'locutus est dominus per Moyses et Aaron in ordine laycorum per Petrum et Paulum in ordine clericorum, novissime vero diebus in ordine monachorum locutus est.'

5   See, for instance, the joint encyclical by the generals of the Dominican and Franciscan Orders in 1255 (quoted Reeves, *Influence*, 146, from Wadding, *Annales*, iii, p. 380) and the opening words of St Bonaventura's *Legenda maior*, quoted E. R. Daniel, *The Franciscan Concept of Mission* (Lexington, Ky., 1975), 26.

6   Quoted in Daniel, *The Franciscan Concept*, 28.

7   Roger Bacon, *Opus Majus*, ed. J. Bridges (London, 1900), i, pp. 268–9.

8   Quoted from *De Periculis novissimi temporis* in Reeves, *Influence*, 62.

9   For references, see Reeves, *Influence*, note to pp. 60–3 and bibliography, new edn.

10   See especially J. Ratzinger, *The Theology of History in St Bonaventure*, tr. Z. Hayes (Chicago, 1971).

11   See especially D. Burr, *The Persecution of Peter Olivi: Transactions of the American Philosophical Society*, n.s. 66, pt. 5 (1976) (Philadelphia, 1976); id., 'Olivi's apocalyptic timetable', *The Journal of Medieval and Renaissance Studies*, 11, 2 (1981), 237–60.

12   For references, see Reeves, *Influence*, notes to pp. 242–7.

13   For references, see ibid., note to pp. 203–7.

14   H. Lee, M. Reeves and G. Silano, *Western Mediterranean Prophecy: The School of Joachim of Fiore and the Fourteenth-Century Breviloquium* (Toronto, 1988).

15   F. Tocco, *Studii Francescani*, iii (Naples, 1909), 515. On the Fraticelli, see R. Rusconi, *L'Attesa della Fine: Crisi dell societa, profezia ed Apocalisse in Italia al tempo del grande scisma d'Occidente* (1378–1417) (Rome, 1979), 39–84.

16   For references, see Reeves, *Influence*, 54–5.

17   'Dies irae, dies illa, / solvet saeclum in favilla / teste David cum Sibylla. / Quantus tremor est futurus / quando iudex est venturus, / Cuncta stricte discussurus! / Tuba, mirum spargens sonum / per sepulchra regionum . . .' E. Ermini, 'Il "Dies Irae"', *Biblioteca dell' Archivum Romanicum*, ii (Geneva, 1928), 62ff.

18   Arnold of Villanova, *De tempore adventus Antichristi*, ed. in part by H. Finke, *Aus den Tagen Bonifaz VIII* (Munster, 1902), pp. cxxix–clix.

19   F. Pelster, 'Die Quaestio Heinrichs v Harclay ueber die Zweite Ankunft Christi u. die Erwartung der Baldigen Weltendes zu Anfang der XIV Jahrhunderts', *Archivio italiano per la storia della pietà*, i, pp. 53–82.

20   Ibid., 44.

21   John Quidort, *Tractatus de Antichristo* (Venice, 1516), fos 35V–42V.

22   Lee, Reeves and Silano, *Western Mediterranean Prophecy*, 55–7; R. Lerner, 'On the Origins of the Earliest Latin Pope Prophecies; A Reconsideration', *Fälschungen im Mittelalter, MGH Scriptores*, 33, v (Hanover, 1988), 29–30.

23   Edited H. Lee, G. Silano in *Western Mediterranean Prophecy* (ref. n. 13), pp. 148–322.

24   See M. Reeves, 'The Vaticinia de Summis Pontificibus: A Question of Authorship', in *Intellectual Life in the Middle Ages: Essays presented to Margaret Gibson*, ed. L. Smith and B. Ward (London and Rio Grande, 1992), 145–56, on the debate concerning their origins. See also Lerner, 'On the Origins', 611–35.

25   Professor Martha Fleming is preparing an edition of the *Vaticinia*.

26 On the origins and history of the Last World Emperor prophecy, see P. Alexander, *The Byzantine Apocalypse Tradition*, ed. D. Abramse (Berkeley, Los Angeles and London, 1985).

27 Reeves, *Influence*, 309–12.

28 Pierre Dubois, *De recuperatione Terre Sancte*, ed. C. Langlois (Paris, 1929), 98–9.

29 H. Grundmann, 'Die Liber de Flore', *Historisches Jahrbuch*, 49 (1929), 33–91.

30 This was in part a commentary on the pseudo-Joachimist *Oraculum Cyrilli* and is known under the titles *Expositio magni prophete Joachim in librum beate Cyrilli* . . . or *Liber de magnis tribulationibus* . . . or (in the first printed edn, Venice, 1516) *Libellus fratris Theolosphori de Cusentia* . . . The main authority on Telesphorus and the various mss. and redactions of his work is still E. Donckel, 'Die Prophezeiung des Telesforus', *Archivium Franciscanum Historicum*, xxvi (1933), 29–104.

31 Quoted Reeves, *Influence*, 328.

32 See ibid., 425–7.

33 Quoted ibid., 425. The original text: 'Aestimo igitur mundum dictum decrescere in pravis moribus, usque ad profundum delictorum, quousque veniat filius perditionis.'

34 Quoted Rusconi, *L'Attesa della Fine*, 68.

35 On Giovanni delle Celle and the Santo Spirito circle, see ibid., 57–71. See also Reeves, *Influence*, 253–4. The original text: 'questa bestia è Anticristo, e di vero che alcuno m'ha detto, che dee essere un altro papa; per la qual cosa delle due cose è l'una: o che il libro, che vidi, è corrotto, o alcuno v'ha aggiunto di suo proprio senso; e però sto a videre.'

36 Rusconi, *L'Attesa della Fine*, 101–8.

37 Reeves, *Influence*, 173, 343–6, 431–3; B. McGinn, 'Circoli gioachimiti veneziani (1450–1530)', *Cristianesimo nella storia*, 7 (1986), 19–39.

38 Reeves, *Influence*, 433–4.

39 McGinn, 'Circoli', 28–30.

40 Reeves, *Influence*, 251–67.

41 See below, pp. 103–5, on Egidio of Viterbo.

42 In the original: 'hinc timet, inde cupit; hinc dominatum amittere formidat, inde coronandi Caesaris gloriam expetit.'

43 Quoted Reeves, *Influence*, 334–5. The original text: 'Mea intentio pro Ecclesia Dei bona et recta est; si Deus aliud de me aut per me ordinare voluerit, in ipsius potestate est, qui solus omnia novit, potest et disponit secundum suam rectissimam voluntatem.'

44 On Savonarola and prophecy, see D. Weinstein, *Savonarola and Florence: Prophecy and Patriotism in the Renaissance* (Princeton, 1970).

45 Marsilio Ficino, *Opera* (Basle, 1576) i, p. 944.

46 Giovanni Nesi, *Oracolo de novo saeculo* (Florence, 1497), sig. c. vii^v.

47 See the sources cited in Reeves, *Influence*, 355–7.

48 Ibid., 430.

49 On the *Apocalypsis Nova*, see A. Morisi, *Apocalypsis Nova: richerche sull' 'origine e la formazione del testo dello pseudo-Amadeo'* (*Istituto Storia Italiano per il Medio Evo. Studi Storici*, 77; Rome, 1970); A. Morisi-Guerra, 'The *Apocalypsis Nova*: a Plan for Reform', in *Prophetic Rome in the High Renaissance Period*, ed. M. Reeves (Oxford, 1992), 27–50.

50 N. Minnich, 'The Role of Prophecy in the Career of the Enigmatic Bernardino López de Carvajal', in *Prophetic Rome*, 111–20.

51 Ibid., 120.

52 See C. Vasoli, 'Giorgio Benigno Salviati (Dragišić)', in *Prophetic Rome*, 152–3 and the references given there.

53 J. Jungić, 'Prophecies of the Angelic Pope in Sebastiano del Piombo's Portrait of Cardinal Bandinello Sauli and Three Companions', in *Prophetic Rome*, 345–70.

54 Ibid., 368–70.

55 N. Minnich, 'Prophecy and the Fifth Lateran Council (1512–1517)', in *Prophetic Rome*, 75–80.

56 Ibid., 66–7.

57 Ibid., 81–4.

58 Ibid., 87.

59 M. Reeves, 'Cardinal Egidio of Viterbo: A Prophetic Interpretation of History', in *Prophetic Rome*, 95–6. On Egidio, see J. O'Malley, *Giles of Viterbo and Reform* (Leiden, 1968); id., *Rome and Renaissance: Studies in Culture and Religion* (London, 1981).

60 For the material in this paragraph, see Reeves, ibid., 99–103. See also F. X. Martin, 'The Writings of Giles of Viterbo', *Augustiniana*, 29, 1–2 (1979), 170.

61 M. Reeves, *Influence*, 347–54. On Lichtenberger, see D. Kurze, *Johann Lichtenberger: Historische Studien*, 379 (Lübeck and Hamburg, 1960); id., 'Popular Astrology and Prophecy in the Fifteenth and Sixteenth Centuries: Johann Lichtenberger', in *'Astrology Hallucinati': Stars and the End of the World in Luther's Time*, ed. P. Zambelli (Berlin and New York), 1986, 177–93.

62 On Gattinara, see J. Headley, 'Rhetoric and Reality: Messianic, Humanist and Civilian themes in the Imperial Ethos of Gattinara', in *Prophetic Rome*, 241–69, and further references given there.

63 Ibid., 255.

64 Ibid., 264–5.

65 Quoted M. Reeves, 'Roma Profetica', in *La Città dei Segreti: Magia, astrologia e cultura esiterica a Roma (XV–XVIII)*, ed. F. Troncarelli (Milan,

1985), 294. See R. Rusconi's fuller study of Galatino in *Prophetic Rome*, 157–87.

66 A. Chastel, *The Sack of Rome*, tr. B. Archer (Princeton, NJ, 1983), 82.

67 Quoted from Chastel in M. Reeves, 'A Note on Prophecy and the Sack of Rome', in *Prophetic Rome*, 275.

68 Reeves, ibid., 275–6.

69 Egidio of Viterbo, *Scechina e Libellus de litteris hebraicis*, ed. F. Secret (Rome, 1959). On this work, see O'Malley, *Church and Reform*, 118–20.

70 Viterbo, *Scechina*, 69.

71 Wolfgang Lazius, *Fragmentum vaticinii cuiusdam . . . Methodii* (Vienna, 1547). On this work, see Reeves, *Influence*, 369–72.

6

Seventeenth-Century Millenarianism

Richard Popkin

At the end of the sixteenth and the beginning of the seventeenth centuries many religious thinkers, especially in Protestant countries, began to suspect that the events taking place before their very eyes were the actual ones leading the beginning of the millennium, the return of Jesus as a political Messiah, and the commencement of his thousand-year reign on earth, to be preceded or followed by Judgment Day, when the reformed true believers would be saved. The emergence of Protestant political powers in England and in the Netherlands, which had defeated the Spanish Catholic forces, the victory of Gustavus Adolphus in the Thirty Years War, the Union of Crowns between Scotland and England,[1] and many other events were taken as signs that God was acting in history preparing the way for the glorious millennial events. Various countries saw themselves as the New Israel where the decisive Providential events would occur.

The Reformation itself had revealed, for those anticipating the millennium, that the Bishop of Rome was Antichrist. New ways of studying Scripture as applied to current events grew out of the study of the Bible in Hebrew and Greek, out of the contact with Jewish readers and the Jewish interpretative tradition, and out of the exciting discoveries being made of divine secrets embedded in Hebrew characters through study of the cabbala.

Millenarian expectations had been expressed at many times in the past. Important millenarian movements existed in Spain, Portugal, and Italy within the Catholic world in the fifteenth and sixteenth centuries.[2] What sets off seventeenth-century millenarianism from previous developments is (a) that it took place primarily within the Protestant world; (b) that it was rooted in a new way of deciphering the symbols and prophecies in Scripture, especially in the Books of Daniel and Revelation, by relating them to historical persons and institutions; and (c) that it saw crucial social and political events of the time as intimately linked to penultimate steps that would occur before the onset of the millennium, and the establishment of the Fifth Monarchy foretold by Daniel, such as the identification of and overthrow of Antichrist,[3] the reunion of all true Christian churches, the Conversion of the Jews, the reappearance of the Lost Tribes, the rebuilding of the Temple in Jerusalem and the reestablishing of the Jews in the Holy Land.[4]

Shortly after the defeat of the Spanish Armada, and the first victories of the Dutch rebellious forces against Spain, several religious writers began working out their millenarian theories. This group included Sir John Napier, a Scot,[5] Thomas Brightman,[6] an exile in the Netherlands, Johannes Alsted,[7] and Joseph Mede, a professor at Cambridge.[8] The Protestant authorities of the time regarded millenarian expression as dangerous and subversive to established society (since it pointed to the imminent replacement of the present social and political world with a totally different one). Hence the key works on the subject were not allowed to be printed in England until the beginning of the Puritan Revolution. Some were published in the Netherlands, where control of the press was much more lenient, and where there was no strong central government. But a serious effort was made to keep these works from being imported into England. Expressions of millenarian views by preachers and teachers were also severely restricted in England up to 1640. Some men were arrested, imprisoned, and/or exiled for their views.

When the Puritans took control in 1640 all sorts of millenarians appeared openly on the scene in England: Ranters, Diggers, Levellers, and so forth,[9] prophesying the oncoming millennium, the Kingdom of God on Earth, and the Fifth Monarchy. Books expounding this suddenly appeared in print, from Joseph Mede's *Clavis Apocalyptica* and assorted hitherto unpublished tracts by him, Francis Potter's *666* (showing by mathematical calculations that the "666" on the head of the beast in *Revelation* is actually the address of the Bishop of Rome[10]), and the works of Brightman, Alsted and others.

Mede had found the answer to the pervasive sceptical doubt all around him in the certainty he discovered in biblical prophecies.[11] He offered a synchronism between the prophecies that appear in Daniel

and those offered in Revelation so that both works could be interpreted together as forecasting future providential events. Based on this,
he had argued with much scholarly ammunition that the millennium
would begin 1,260 years after the fall of the Roman Empire. Hence,
all one had to do to determine when the crucial millennial event
would take place was to figure out exactly when Rome fell. In Mede's
time it was considered to have happened *circa* 400 AD. Thus, the
believers realized that the end of days was close at hand. In fact one,
Mary Cary, announced that the onset of the millennium would be in
1655–6.[12]

Three leading European millenarian thinkers, John Dury, a Scot
trained in Leiden, Samuel Hartlib, a German émigré in England, and
Jan Amos Comenius, the exiled leader of the Moravian Brethren, got
together in London in 1641 to figure out what had to be done to
prepare for the great events to come.[13] Comenius was already engaged
in revising and reforming the educational system, and writing new text
books. Dury was a minister who became an active correspondent of
Mede's when he learned from the Revd William Twisse, now leader
of the Westminster Assembly of Divines, about the quiet Dr Mede
who knew when the present world would end. Dury began what was
to be a lifelong crusade to reunite all of the Protestant churches by
formulating a harmony of confessions. He was also actively involved in
finding ways of converting Jews and bringing Jews and Christians
together. Samuel Hartlib, a curious German refugee, had come to
England in the 1620s and sought to bring together like-minded people
to improve learning, social activities, and Christian knowledge. He had
hundreds of reform projects that would prepare the human scene for
the imminent Second Coming.[14]

The Comenius–Dury–Hartlib proposals of 1641 are truly an amazing set of plans to transform the intellectual, religious, economic, and
social life of England into a pure Christian pre-millennial world,
awaiting the appearance of the Messiah. Their plans would appear
utterly preposterous were it not for the fact that they had the ears of
the people running England at that point.[15] When the funds for some
of their reforms did not immediately become available, Comenius left
for the Continent and carried on his educational reforms from there,
accompanied by his personal prophet, Drabnik, who interpreted unfolding events for him in the millenarian scenario. Dury was appointed
by the Assembly of Divines as their representative to negotiate the

reunion of the churches all over the world. (He carried their authorization with him for decades, and acted accordingly, discussing reunification with Lutherans and Calvinists and other groups in The Netherlands, Germany, Sweden, Switzerland, and France.) He and Hartlib looked for ways of facilitating the conversion of the Jews and bringing Christianity to Muslims, and to American Indians.

They proposed setting up a college of Jewish studies in London to help in their millennial preparations. The college would make Judaism better known to Christians and Christianity less offensive to Jews, and would prepare both groups for their roles in the approaching millennium.[16] The proposed staff of this college (for which Dury and Hartlib asked Parliament to appropriate one thousand pounds annually) was to be Rabbi Menasseh ben Israel of Amsterdam, Adam Boreel, the leader of the Dutch religious group, the Collegiants, and Professor Constantine Ravius of Berlin.[17] The projected college never came into being but it led to a remarkable interaction of Jewish and Christian intellectuals aimed, at least from the Christian side, at furthering their millenarian projects. For forty years or more there was active cooperative work by rabbis and Dutch and English Christian theologians in producing a new edition of the *Mishna* with Hebrew vowel points, plus Spanish and Latin translations.[18] There was active cooperation in constructing an "exact" model of Solomon's Temple, the microcosm of the universe. (The model was on exhibition next to the Amsterdam Synagogue until it was taken to England to be offered as a gift to Charles II.[19])

England at the time had no legal Jewish residents, the Jews having been expelled in 1290. The Netherlands had free Jewish communities made up principally of Spanish and Portuguese Jews, who had been forced converts to Catholicism in Iberia, and found religious freedom in the Dutch Republic. They were able to set up synagogues and schools, publish books, and debate with Christians about the truth of their religion. Most of them had been raised as Catholics in Spain or Portugal. They were able to interact with Dutch theologians, and some, like Menasseh, became the Hebrew teachers of Dutch Protestant scholars.

Among the Jews there was a growing Messianic conviction that God would soon redeem them after their many tragedies culminating in the Expulsion of the unconverted Jews from Spain in 1492 and from Portugal in 1497. Cabbalistic calculations had led them to expect this redemption (in the form of the appearance of the Jewish Messiah) to take place in 1648. Most unfortunately what took place then was the worst pogrom in eastern European history before Hitler. Hundreds of thousands of Jews were massacred, raped, and robbed in Poland and the Ukraine. This seems to have led to some Jewish reconsideration of the course of Divine History, and recalculation of when redemption might occur, settling on 1666 as the crucial year.

Rumors about this reconsideration seem to have led to one of the bizarre expressions of English millenarian expectation, the account of a supposed Jewish Council that was alleged to have met outside of Budapest in 1650 to consider whether in fact the Messiah had already come. This document circulated in the Hartlib–Dury circle and was published in 1655.[20] Its point was the Jews would have converted then if they had been confronted with the pure Christianity that existed in Puritan England rather than the false and corrupt Christianity of the Church of Rome.

A more exciting "sign of the times" occurred when rumors got to England from Puritans in New England that the natives in New England might be the Lost Tribes of Israel. Mede and his student, Henry More, had taken a very dim view of the Indians, and even considered them as children of Satan.[21] Dury, on the other hand, was ready to believe that the Indians were a crucial part of the Providential drama. Dury was preparing the introduction to a book on the subject, and recalled that Menasseh ben Israel had told him of a Portuguese Jewish explorer who said he had encountered an Indian tribe in the Andes mountains who were carrying on a Jewish religious service! Dury asked Menasseh for the details and then asked him about the Jewish view about the reappearance of the Lost Tribes. This led Menasseh to write his most famous work, *The Hope of Israel*, in 1650. The work, written in Spanish, was quickly translated into English by a wild-eyed millenarian, Moses Wall, and was dedicated (by Dury) to the English Parliament. Menasseh had carefully tried to minimize the excitement that Dury was generating about the American Indians by stating that it seemed that part of a Lost Tribe had been found in South America, but that the Indians were mostly people from Asia who crossed over by a land bridge. Menasseh then gave an account of his own Messianic expectations. (A leading Portuguese Jesuit, Antonio de Vieira, rushed back from Brazil where he was converting Indians to confer with Menasseh in Amsterdam about the significance of the report of Lost Tribes in the Andes. Vieira then wrote his own millenarian work, *The Hope of Portugal*, describing his expectations, that the Jews would be returned to Portugal and reunited with their converted brethren. Then Jesus would come to Portugal, and take the Jews thence to the Holy Land. Vieira was later arrested by the Inquisition, and was charged with "conspiring with a rabbi." The Jesuit was finally released to carry on his millenarian activities.[22])

Menasseh, after the success of *The Hope of Israel* among the millenarians, next wrote a humble address to Cromwell, explaining that almost all of the prophesied events that would take place before the arrival of the Jewish Messiah had in fact already occurred. The main one missing was the complete dispersion of the Jews to the four corners of the world. From Menasseh's knowledge, the one corner that had no Jews was England. So the Jews had to be recalled to England before the end of days. This news led to the British government appointing a delegation to negotiate with Menasseh about the conditions of the Jews returning to England.[23] The millenarians were convinced that if the Jews could be brought back to England, and there experience the pure Christianity of the Puritan world, they would of course convert, and then the millennium would begin. Cromwell had opened the Parliament in 1653, calling them the Parliament of Saints, who would bring about the New Israel in England. The popular millenarian movements of Ranters, Diggers, Levellers, and so forth agitated to create the preconditions for the millennium in a classless society.[24]

Many of the millenarians believed that the conversion of the Jews would take place in 1655–6, so there was not much time to waste.[25] Another element involved in this was the answer the "very learned and pious" Joseph Mede had given to the Revd William Twisse about what the actual Conversion of the Jews would be like. Twisse had wondered whether every Jew everywhere in the world would have to be converted as a prelude to the millennium. Mede told him that perhaps only a token conversion would occur, and that would suffice. Saul of Tarsus had converted in biblical times, becoming the Apostle Paul. Perhaps there would be another such token, a prominent convert, who would represent all of the Jews.[26] (Menasseh either purposely or inadvertently contributed to this possible scenario, by appointing himself "agent of the Jewish world" just before he went to England.)

What seems to have been a critical moment in Menasseh's planning was the visit he made to Brussels in 1654 to meet Queen Christina of Sweden, who had just abdicated her throne. She apparently believed that she was to play a crucial role in the millennium.[27] In fact, on her first stop on leaving Sweden, she went to the home of her Jewish banker, Diego Teixeira, in Hamburg. There she was greeted by Juan de Prado, a recent Marrano refugee from Spain, who said to her, "hail to the new messiah – but who would have expected it would be a woman!"[28]

In Belgium, Christina was living next door to the secretary of the Prince of Condé, Isaac La Peyrère, a leading French millenarian. (La Peyrère was supposed to arrange a marriage of Christina with the Prince.) He had written a wild millenarian work, *Du Rappel des Juifs*, published in 1643, in which he envisaged the Jews being brought back to France (from which they had been expelled at the end of the fourteenth century), then converted to Jewish-Christianity, and next led to rebuild the Holy Land by the King of France, who would rule the world with the Jewish Messiah, whose arrival was imminently expected.[29] In a work that he had not yet published, *Prae-Adamitae*, La Peyrère set forth a radically heretical system of Bible interpretation to support his millenarian vision ("addressed to all of the Jews and all of the Synagogues in the world, by one who wishes to be one of you").[30] Menasseh, who was extremely familiar with what Christian millenarians were thinking about Jewish matters, had apparently not heard of La Peyrère's views until this visit. The rabbi rushed back to Amsterdam, where he went to the home of a leading Dutch millenarian, Peter Serrarius, and told an assembled group there that the coming of the Messiah was imminent. This led the Czech millenarian, Paul Felgenhauer, to put out a work, *Good News for the Jews*, dedicated to Menasseh.[31] In the book, Menasseh added a letter in which he listed four people who knew that the Messiah would soon be here, plus the author of *Du Rappel des Juifs*.[32] Menasseh then wrote his most Messianic work, *Piedra gloriosa*, which was illustrated by Rembrandt, and next prepared to set out for England to petition for the readmission of the Jews. Before leaving he encountered La Peyrère in Amsterdam. The latter was there to have his most heretical work, *Prae-Adamitae* published (at Christina's expense). Menasseh and Felgenhauer wanted to argue with him about the theory that there were men before Adam. They both wrote refutations of his book, but

Menasseh seems to have accepted some of La Peyrère's French-oriented millenarianism.[33]

In England there was great millenarian expectation in the summer of 1655. Reports indicate that all sorts of people in the government, in business, in the churches, seriously thought the "end of days" was at hand, and saw Menasseh's coming as evidence of this.[34] (Perhaps Menasseh was seen as the token Jew, the "convertible Jew."[35]) In the first glimpse we have of his arrival, he was met by a Welsh royalist millenarian, with the unlikely name Arise Evans, who believed that the exiled Charles Stuart was the Messiah or the king who would rule the world with the Messiah. Evans had read Menasseh's *Hope of Israel*, and wanted to impart his great news to the rabbi. We have a report of the conversation, apparently written down since they had no common language. When Evans asked Menasseh if he thought Charles Stuart could be the Messiah, the rabbi said no, but he thought the King of Sweden, or, as an important Frenchman has said, the King of France could be he.[36] Menasseh seems to have adopted La Peyrère's form of millenarianism. In the one book he wrote and published in England, Menasseh specifically quoted from the *Rappel des Juifs* to justify a way of reconciling Judaism and Christianity. The difference between the religions was just over a matter of fact of what happened in the first century. They agreed about what was to happen, namely that a Messiah in the flesh was about to arrive, who would transform the world. So, the Jews and the Christians should focus on the present and future and let the minimal difference about the past alone.[37]

In the fall of 1655 Menasseh met with many prominent English millenarians. The commission Cromwell appointed considered the pros and cons of readmitting the Jews to England, without coming to any conclusion. They talked about the theological, economic, and social implications of the readmission of the Jews.[38]

Despite all of the millenarian enthusiasm, the Jews did not in fact convert in 1655–6, and neither the Jewish Messiah nor the Christian political Messiah appeared on the scene. However, two developments indicate the force of millenarianism in England at the time.

One of Cromwell's agents, the Revd Jean Baptiste Stouppe, of the French Reformed Church in London, seems to have been part of a theological-political conspiracy to create a Protestant millennial kingdom in Europe. He, plus Queen Christina, plus the Prince of Condé, plus Menasseh, were involved in the planning. Stouppe was trying to get the Protestants in France to rebel, and to convince Condé to be their leader. Cromwell would send an army into France. Then an alliance would be made between Mazarin and Cromwell. Christina would become regent of Belgium. The justification for the English invasion of France was that the French Catholic authorities were persecuting the Grisons in Savoy, a surviving remnant of the faithful elect, the Waldensians, a proto-Protestant group. Revd Stouppe wrote fervent, millenarian pamphlets urging the rescue of the Grisons (he was one himself). Then he went to France to enlist Protestant support, and escaped to the Netherlands where he actually offered Condé the throne of France on behalf of Cromwell, if he would lead the revolt, after which Cromwell would invade, and the Protestant millennial state would then be created. Condé cautiously said that he could only act *after* Cromwell invaded. So nothing came of all of this theological-political plotting, which appears in lots of intelligence reports from agents in Belgium and elsewhere.[39]

The other development, which may have had more effect, was that *a* Messiah did appear in England. The Quakers had taken over some of the popular millenarian fervor in the 1650s.[40] In October 1656 the Quaker leader, James Nayler, a former army officer, announced that Jesus was within him, and that he was Jesus. He paraded into Bristol on the back of an ass, with his followers proclaiming him "the King of the Jews" and singing "Hosanna in the highest." He was reported to have raised a woman from the grave. Nayler's actions caused great excitement. He was arrested by the authorities, and was tried for blasphemy by the House of Parliament.[41] Before the trial Margaret Fell, "the mother of the Quakers," wrote a pamphlet urging Menasseh to have all of the Jews convert.[42] Nayler was convicted, even though Cromwell defended him. He was brutally punished and jailed for four years. His unrepentant followers fled to Holland and to the outposts of Quaker trading in the Levant, and in the Western Hemisphere, and they seemed to have carried their millenarian message with them.

The leading Dutch and English millenarians were disheartened by the failure of great events to occur in 1655–6. They kept seeking clues in astrology, in strange historical developments, and in cabbalistic calculations. When a rabbi from Jerusalem came to Amsterdam in 1657, and they found him "sympathique" in that he seemed to hold pro-Christian views on various subjects including whether Jesus could be the Messiah, they immediately saw his appearance and his attitude as a Providential sign that the Jews would soon convert.[43] Dury put out an excited pamphlet about it, citing the amazing pro-Christian remarks of the rabbi.[44] Dutch and English millenarians collected a large amount of charitable contributions for the rabbi's brethren in the Holy Land, the first such pro-Jewish Christian venture in recorded history, and they gave the rabbi a New Testament to have translated into Hebrew for the benefit of his brethren. (Needless to say, the rabbi did not convert, and when he returned to Jerusalem he was condemned by his co-religionists for taking alms from gentiles.[45])

Several of the millenarians regularly attended services at the Amsterdam synagogue and kept conferring with Jewish scholars about possible clues as to when the Messiah might arrive. Strange natural events like comets, and human events like sudden deaths and monstrous births, had to be studied to determine if they were signs of what was to come.[46] Clues about when the Messiah would come were sought in the mystical Jewish writings.[47] The publication in Latin of the *Kabbala Denudata*, a collection of such works from the Zohar up to seventeenth-century cabbalistic writings, provided much material for those carrying on this search.[48]

The Restoration of Charles II may have ended the millennial expectations of many of those connected with the Commonwealth government and with the heady expectations of the Puritans. (Some were executed, some exiled, and some driven to early retirement.) John Dury, who was trying to avoid being condemned as a regicide, wrote to Charles II telling him that a student of Peter Serrarius's in Amsterdam had had a dream in which he foresaw that Charles would be restored and that he, Charles, would convert the Jews.[49] Charles was not impressed with being given this millenarian role and sent Dury into permanent exile on the Continent (where he continued trying to reunite the Christian churches in preparation for the millennium).

Others tried to temper their millenarianism so that it was not seen as a threat to either church or state, but still preserved the great expectation that monumental events would occur within a decade or two. Many involved in the formation of the Royal Society of England had such views.[50] And still others refused to accept the Restoration and its re-establishment of the now broad-based Church of England. They survived underground, or in marginalized religious groups like the Sabbatarians.[51]

Developments in the Catholic world, such as the changes of popes, and the Turkish attacks on the Catholic Austro-Hungarian Empire, continuously produced "evidence" that the end was near, that Divine Redemption was about to take place. Radical Protestant groups in Poland and Transylvania stirred up millennial expectations. Their anti-Trinitarianism was coupled with a literalist interpretation of the Old Testament picture of the expected Messiah. Some of these groups in fact went so far as to adopt Jewish practices in preparation for the Jewish political Messiah who would soon appear.[52]

In this state of affairs, another chapter in seventeenth-century millenarianism began when news reached central and western Europe that amazing events were occurring in the Jewish world in the Ottoman Empire. A mystical Jew in Smyrna, Sabbatai Zevi, on Jewish New Year's Day, 1665–6, announced that he was the Messiah![53] He may have been influenced by the earlier Quaker Messianic claimant. His father worked for Quaker merchants. And he was soon denounced as a "Quaker-Jew."[54]

Sabbatai Zevi started performing acts that were reserved only for the long-awaited Messiah. He changed Jewish ritual. He declared that his birthday, the ninth day of the month of Ab (in the Jewish calendar), traditionally celebrated as a somber fast day commemorating the fall of the first and the second Temple, and the expulsion of the Jews from Spain, would now be a feast day! And he appointed new kings of the earth, a group of friends and followers.

Instead of being regarded as a crank and a madman, Sabbatai Zevi was quickly accepted by well over ninety percent of the Jewish population all over the world. The Amsterdam Jewish community was almost entirely carried away. Some of its leaders rushed to Palestine to take part in the return of the Jews to Zion.[55] And one finds reverberations of the Jewish Messianic excitement among millenarians in the Netherlands, England, and America. Peter Serrarius became a follower and wrote a lot of pamphlets in English and Dutch about the wonderful events that were unfolding.[56] It was reported that a ship with silken sails and Hebrew flags announcing the return of the Lost Tribes had landed near Aberdeen. It was also reported that Jews and the Lost Tribes were besieging Mecca, and that soon the Sultan would give his crown to Sabbatai Zevi.[57] Instead, the next stage in this "petit drame" was that Sabbatai Zevi became a Muslim. The Sultan had seized him, and placed him in a castle in the Dardanelles. There Sabbatai Zevi held court for Jewish pilgrims from all over. A Polish rabbi came, and soon decided that Sabbatai Zevi was an impostor, and told the Turkish authorities so. Then the Sultan had Sabbatai Zevi brought before him, and told him that a test would be performed to see if he was the real Messiah. The Sultan's archers would shoot arrows at him. If he was the Messiah he would be able to stop the arrows. If not, then . . . At that moment Sabbatai renounced his claims, and turned Muslim. He became a minor official in the Ottoman Empire. During his last ten years of life he gave hints and signs to his followers that he had only converted in body, but not in spirit. A Jewish millenarianism developed of those who are now awaiting the return of Sabbatai Zevi in glory as the true Messiah. There are still followers in Greece, Turkey, and Palestine.[58]

As might be expected there was tremendous shock in the Jewish world, shock that continues to the present day. Followers of Sabbatai Zevi were forced to renounce their beliefs or be cast out. In Amsterdam many followers became secret believers, and remained so into the early eighteenth century.[59] Some Christian followers, including Serrarius, managed to accept Sabbatai Zevi's conversion as part of the Divine plan. Serrarius told Henry Oldenburg that it shows that God works in mysterious ways.[60] Serrarius died in 1669 on his way to see the new Messiah. There is reason to believe that Comenius remained a believer until his death in 1670.

Some millenarians remembered that Menasseh ben Israel had told them that there would be two Messiahs, one from the house of Joseph and one from the house of David.[61] So Sabbatai Zevi could be one of the two. Other millenarians like Dury and Jean de Labadie tried to figure out where Sabbatai Zevi fitted in their millenarian cosmos. Dury first tried to minimize Sabbatai Zevi's importance. He saw him as a minor potentate, King of the Jews, within the Ottoman Empire. Then, as he and Labadie considered the matter, they offered the view that since the Christians had not sufficiently reformed, God was first rewarding the Jews by giving them their Messiah, before the Christians would receive theirs.[62]

After the debacle of the Sabbatian movement, a sequel occurred centered around a Danish Messiah pretender, Oliger Pauli, who claimed to be a descendant of Abraham and to have had a Jewish grandfather. Pauli, an important merchant, gathered a group of rabbis around him, and tried to get the political rulers of the world to accept him.[63] His leading publicist was Moses Germanus, a rabbi in Amsterdam who had begun his intellectual career as a German Catholic, studying with the Jesuits. He became a Lutheran, an associate of the Pietist Jacob Spener, then a Mennonite, a radical Protestant, before converting himself to Judaism and moving to Amsterdam. He had worked on the *Kabbala Denudata* and was involved with the millenarianism of Knorr von Rosenroth and Van Helmont, friends of Leibniz.[64] In his writings, Moses Germanus sought to transform the image of Jesus into that of a Jewish moral teacher who had been foolishly portrayed as a divine figure some centuries after his death. The real Messiah was just appearing now in the figure of Oliger Pauli.[65] Further Messianic and millenarian movements, centered around significant or insignificant individuals, continued and still continue up to the present day.

A kind of millenarianism had been developing among some of the scientists from the 1640s onward. They saw the increase of knowledge as a Providential sign that the climax of history was near, and saw themselves as helping in God's work by fathoming the secrets of Nature. A spiritual brotherhood of scientists, religious thinkers, and Bible interpreters developed first around Robert Boyle, Hartlib, and others, and then led to such avant-garde institutions with a millenarian bent as the Royal Society of England and the Rosicrucians.[66] Such millenarianism was divorced from immediate political events, and was developed by two of England's leading intellectuals, the Cambridge Platonist Henry More, and the great scientist-mathematician, Isaac Newton.

During the Commonwealth period, More attacked what he called "enthusiasm," the attitude of many around him who were sure they knew the divine message when in fact they did not. He regarded Quakers, Ranters, and others as emotionally disturbed. Instead he proposed a calmer, somewhat detached and ahistorical understanding of the meaning of the Revelation. More was distanced from the political activists and advocated spiritual improvement as a preparation for the great events that someday were to come.[67] He worked for a while with his younger contemporary at Cambridge, Isaac Newton, on interpreting the symbols in Revelation and Daniel. Both were heavily influenced by the work of Joseph Mede. They had a falling-out over how literally to take some of the text.[68]

More died in 1687 having published two works on Revelation.

Newton, who gained his great reputation in 1687 with the publication of *Principia Mathematica*, had been working since his college days on deciphering God's message, especially in the two prophetic books. Unknown to most of his contemporaries, he spent an inordinate amount of time working on biblical history, church history, and Scriptural interpretation. Newton had come to the conclusion that the forces of Antichrist had taken over the Christian Church in the early centuries, and that the true church would have to be restored before the Second Coming. The doctrine of the Trinity, he regarded as a great falsity that Fathers like St Athanasius had inflicted on the community of believers.

In realizing the great iniquity of the prevailing church, Newton saw that his own anti-Trinitarian version of God's message would be considered heretical, and that he would lose his position in society, or worse, if he allowed his views to become generally known. Therefore, though he wrote an enormous amount (more than half of his writings) on religious subjects, he published none in his lifetime. Shortly after his death, one of the several versions of his *Observations on Daniel and the Apocalypse of St. John* was published. Two decades later two letters he had sent John Locke against the Doctrine of the Trinity were published. The rest of his very large corpus of theological writings has remained unpublished. The manuscripts were auctioned off at Sotheby's in 1936, and are now scattered across the globe. The largest collections are in the National Library of Israel in Jerusalem and in King's College, Cambridge.

The papers reveal Newton to have been a very learned scholar of church history. He was convinced that the Book of Nature and the Book of Scripture were each written in code, to be deciphered by the wise when God so willed. In his own lifetime both books were gradually being decoded, revealing the Divine domination of the physical and human universes. Newton realized from his studies that the dating of the fall of the Roman Empire had to be revised since, in truncated form, the Empire survived into the sixth and seventh centuries in the Exarchate of Ravenna. Hence, using Mede's calculus, the millennium would not begin until the late nineteenth or early twentieth centuries.

Newton also insisted that we were not in a position to determine with any accuracy when the prophesied events would occur. God did not intend for each of us to be prophets. We can only determine when the prophesied events have occurred, when the prophecies have been fulfilled. We cannot predict, we can only tell *post factum* that God is active in history. Just the same, in view of all of the prophecies that have been or are presently being fulfilled, we realize that those connected with the millennium will be fulfilled in the near or relatively near future.[69]

Newton's chosen successor at Cambridge, William Whiston, put this all together in his Boyle Lectures on the fulfillment of biblical prophecies, combining the best scientific information of the time with calculations predicting Providential events. Newton kept his millenarianism secret, revealed only to a few chosen disciples. Whiston went public, denouncing the doctrine of the Trinity and the established church. He had to give up his chair of mathematics at Cambridge, and became an outcast, offering his predictions in coffee houses. He became notorious for interpreting unusual natural events like earthquakes, comets, and storms as signs that the events in Daniel and Revelation were about to take place.[70]

A forceful millenarian interpretation of current events was offered by the French Protestant leader, Pierre Jurieu. He, like many Huguenots, had fled to the Netherlands. There he was much involved in trying to restore the situation of the French Protestants through human and divine action. He was involved with the Jews in Holland, and with William of Orange. He saw that the accomplishment of all of the prophecies in Scripture, including those that relate to the Jews, were being fulfilled at the very moment. Jurieu hoped that by befriending the Jews, they might be led to recognize the truth of Christianity, that the Messiah had already come. Jurieu's great work, *The Accomplishment of the Scripture Prophecies, or the Approaching Deliverance of the Church*,[71] is dedicated "To the Nation of the Jews." He told the Jews that the prophecies about the rebuilding of Jerusalem and their gathering in their own land would soon be fulfilled.[72] In the crucial section on what will happen to the Jews, Jurieu said, "There must therefore come a *time*, that shall be the reign of the *Messiah* and the Iews, in which this Nation shall be exalted (as hath been promised them) above all *Nations*."[73] The Jews will be the last peoples converted, and it will be by Divine intervention. "*Christ* will *convert* them by some glorious and surprising *apparition*."[74] The beginning of the Divine events that would lead to the conversion of the Jews and the millennium would commence, Jurieu said, around 1710 or 1715.[75]

After William's victory in England, Jurieu saw God actively operating in current history, restoring his chosen people and bringing about the millennium. He predicted that the Antichrist would soon be overthrown, that the King of France would also be overturned and that the millennial kingdom would begin.

Pierre Bayle mercilessly ridiculed Jurieu's predictions and his millenarianism. But Jurieu's views were most important for the Huguenots still living in France, whose world was increasingly restricted as official policy tried to force them to convert to Catholicism. The die-hards who hid in caves in the Cevennes saw their salvation in terms of Divine intervention. Jurieu's ideas convinced them that by remaining true witnesses to the faith they would play an important part in the world to come. Some became prophets of this, and began predicting what was soon to happen. When some of these French prophets escaped to England in the early eighteenth century they became leaders of a new millenarian movement, that quickly captured the imagination of both intellectuals, aristocrats, and simple believers. In fact, one of Newton's closest disciples, the Swiss mathematician, Fatio du Vallier, became one of the their leading figures. The French prophets became genuinely disruptive, and were severely persecuted.[76]

The millenarian ideas that developed in the seventeenth century continued to percolate in later times, some on a theoretical level like those presented by Bishops John Clayton and Thomas Newton, and by David Hartley and Joseph Priestley. Others appeared in popular movements like the French prophets, the convulsionaries in France, and in millenarian communities in America. Millenarianism rose again as a major intellectual and political force when the revolutions occurred in America and then in France, leading to religious and political movements that have been important ever since. Seventeenth-century millenarianism provided the basis for interpreting the key Scriptural texts, and relating them to historical events then taking place. One outcome has been a Christian Zionism that has played an important part in encouraging the return of Jews to Palestine, and the construction of a Jewish homeland there.[77] This view sees its origins in the thought of seventeenth-century philo-Semitic millenarian thinkers.[78] Millenarian thought in the seventeenth century has cast a long shadow in subsequent centuries, and has spawned many of the later millenarian fundamentalist movements, or provided a theological and interpretative basis for them.

NOTES

1 On this see Arthur H. Williamson, "The Jewish Dimension of the Scottish Apocalypse: Climate, Covenant and World Renewal," in Y. Kaplan, H. Mechoulan, and R. Popkin, eds, *Menasseh ben Israel and his World* (Leiden, 1989), 7–30.

2 Cf. Marjorie Reeves, *The Influence of Prophecy in the Later Middle Ages* (Oxford, 1969); Norman Cohn, *The Pursuit of the Millennium, Revolutionary Millenarian and Mystical Anarchists of the Middle Ages* (New York, 1961); and Marion Kuntz, *Guillaume Postel, The Prophet of the Restitution of all Things* (The Hague, 1981).

3 On this theme see Christopher Hill, *Antichrist in Seventeenth-Century England* (London, 1971).

4 There is a wealth of literature on the subject. Besides works cited later on in this essay, one should look at Peter Toon, ed., *Puritans, the Millennium, and the Future of Israel, Puritan Eschatology, 1600–1660* (Cambridge, 1970); Meir Verete, "The Restoration of the Jews in English Protestant Thought, 1790–1840," *Middle Eastern Studies*, VIII (1972), 3–50; B. S. Capp, *The Fifth Monarchy Men: A Study in Seventeenth Century English Millenarianism* (London, 1972); E. L. Tuveson, *Millennium and Utopia* (Gloucester, Mass., 1972); and R. Popkin, ed., *Millenarianism and Messianism in English Thought, 1650–1800* (Leiden, 1988).

5 See John Napier, *A Plaine Discovery of the whole Revelation of Saint John* (Edinburgh, 1593).

6 Thomas Brightman, *The Revelation of St. John Illustrated*, 4th edn (London, 1644). See also David S. Katz, *Philo-semitism and the Readmission of the Jews to England 1603–1655* (Oxford, 1982), 91–4; and Avihu Zakai, "Thomas Brightman and English Apocalyptic Tradition," in Kaplan et al., eds, *Menasseh ben Israel*, 31–44.

7 J. H. Alsted, *The Beloved City* (London, 1643).

8 On Mede see Katherine R. Firth, *The Apocalyptic Tradition in Reformation Britain, 1530–1645* (Oxford, 1979).

9 On this see Christopher Hill, *The World Turned Upside Down* (London, 1972).

10 Francis Potter, *An Interpretation of the Number 666* (Oxford, 1642). In the introductory remarks, taken from Mede's *Apostasy of the Latter Times*, it was said that Potter had made "the greatest discovery that hath been made since the world began."

11 Mede reported that when he first came to Cambridge in 1603 he came across the works of the ancient sceptic, Sextus Empiricus, and was cast into doubt about all subjects. He sought for truth and certainty in what

was taught at Cambridge, and finally found it in biblical prophecies. Cf. John Worthington, "The Life of the Reverand and most learned Joseph Mede," in *The Works of the Pious and Profoundly-Learned Joseph Mede* (London, 1664); K. Firth, *Apocalyptic Tradition*, ch. 6; and Richard H. Popkin, "The Third Force in Seventeenth Century Thought: Scepticism, Science, and Millenarianism," in Popkin, *The Third Force in Seventeenth-Century Thought* (Leiden, 1992), 92–3.

12 Mary Cary, *The Little Horn's Doom & Downfall* (London, 1651).

13 They seem to have known each other from the period before 1630 when Dury was a minister at Elbing, and Hartlib and Comenius attended his church. See J. Minton Batten, *John Dury, Advocate of Christian Reunion* (Chicago, 1944); and G. H. Turnbull, *Hartlib, Dury and Comenius* (London, 1947).

14 Hugh Trevor-Roper, "Three Foreigners: The Philosophers of the Puritan Revolution," in *Religion, the Reformation and Social Change* (London, 1967).

15 Cf. Turnbull, *Hartlib, Dury and Comenius*, where lists of their proposals are given.

16 Cf. Popkin, "The First College of Jewish Studies," *Revue des etudes juives*, 143 (1984), 351–64.

17 Ibid., 353.

18 On this joint project to edit and publish the *Mishna* see Popkin, "Some Aspects of Jewish–Christian Theological Interchanges in Holland and England 1640–1700," In J. Van den Berg and E. van der Wall, eds, *Jewish–Christian Relations in the Seventeenth Century* (Dordrecht, 1988), 3–32; and David S. Katz, "The Abendana Brothers and the Christian Hebraists of Seventeenth-Century England," *Journal of Ecclesiastical History*, 40 (1989).

19 On the Temple model, see A. K. Offenberg, "Jacob Jehuda Leon and his Model of the Temple," in Van den Berg and van der Wall, *Jewish–Christian Relations*, 95–115.

20 Cf. Popkin, "The Fictional Jewish Council of 1650: A Great English Pipedream", *Jewish History*, V (1991), 7–22.

21 Mede's view on the Satanic origin of the American Indians appears in his letter to the Revd William Twisse, March 23, 1634/5, in *Works*, 980–1. Henry More, in *An Explanation of the Grand Mystery of Godliness* (London, 1660), Book III, chs 3, 13, and 14, dealt with the demonic practices of the savages in America. See also, Popkin, "The Rise and Fall of the Jewish Indian Theory," in Kaplan et al., eds, *Menasseh ben Israel*, 63–82.

22 On Vieira see R. Cantel, *Prophètisme et Messianisme dans l'oeuvre du Pere Vieira* (Paris, 1960); and A. J. Saraiva, "Antonio Vieira, Menasseh ben

Israel et le Cinquième Empire," *Studia Rosenthaliana*, VI (1972), 26–32.

23 On this see Katz, *Philo-semitism*, chs 4–6.

24 On this see Hill, *The World Turned Upside Down*, and Katz, *Philo-semitism*, ch. 3.

25 Pope Alexander VII seems to have held a similar view. One of the first things he did as Pope was to commission a Hebrew translation of the writings of St Thomas Aquinas, so that the Jews, when they converted, would immediately have access to an explanation of Christianity. One volume of this undertaking appeared, with a 200-page account of the project in Latin. Copies exist in the Vatican Library and the Hebrew Union Library in Cincinnati, Ohio.

26 Cf. Mede, *Works*, epistles to William Twisse, 928–40.

27 Cf. Susanna Akerman, *Queen Christina of Sweden and Her Circle* (Leiden, 1991).

28 Cited in Yosef Kaplan, *From Christianity to Judaism. The Story of Isaac Orobio de Castro* (Oxford, 1989), 128, from a poem in honor of Prado by Conde Bernadino de Rebolledo, the Spanish ambassador in Copenhagen.

Christina was again in Teixeira's house in 1666 when the news was received of the appearance of the Jewish Messiah, Sabbatai Zevi. Christina joined in the frenzied religious dancing in celebration of the great event.

29 On La Peyrère, see Popkin, *Isaac La Peyrère (1596–1676). His Life, Work and Influence* (Leiden, 1987).

30 La Peyrère, *Men before Adam* (n.p., 1656), dedication.

31 Paul Felgenhauer, *Bonum Nuncium Israeli quod offertur Populo Israel &c Judae in hisce temporibus novissimis de Messia . . .* (Amsterdam, 1655).

32 Ibid., 89–90.

33 See Popkin, "Menasseh ben Israel and La Peyrère" I and II, *Studia Rosenthaliana*, VIII (1974), 59–63 and XVIII (1984), 12–20.

34 See, for instance, the report of the Swedish diplomat, Bonde, for August 23, 1655, in Michael Roberts, *Swedish Diplomats at Cromwell's Court, 1655–56: The Missions of Peter Julius Coyet and Christian Bonde*, Camden Fourth Series, Office of the Royal Historical Society (London, 1988), 142.

35 See Popkin, "Spinoza, the Convertible Jew," Cortona Conference 1991 on Spinoza, forthcoming.

36 Arise Evans, *Light for the Jews, or the Means to Convert them, in Answer to a Book of theirs, called the Hope of Israel, written and Printed by Manasseth Ben Israel, Chief Agent for the Jews here* (London, 1664), 1–20.

37 Menasseh ben Israel, *Vindiciae Judaeorum* (London, 1656), 18. "For, as a most learned Christian of our time hath written, in a French book,

which he calleth the *Rappel of the Iewes* (in which he makes the King of France to be their leader, when they shall return to their country), the Iewes, saith he, shall be saved, for yet we expect a *second* coming of the same Messiah, and the *Iewes* believe that that coming is the *first* and not the second, and by that faith shall be saved; for the difference consists only in the circumstance of time."

38   On the Whitehall Commission, see Katz, *Philo-semitism.*

39   On this see Gilbert Burnet's report of what Stouppe told him about his involvement with Cromwell in Burnet's *History of My Own Time.* See also the references to Stouppe in the correspondence of John Thurloe, Cromwell's intelligence chief. See also Stouppe pamphlets on the persecutions of the Grisons from the beginning of 1655. And see the letter of Louis de Bourbon, Prince of Condé, Rocroy, Dec. 6, 1653, published in *Mémoires de Henri-Charles de la Tremoille, Prince de Tarante* (Liege, 1767), 169–71. Susanna Akerman and I are planning a study of this theological-political conspiracy.

40   The Quakers, as a movement, began in 1652, and attracted some of the former Ranters, Levellers, Diggers, etc. See William C. Braithwaite, *The Beginnings of Quakerism,* 2nd edn, revised by Henry J. Cadbury (Cambridge, 1955).

41   On Nayler see Mabel R. Brailsford, *A Quaker from Cromwell's Army* (London, 1927), Emelia Fogelkou, *James Nayler, the Rebel Saint* (London, 1931), and Hill, *The World Turned Upside Down,* ch. 10.

42   Margaret Fell, *For Menasseth Ben Israel: The Call of the Jews out of Babylon* (London, 1656).

43   See Popkin, "Rabbi Nathan Shapira's Visit to Amsterdam in 1657," in J. Michman and T. Levie, eds, *Dutch Jewish History* (Jerusalem, 1984), 185–205.

44   *An Information Concerning the Present State of the Jewish Nation in Europe and Judea. Wherein the Footsteps of Providence preparing a way for their Conversion to Christ, and for their Deliverance from Captivity are Discovered* (London, 1658).

45   See David Katz, "English Charity and Jewish Qualms: The Rescue of the Ashkenazi Community of Seventeenth-Century Jerusalem," in A. Rapoport-Albert and S. J. Zipperstein, eds, *Jewish History: Essays in Honour of Chimen Abramsky* (London, 1988), 245–66.

46   See, for instance, the millenarian interpretations of the eclipse of 1654 in Elisabeth Labrousse, *L'Entrée de Saturne au Lion. L'Eclipse de Soleil du 12 Aout 1654* (The Hague, 1974).

47   See Popkin, "Two Unused Sources about Sabbatai Zevi and his Effect on European Communities," *Dutch Jewish History* II, ed. J. Michman (Jerusalem, 1989), 67–74.

48   Christian Knorr von Rosenroth, *Kabbala Denudata* (Sulzbach, 1677–8).
     The collection begins and ends with claims that this body of material will
     help bring about the Conversion of the Jews, and hence begin the
     millennium. See Allison Coudert, "The Kabbala Denudata: Converting
     Jews or Seducing Christians?," in R. H. Popkin and Gordon Weiner,
     eds, *Jewish Christians and Christian Jews from the Renaissance to the Enlight-
     enment* (Dordrecht, 1994), 73–96.

49   On this see Ernestine G. E. van der Wall, "Prophecy and Profit: Nicolaes
     Van Rensselaer, Charles II and the Conversion of the Jews," in C.
     Augustin et al., *Essays on Church History, Presented to Prof Dr Jan van den
     Berg* (Kampen, 1987), 75–87.

50   Michael Hunter, *Science and Society in Restoration England* (Cambridge,
     1981); James R. Jacob, *Robert Boyle and the English Revolution* (New
     York, 1977); Margaret Jacob, *The Newtonians and the English Revolution*
     (London, 1977); and R. Kroll, R. Ashcroft, and P. Zagorin, eds, *Philoso-
     phy, Science and Religion in England, 1640–1700* (Cambridge, 1992).

51   See David S. Katz, *Sabbath and Sectarians in Seventeenth Century England*
     (Leiden, 1988).

52   See George H. Williams, *The Radical Reformation* (Philadelphia, 1962);
     and Dan Robert, *Az Erdelyi Szombatosok es Pechi Syimon, The Transylva-
     nian Sabbatarians and Simon Pechi* (Budapest, 1987).

53   The details of his case and career appear in Gershom Scholem, *Sabbatai
     Sebi: The Mystical Messiah* (Princeton, NJ, 1973).

54   Cf. Hanna Swiderska, "Three Polish Pamphlets on Pseudo-Messiah
     Sabbatai Zevi," *British Library Journal,* 15 (1989), 212–16.

55   On what happened in the Amsterdam Jewish community, see Yosef
     Kaplan, *From Christianity to Judaism. The Story of Isaac Orobio de Castro*
     (Oxford, 1989), ch. 8.

56   Cf. Ernestine G. E. van der Wall, *De Mystieke Chiliast Petrus Serrarius
     (1600–1669) en zijn Wereld* (Leiden, 1987), esp. chs 9–12. Serrarius
     was a leading millenarian closely associated with Dury, Boreel, and
     Oldenburg, and was the patron of Spinoza.

57   Cf. Michael McKeon, "Sabbatai Sevi in England," *Association of Jewish
     Studies Review,* 3 (1977), 131–69.

58   On this see Scholem, *Sabbatai Sebi,* and his article on the Donmeh in the
     Encyclopedia Judaica.

59   Studies that will soon appear by Matthew Goldish based on recently
     discovered manuscript materials indicate that there were active followers
     in London and Amsterdam. Marsha Keith Shuchard has found active
     Sabbatians involved with Free Masons and Swedenborgians in London
     throughout the eighteenth century. See her "Swedenborg, Jacobitism,
     and Freemasonry," in Erland Brock and Jane Williams-Hogan, eds,

Swedenborg and his Influence (Bryn Athyn, 1988), 159–79, and her forthcoming book on the subject.

Another movement emerged in the late eighteenth century, led by one Jacob Frank, who claimed to be the reincarnation of Sabbatai Zevi.

60 See *The Correspondence of Henry Oldenburg*, eds Marie Boas Hall and Rupert Hall (Madison and Milwaukee, 1974), vol. III, 446–7, and E. G. E. van der Wall, "A Precursor of Christ or a Jewish Impostor," *Pietismus und Neuzeit*, 14 (1988), 109–24.

61 See, for example, Nathaniel Homes, "Some Glimpses of Israel's Call Approaching," in *Miscellanea* (London, 1666).

62 Popkin, "The End of the Career of a Great 17th Century Millenarian: John Dury," *Pietismus und Neuzeit*, 14 (1988), 203–20, and "Jewish Christian Relations in the 16th and 17th Century: The Concept of the Messiah," *Jewish History*, 6 (1992), 163–77; and van der Wall, "A Precursor of Christ."

63 On Pauli see Hans Joachim Schoeps, *Philosemitismus im Barock* (Tübingen, 1952), 53–67.

64 On this see the study by Allison Coudert, *Leibniz and the Kabbala* (Kluwer, forthcoming).

65 On his career see Schoeps, *Philosemitismus*, 67–81, and the articles on him, listed under his real name "Spaeth, Johann Peter," in the *Jewish Encyclopedia*, 11:484, and in the *Encyclopedia Judaica*, 15:219–20.

66 On this see Charles Webster, *The Great Instauration: Science, Medicine and Reform 1626–1660* (London, 1975), and Frances A. Yates, *The Rosicrucian Enlightenment* (London, 1972).

67 On More see the articles in Sarah Hutton, ed., *Henry More (1614–1687) Tercentenary Studies* (Dordrecht, 1990), and the articles by Sarah Hutton and Robert Iliffe on More's studies on the Book of Revelation in J. E. Force and Popkin, eds, *Spinoza and Newton as Bible Scholars* (forthcoming).

68 On this see Popkin, "The Third Force in Seventeenth-Century Thought: Scepticism, Science and Millenarianism," in *The Third Force*, 90–119. Their falling-out over interpreting Revelation is described in More's letter to Dr John Sharp, Aug. 16, 1680, in *The Conway Letters*, Marjorie Hope Nicolson and Sarah Hutton, eds (Oxford, 1992), 478–9.

69 Cf. James E. Force and Richard H. Popkin, *Essays on the Context, Nature, and Influence of Isaac Newton's Theology* (Kluwer, 1990), and Popkin, "Newton's Biblical Theology and his Theological Physics," in P. B. Scheurer and G. Debrock, *Newton's Scientific and Philosophical Legacy* (Kluwer, 1988), 81–97.

70 On Whiston, see James E. Force, *William Whiston, Honest Newtonian* (Cambridge, 1985).

71 London, 1687. The French original appeared in the same year.

72 p. *2r–v.

73 Ibid., Book II, ch. 17, p. 299.

74 Ibid., 309–10. Jurieu's view of what will happen seems to be a combination of Mede's and La Peyrère's expectations.

75 Cf. ibid., Book II, p. 48.

76 See Hillel Schwartz, *The French Prophets: The History of a Millenarian Group in Eighteenth-Century England* (Berkeley, 1980).

77 On this see Popkin, "The Christian Roots of Zionism," *Contentions*, vol. II (1993), 99–125.

78 See Nahum Sokolow, *The History of Zionism 1600–1918* (London, 1919).

7

Secular Apocalypse: Prophets and Apocalyptics at the End of the Eighteenth Century

Elinor Shaffer

A dramatic scene about 'The End of the World' was staged at the *fin-de-siècle* by Christian Morgenstern, the well-known poet of 'The Gallows Songs', about the evil genius who triumphantly announces he has engineered the end of the world – and then is brought up short when he realizes that once his plan is carried out no one will be left to celebrate his fame:

> 'Tonight I shall carry it out. Tonight, just as the 14th of November has ended and the 15th of November has begun, it will take place, after which nothing will take place ever again, anywhere.
> 'But I'd like to tell you how I came to my decision – although – yes, yes, yes, certainly, it's true – to what end should I tell the story, after all? I have just pointed out that tonight everything will come to an end, and so this story too will end, and also every reader of my story.'[1]

Lighthearted though this brief playlet or 'ten-minute sizzler' is, it reveals an important truth. The human will to believe that the End of the World is not the end of the world is as powerful as the hope or the fear of the End. 'The End of the World' as traditionally understood is the end of the others, the enemy, the unworthy, the present oppressors – but not of ourselves. The end of the world ushers in a new world, preferably on earth. The convinced millenarian, as Norman Cohn has vividly shown, believed that the apocalypse would usher in a thousand-year rule of the Saints – that is, the rule of the believers – on earth – before the Day of Judgement actually took place.[2]

Drawing directly, like so much literature, on the apocalyptic scenes of the Book of Revelation, John Donne put the desire for deferral not from the point of view of the architect of the end, but from that of the individual subject to it. First impatiently summoning up the angels to give the signal for the dead to arise for the Last Judgement –

> At the round earth's imagined corners, blow
> Your trumpets, Angels

and then envisioning the souls of the dead reunited with their bodies in order to rise from their graves:

> and arise, arise
> From death, you numberless infinities
> Of souls, and to your scattered bodies go

and only when the risen dead are to stand to be judged, in terror silencing the trumpets again:

> But let them sleep, Lord, and me mourn a space . . .

Before the end, 'Teach me how to repent', he asks; but the space required to learn how to repent may be immeasurable.[3] Dr Donne is pleased to be witty as well as learned, even when meditating on Last Things.

If, however, in the millenarial scenario the world does not end but only *this* world, or even this era or phase of the world – if the world ends only to be renewed or replaced, introducing radical discontinuity but not the definitive end, both its end and its renewal may be envisaged in a variety of ways. Even after the Last Judgement itself (in the Book of Revelation scenario), it is a new world that comes: the New Jerusalem, which may be interpreted as transcendent, or once again as secular. The New Jerusalem has no End. As a recent critic puts it in an essay entitled 'Why Destroy the World?', 'There are virtually no tales of the end of the world in which all of creation ends.'[4]

The traditional apocalypse ('unveiling' or, simply, 'disclosure') thus reveals and signifies as much the new beginning or renovation as the end. Each period, however, redefines its notion of the end and its mode of deferring it.

In our own time the apocalyptic end is primarily a natural one, or one predicted or explicable by science, and is defined simply as a catastrophe or violent destruction. In this simplified and reduced scenario we have considerable if reluctant faith. The utopian hope of renovation, by contrast, is, at this particular moment, at a very low ebb. In returning to the end of the eighteenth century we may find it especially difficult to entertain or recapture the millennial hope that the prospect of the French Revolution raised. Even by the end of the nineteenth century, apocalypse had descanted into 'fin-de-siècle', decadent, degenerate, and at times already beckoning to a natural or pseudo-scientific apocalypse in the form of biological exhaustion or entropic dissipation. 'Fin-de-siècle' was defined by Barbey d'Aurevilly as 'the dress rehearsal of the Last Judgement without king or god'.[5]

At the end of the eighteenth century both King and God were present on the opening night, and the shades, at least, of King and God were still vivid throughout the run. The ambiguity attaching to a secular Enlightenment apocalypse, however, was already visible at the time of the French Revolution. The state of affairs eloquently described by Christopher Hill as obtaining in the English Revolution – 'It is difficult to exaggerate the extent and strength of millenarian expectations among ordinary people in the 1640s and early 50s' – had been much altered.[6] England by the middle of the next century was no longer that 'nation of Prophets'.

The ambiguity that arises in the eighteenth century stems from the new movement of criticism or critique, which called in question the literal belief in prophecy and its fulfilment. The rational Enlightenment scrutiny of the biblical texts was itself part of the political movement that questioned the basis of authority in church and state. Yet the literal application of the apocalypse to historical events became once again, as the French Revolution proceeded, almost irresistible. Enlightened scepticism and millennial enthusiasm seemed for a moment in the 1790s to inhabit the same individuals. New variants on the genre of literary apocalypse emerged amidst a flood of apocalyptic imagery. But the battle over what was authentic and inauthentic intensified.

As Franco Venturi has written of the Europe-wide influence of the English Commonwealthmen and especially the Deist John Toland, 'It is certainly true that, as always in the German Enlightenment, the moral and aesthetic temptations made the call for political freedom of the British thinkers less active.'[7] Venturi argued twenty years ago that 'the history of this process has still to be written'. In fact, the German critic Reinhart Koselleck has recently done much to show the power of these very 'moral and aesthetic temptations' in the formulation in both France and Germany of the essential notion of the independence from the state of an institution of criticism or the Republic of Letters, first in a Spinozist defence against state power holding that comment on moral and aesthetic matters had nothing to do with the state, and should therefore be free; and then, in a further claim to autonomy making moral and aesthetic criticism a political base and springboard.[8] The critical claim to autonomy – a word that has come in for some lambasting recently – was in the first instance precisely not what the lambasters, among them 'new historicists' and 'deconstructionists', call it, a mode of evasion or withdrawal from the world of political implication and action, but on the contrary the claim to a high ground from which they could launch the critique of church and state.

Kant, the theorist of autonomy in the moral and aesthetic spheres, also laid the foundations for the actual institutions of critique. Taking an example close to us, the principle of academic freedom, that is, the autonomy of the University as the place of independent inquiry, was formulated by Kant in the *Conflict of the Faculties* (1798) and embodied in the plans for a new University presented by Wilhelm von Humboldt to the King of Prussia in 1808. Humboldt boldly demanded not only intellectual autonomy, but financial autonomy from the state: only by guaranteeing an independent income to the university could the state that aspired to be honoured in the history of humankind prove its own stature in matters of culture and education.[9]

Yet the weapon of critique was also turned against any literal religious interpretations of the apocalypse whether of left or right. Kant stated the philosophical case vigorously. The hope of 'deferral' of the end may be a natural one; but the critical spirit of the Enlightenment was not slow to perceive and to capitalize on the fact that there are also philosophical problems in the notion of the end of time that nevertheless ushers in a new time. As Kant pointed out in his essay *The End of All Things* (1794), 'the notion that a time will come when all change (and with it time itself) ceases, is offensive to the imagination.'[10] The human mind cannot grasp the notion of the end of time, because the mind's medium is time. It cannot grasp eternity except as the negative of time. A life without time (if it can be called life) can only appear as extinction. Our minds fall unavoidably into contradictions, when we try to take a single step out of the world of the senses into that of the intelligible. 'The instant that forms the end of time, should also be the beginning of eternity, with which then the two are brought into the same time series, which is self-contradictory.'[11]

As a result, the mind keeps transforming eternity back into time terms. The angel of the apocalypse is always driven back by the high winds of history. The eternal hallelujahs of heaven and the eternal outcry of the tormented in hell are translated into repetition, a conception belonging to time. Instead, Kant suggests, we should convert the notion of 'the end' to moral uses by viewing the unending progression from good to better as if it were subjected to no changes in time.

To comprehend the clash between the enabling of movements of reform and revolution, on the one hand, and the scepticism attaching to traditional prophecies of the apocalypse, on the other, both arising from the critical movement towards autonomy, we need to go back a step. The critical impulse had from the beginning of the eighteenth century trained the eye of reason on Scripture, enabling new claims to independence and free thought, but undermining the literal millennial visions of the English Revolution.

The critique of the Book of Revelation was one of the main vehicles of the new criticism. The role of prophecy was central to religion: as the Nicene creed put it (third article), 'We believe in the Holy Spirit . . . who spoke through the prophets.' By the same token criticism focused on prophecy. The prophets of every religion began to be seen as deceivers, seeking power for themselves or securing that of their overlords. The English Deists subjected the claims of prophecy to sceptical examination; Anthony Collins in *A Discourse of the Grounds and Reasons of the Christian Religion* (1724) and *The Literal Scheme of Prophecy Considered* argued that no prophecy, if taken at the literal level, could be regarded as having been fulfilled except by elaborate interpretation by allegory and type. Mid-eighteenth-century writers initiated a form of apology for discredited prophecy; Robert Lowth, for example, held biblical prophecy to be the central example of 'the primeval and genuine poetry'.[12] Lowth also wrote a disquisition on Isaiah which had a far-reaching influence on the notions of prophetic style. The Book of Revelation was almost universally acknowledged to be the most perfect embodiment of biblical prophecy, and in suggesting a style of apparent disorder and bold transitions, multiple perspectives, and visionary theatre, did much to introduce a new notion of what poetry should be. This new-model 'prophetic voice' exerted an immense attraction in the later eighteenth century, and is the source of much that we know as Romantic poetry.

The inquiry into the nature of prophecy impinged directly on the genre of apocalyptic, which had been 'grafted onto the prophetic trunk'. In fact, though, the close inquiry into prophecy did not undo the graft but had the effect of moving prophecy closer to apocalyptic, indeed, redefining prophecy in terms of apocalyptic. The Deists had attacked so-called prophecy on the grounds that it was written after the events it pretended to prophesy and predict; religious leaders, they concluded, are not to be trusted. If the Book of Daniel was written later than the events it prophesies (as Collins suggested), what do we mean by 'prophecy'?

But this is the very definition of 'apocalyptic': that it is written after the date of the end it predicts. Apocalyptic as a literary genre practised by the Jews and the early Christians between 250 BC and 150 AD is distinguished both from prophecy and from the more general 'apocalyptic pattern of thought'. Historically the genre of apocalypse represents a visionary restatement of the cosmic power of God (Jehovah), as opposed to the prophetic genre in which God's power is seen working itself out in history. The apocalyptic writings are attached to the names of wise men or scribes, not prophets, and derive from a need to restate the true form of divine regime in an actual situation of a loss of control over current historical events.[13] Many influential prophecies were in fact instances of apocalyptic. The most important of the Sibylline Oracles, for example, though written in the seventh century, was issued under the name of the fourth-century bishop and martyr Methodius of Patara and purported to be a prophecy. The more outspoken free-thinkers were not slow to call this 'forgery'. Nevertheless, as the history of the best-known example, the Book of Revelation, vividly shows, the revelation of eschatological salvation in a narrative frame by an otherworld mediator can easily be mistaken for a prophecy of future intervention of the divine in the affairs of history, and that future may often be understood as imminent. This is not least the case if the revelation is presented to a group with an experience of alienation and deprivation, and a felt need for redress, as happened again at the time of the French Revolution.

It was not difficult to make the dates fit the new Revolutionary timetable. The traditional calculation of when the apocalypse would take place had not been altogether accurate: the early Christians, puzzled as to why the apocalypse promised by 'John' had not come, calculated on the basis of Scripture (Genesis and Psalm 90) that to God a thousand years is like a day, and thus on analogy with the six days of creation the world would end after six thousand years, and the new Sabbath or the Millennium, the last thousand years, begin; and if (on the estimate of the lifespans given in Genesis) the world began in the year 4004 BC then it must end in the year 2004 AD. But there was a flaw in this timetable: for the Jewish calendar reckons in lunar months, which are shorter, so that the allotted time would be up sooner: in fact, some calculated, at the time of the French Revolution. Blake, in his early Prophetic Book *America*, used a calculation of the epochs of history based on Matthew 1.17 – 'So all the generations from Abraham to David are fourteen generations; and from David until the carrying away into Babylon are fourteen generations; and from the carrying away into Babylon unto Christ are fourteen generations' – to arrive at the time, fourteen generations from Christ, of the American Revolution.[14] Thus once again the Revolution seemed both to call in question the apocalyptic view and to bear it out, even to carry it out. We today may take note: the more traditional date of 2004 is very near.

Apocalyptic is a genre in its own right; but in the context of critique and of encroaching revolution a clash between rational critique and the forces it had helped to unleash was inscribed in the difference between literally interpreted prophecy and poetic apocalypticism. Apocalyptic was inauthentic prophecy: only he who had already lived past the 'sell-by' date of the End could prophesy it retrospectively.

Thus the very movement of criticism which seemed to endow poets with the dignity of prophets and empower them with a new style in fact turned them to apocalyptics, who were deprived of the power to see into the future, deprived of prophetic inspiration. The critical movement could turn poets into prophets only because it had turned prophets into poets.

The analysis of the authorship and dating of the OT and NT had a powerful influence also on the notion of authorship itself, as I have argued elsewhere.[15] If the author of the Book of Revelation was not the Apostle John nor the Evangelist John (as was powerfully argued both on dating and stylistic grounds), who was he? In the loss of belief in the direct inspiration of the Scriptures from God greater stress was placed on the mode of authorship, on the genres of authorship, and on the literary conduct of the text. The sense in Revelation of the 'double authorship', as Paul Ricoeur has put it – the voice of God speaking through the visionary's – was too narrow; 'the explicit form of double speaking tends to link the notion of revelation to that of inspiration conceived as one voice behind another.'[16] The author discerned behind the traditional name ('John') begins to pull away from the condition of mere dictation, of double speaking, of insufflation, and to occupy a ground of 'autonomy'.

But if the assertion of independence on behalf of, and on the part of, the author gives him new critical purchase, it also weakens him; for he no longer has the conviction lent by the assurance that the voice of the Holy Spirit speaks through him. He becomes self-conscious, reflective, assailed by self-doubt; he is belated, too late to be a true prophet; his voice unaided and alone is a feeble instrument. The conditions of political extremity, while initially they feed the prophetic afflatus, may not be favourable to his talents.

The further Kantian claims of autonomy, to have lodged within consciousness the true Kingdom of Ends (the realm of morality), and the free and harmonious play of the faculties (the realm of aesthetics) gave the poet new, inner resources. But the claim of the self-consciousness to found itself, as Ricoeur puts it, 'makes a scandal of the notion that a particular moment of history can be invested with an absolute character'.[17] Thus, paradoxically, the modern apocalyptic consciousness is precisely the consciousness unable to envision a particular moment of history as either the First Coming – or the Second Coming. The modern apocalyptic cannot see the apocalypse.

Yet for a time the progress of rational critique and the outbreak of events that could be interpreted as the apocalypse, the beginning of the millennium, were strangely intermingled and mutually enabling. The critical impulse that trained the eye of reason on Scripture could in some respects and in paradoxical ways make the belief in a literal apocalypse the more heady, the more dangerous in its effects. We may take the example of Zion Ward, the follower of Joanna Southcott, who embraced his belief in her prophecies because of his encounter with the radical Richard Carlile. Employing the erudite techniques of the higher criticism in a political cause, Carlile declared that the only evidence for the existence of Jesus Christ was the New Testament, and that the supposed 'disciples' had written their gospel 'witness' more than a hundred years after the events of the Crucifixion and the Resurrection they claimed to have seen with their own eyes. The Gospels are an allegory; Jesus stands for Science, the true Word of God, which is always being born again from obscurity, ever persecuted by priests, once more rising from the dead. For Zion Ward, this shattered his faith; but he found his way by these very means to a new faith in the prophecies of Joanna Southcott.[18] His experience is an early and strange example of what became the Victorian genre of conversion explored by Carlyle, Mrs Humphrey Ward (in her fine novel *Robert Elsmere*), and Samuel Butler. For if the Scriptures are not event, not past history, but figures of what is to come, then (Zion Ward reasoned) they might still be coming, still be before us, still to be realized. What did not take place *then* may be about to take place *now*.

Joanna Southcott herself began to have prophetic visions in the momentous year 1792, when she first heard her Voices prophesying war, while Pitt was declaring in his Budget speech: 'there never was a time in the history of our country when from the situation in Europe we might more reasonably expect fifteen years of peace.'[19]

Joanna's Voices have sometimes been suggested as a source for Coleridge's line in 'Kubla Khan', 'ancestral voices prophesying war'; more probably Coleridge and Southcott shared the same biblical resources, though the shared imagery only makes more vivid the contrast between the apocalyptic author and the prophetess. Certainly the young Coleridge himself in 1794 began a poem replete with imagery of the Book of Revelation, in which the events of the end are presided over by a procession of the illustrious ushering in a millennial age, including Milton, Newton, Hartley and Priestley:

> Who of woman born
> May image in his wildly-working thought,
> How the black-visaged, red-eyed Fiend outstretcht
> Beneath th'unsteady feet of Nature groans
> In feverish slumbers – destin'd then to wake,
> When fiery whirlwinds thunder his dread name
> And Angels shout, DESTRUCTION! How his arm
> The Mighty Spirit lifting high in air
> Shall swear by Him, the ever-living ONE
> TIME IS NO MORE![20]

Coleridge did not call these rather windy evocations of the apocalypse 'prophecies' even then, when his enthusiasm for the Revolution had not yet fully waned, but 'religious musings'.

Joanna Southcott, however, believed that she was the 'Woman clothed with the Sun' of Revelation and would give birth to the Son she called Shiloh; after celebrating marriage with her 'Joseph', she died disillusioned in 1814 when her false pregnancy subsided. The image of false pregnancy is a powerful one for the failure of apocalyptic expectation (for the womb of time which, when full, will give birth to the apocalypse is a common apocalyptic expression from the apocalypse of Ezra, much used, for example, by Blake). But her followers lived on in the expectation of the imminent appearance of Shiloh, her child, the new leader. The name derives from Genesis where the King James version has Jacob say, 'The sceptre shall not depart from Judah until Shiloh come' (49.10). The passage is much disputed; but Joanna adopted the name of what is normally a town in Palestine as her son's name, and indeed the Messiah's name.[21] Joanna Southcott's successor, George Turner, heard a voice proclaiming: 'Shiloh lives! When old enough he will return. Then Armageddon will begin. Get ready to play your part in it.' The proclamations continued:

> The Angel of the Lord shall sink all by Earthquake. The whole United Kingdom is to be divided to the People on the Roll. [These were the faithful who had received the 'Seal of the Apocalypse' from Joanna.] Those who are not worth a penny now must be lords of the land. No rents must be paid. No postage for letters. No turnpikes. No taxes. Porter a gallon for one half-penny. Ale the same. The dead must be carried in carts three miles from the city and put into deep pits covered with pigs' flesh.[22]

Finally the voice promised, 'Shiloh My son, shall appear in London on October 14th.' He would come as a boy of six, for he had been born when Joanna died in 1814. First would come fifteen years of struggle, while Shiloh established his Kingdom; then would come the march to Jerusalem, and the millennium, the thousand years of bliss. Turner delivered the prophecy to his followers, and the faithful gathered on the evening of 13 October in a hall hired by Turner to await the Coming. Shiloh might come at midnight, or at any time during the day. There was hardly room to stand; hour after hour ticked away, the air grew hotter and hotter; still they waited and prayed. In a moment they would see him! But midnight came and went, and so did the noon and the evening; and when the clock struck twelve for the third time, a moan went up: they realized that nothing had happened.[23]

Those people who expected the Apocalypse in whatever form, political or religious, or more commonly an intermingling of both, and were thus disappointed, were struck by what E. P. Thompson has called the 'chiliasm of despair'.[24] The term has two applications, to the disappointed enthusiasts for revolution, and to those converted to counter-revolution. As Karl Mannheim put it:

> Chiliasm has always accompanied revolutionary outbursts and given them their spirit. When this spirit ebbs and deserts these movements there remains behind in the world a naked mass-frenzy and a despiritualized fury.[25]

In England, what Thompson identifies as 'authentic millenarialism' – that is, the millenarialism that links 'poor man's dissent' with political revolutionary activity – was short-lived, ending in the late 1790s, with the defeat of English Jacobinism, the onset of the Wars, and the confining in a madhouse of Richard Brothers, a forerunner of Southcott, and author of the *Revealed Knowledge of the Prophecies and Times* (1794).[26] This may be to put it within too narrow historical bounds; on Thompson's own showing, Brothers had already been confined by 1796. But it was part of Thompson's aim to stress how short-lived the moment of 'authentic millenarialism' was in England.

Yet when Zion Ward arose as leader, well after Southcott's death, the faithful remnant were still expectant. For men such as Ward the radical attack on the literal word of the Bible led to a renewed literalism: indeed, Jesus the Messiah had not come, but He would now come. As Ward proclaimed: 'Behold, now Behemoth dasheth in pieces false and counterfeit Christianity.'[27]

Thus the literal belief in the apocalypse, in the pockets where it survived, died hard. If we look to see how the tradition of critique fared in the biblical criticism of the Book of Revelation just after the Revolutionary period, after the fall of Napoleon and the Restoration, we find a review essay in the theological journal (*Theologische Zeitschrift*) edited by leading German theologians Schleiermacher, de Wette, and Lücke in 1820 dealing with new works on the Book of Revelation. The essay opens with the striking statement that 'the interpretation of

the apocalypse stands at the same point to which Eichhorn had brought
it more than thirty years ago'.[28] J. G. Eichhorn, in his Latin *Commentary
on the Apocalypse of John* (1791), had given the visions of its author a
specific historical setting: the Fall of Jerusalem in the year 69–70 AD;
and he had divided the whole into three acts of a grand drama. But
Eichhorn had still maintained that John the Apocalyptic was the same
man as the Evangelist John, that is, that the Book of Revelation was
written by the author of the Gospel of John and the disciple of Jesus.
Now this identification was challenged.[29] In effect, the late dating of
the fourth Gospel well beyond apostolic times had already driven the
Gospel and the Book of Revelation far apart, and Eichhorn's revision
of the rules governing canonicity had made the name of the author in
any case merely traditional. He had already enunciated the principle
that canonicity was not to depend on apostolic authorship, but authorship on canonicity, that is, on tradition within the church, and on the
conformity of the doctrine with apostolic teaching.[30] More important,
for our present purposes, the visions of 'John', in the new view of
thirty years later, are visions not of his own time nor of a past time
revisited and still less of the future, but visions he had while writing:
aesthetic visions of a creative present.[31] The ostensible place of the
visions, Patmos, Eichhorn had already seen as a 'poetic fiction' rather
than an actual geographical location.[32] Time is historicized, yet it is not
thereby fixed in time, on the contrary, it is made movable, at the beck
and call of the visionary, in so far as it refers to the period of writing.
Moreover, according to the reviewer, these are not 'visions' in the
sense of visualizable images; the vision is specifically a poetic, a literary
form.[33] 'John' – whoever he may have been – is unequivocally and
wholly a poet. History becomes the medium – it is neither what must
be denied, as by Augustine, in favour of an ideal, timeless view of
divine order, nor is it the mistaken literal chronology of those who
interpreted the angel of Revelation's words, 'The time is at hand', as
setting the alarm for the millennium at twelve o'clock tomorrow.

The reviewer, Friedrich Bleek, later gave lectures on the Apocalypse, and the translation into English was offered by subscription to
'persons of liberal thought'.[34] The section entitled 'On the Literary
Envelope of the Book, especially the Mode of Description in Visions'
throws some further light on the matter. While the writer still attributed genuine prophecy to the earliest Old Testament prophets, and
even granted that in a later age the apostles Peter and Paul may have

'been put into an ecstatic condition, in which symbolical images were brought before their spiritual eye for the revelation of religious truth', the writer of the Apocalypse was not in a state of ecstasy while writing:

> We must either look upon the whole representation in visions merely as a free literary envelope, such as is often found in Jewish and Christian writers of that and later times; . . . or, if visions were actually communicated to the author with symbolic images referring to the future and ulterior development of the kingdom of god, that he carried them out afterwards with poetic freedom in individual parts, and their connection with one another. In either case it is understood that the writer is not constant in the mode of representation by visions, but uses the future tense for prophecy several times; soon returning, however, to another mode, where the future presents itself as present to his eye.[35]

We may see Coleridge's words in the preface to 'Kubla Khan' (1816) – 'the words rose up before me as things' – in this light: the visionary images of the poet are instantly realized as words. Coleridge's preface is notoriously a piece of apocalyptic; for it was written twenty years after the poem itself, repositioning the apocalyptic's vision before the event. Indeed, the whole setting of the event of writing the visions is closely related to contemporary styles of apocalyptic. One of the more literal-minded 'prophets', William Sharp – incidentally, a friend of Blake's who was in close touch with Joanna Southcott – is described by Thomas Holcroft as 'favoured with a revelation' in a passage strikingly similar to Coleridge's report of his retreat to a farmhouse 'near Linton' that has never been securely identified:

> Last summer Sharp had retired to a lonely place near or at Kilburn; and there he himself had been absolutely favoured with a revelation, communicating to him personally, beyond all doubt, the revolutions that are immediately to happen.[36]

Coleridge wrote in the same vein:

> In the summer of the year 1797, the Author, then in ill health, had retired to a lonely farm-house between Porlock and Linton, on the Exmoor confines of Somerset and Devonshire . . . The Author continued for about three hours in a profound sleep, at least of the outward senses, during which time he has the most vivid confidence, that he could not have composed less than from two to three hundred lines; if

that indeed can be called composition in which all the images rose up
before him as things, with a parallel production of the correspondent
expressions, without any sensation or consciousness of effort.[37]

At this moment, we recall, the notorious 'person from Porlock' 'de-
tained' him, dissipating the vision. Coleridge's apocalyptic 'preface'
may then be a political tactic, as Empson has ingeniously argued about
the glosses on 'The Ancient Mariner', added at the same time: the
apocalyptic poet calls attention by these echoes to the failed expectations of the past in justification of his epic *manqué*.

Perhaps the major piece of English apocalyptic poetry in the Romantic period is Wordsworth's account of 'Crossing the Alps' in Book
VI of *The Prelude* – a passage on which all the critics of Romanticism
in the last forty years have cut their eye teeth. Recently there has again
been an outcry against the Romantic 'evasion' of political realities; thus
we are told that Wordsworth is at fault for not placing the vagrants
who were living in the Abbey at the time inside 'Tintern Abbey'
(though those who remember the poem will know that Tintern Abbey
itself is not described in it);[38] and that he ducked the issue of Napoleon
by omitting mention of him in his 'Crossing the Alps' passage (though
of course Wordworth's crossing preceded Napoleon's). Such readings
conclude that Wordsworth's description of his 1790 tour in Book VI
is 'a sustained effort to deny history by asserting nature as the separating
mark constitutive of the egotistical self'.[39] More sweepingly still, 'the
theory of denial is the Imagination'.[40]

Yet in the new critical apocalyptic it was not the contents – the
occult secrets of the End revealed by superstitious 'oracles' as God's
plan[41] – that the poets employed, but the aesthetic forms suggested by
it and their associated imagery: dreams, visions, the journey to Hell,
apocalyptic marriage, and perhaps above all the form of the 'premon-
ition of the future', or what Coleridge called 'presentiment'. The
presentiment of the future encourages the intervention of the narrator/
author, just as the narration of a past historical event, as Benveniste tells
us, tends to exclude such intervention, as the past tells itself and is
beyond intervention.[42] The apocalyptic stance allows the person of the
narrator/author to intervene in the past. But just as the apocalyptic
loses the authenticity of the prophet's voice inhabited by the Holy
Spirit, so he loses the certainty of the enacted past. He is already
without the fulfilment of the future that the prophet can claim; he is

left with his 'presentiment'. He becomes fragmentary, disordered, self-conscious, sometimes ironic, in the sense of Romantic irony that places the source of the irony in the recognition of the impossibility of maintaining the vision by the power of art alone.

But Wordsworth here – writing in the year 1802 – employs the apocalyptic form that had become the poet's form *par excellence* to embody the presentiment. Wordsworth, in the company of a fellow student, caught up in enthusiasm for the Revolution (the Fall of the Bastille had occurred on the day of their crossing from England, and *fêtes de fédération* took place all along their route), was crossing the Simplon Pass in 1790. They missed their way, and kept on climbing; only to meet a peasant who instructed them to descend again to the point they had started from, from which point 'all our course / Was downwards with the current of the stream'.[43] Disappointed, Wordsworth realized they had crossed the Alps without knowing it. He is touched with a form of 'the chiliasm of despair': the event towards which all his hopes and expectations were straining lay already in the past. He had prophesied it, and awaited it, and now he could only lamely reconstruct it as a past event. At this point he breaks into the narrative with his invocation of the imagination:

> In such strength of usurpation, in such visitings
> Of awful promise, when the light of sense
> Goes out in flashes that have shewn to us
> The invisible world, doth greatness make abode,
> There harbours whether we be young or old.
> Our destiny, our nature, and our home,
> Is with infinitude – and only there;
> With hope it is, hope that can never die,
> Effort, and expectation, and desire,
> And something evermore about to be. (532–42)

The event that has been missed has been internalized; it is 'a spot of time', and the apocalypse is a permanent aspect of the future. After his moment of disappointment, of 'dull and heavy slackening', he can go on. And going down, not up, he has the moment of the apocalypse with him:

> The immeasurable height
> Of woods decaying, never to be decayed,

The stationary blasts of waterfalls,
And everywhere along the hollow rent
Winds thwarting winds, bewildered and forlorn,
The torrents shooting from the clear blue sky,
The rocks that muttered close upon our ears –
Black drizzling crags that spake by the wayside
As if a voice were in them – The sick sight
And giddy prospect of the raving stream,
The unfettered clouds and region of the heavens,
Tumult and peace, the darkness and the light,
Were all like workings of one mind, the features
Of the same face, blossoms upon one tree,
Characters of the great apocalypse,
The types and symbols of eternity,
Of first, and last, and midst and without end. (556–72)

To understand the current assault on the imagination we need to go back to the point where Paul de Man first restated the importance of Romanticism to our own time, and mounted the attack against Wordsworth through this same passage of the *Prelude*. His article 'Wordsworth and Hölderlin', written in 1956, argued that the study of Romanticism was vital to our time, for 'The main points around which contemporary methodological and ideological arguments circle can almost always be traced directly back to the romantic heritage.'[44] The claim to contemporary relevance has given Romantic studies a peculiar intensity. Romanticism has been the major battleground of theorists and critics.

In de Man's treatment, Wordsworth's experience in the Alps is accorded a powerful reference to historical events, but one that becomes separated from it by the need to overcome failure. 'The moment of active projection into the future (which is also the moment of the loss of self in the intoxication of the instant) lies for the imagination in a past from which it is separated by the experience of a failure.'[45]

This could be taken as referring to the time lapse between the experience (1790) and the writing (1802), during which Wordsworth had come to the conviction that the Revolution had failed, so that his moment of failure to realize that he was at the point of crossing the Alps, which is overcome by his invocation to the imagination, is now seen by the poet as analogous to the historical failure he has lived through and is attempting to transcend in poetry. So much is widely accepted. But de Man goes further: 'The future is present in history only as the remembering of a failed project that has become a menace.' He tries to make the failure and the menace historically concrete, by reading later poems of Wordsworth on the monastery of the Chartreuse (1816–19), later still incorporated into the 1850 *Prelude*, into the Book VI of 1802. The poet's regret that the supporters of the French Revolution may destroy the monastery, is equated by de Man with the failure to attempt to persuade them otherwise, and the analogy of the failure to recognize the crossing-point is made with a specific political failure to counter the worst excesses of the Revolution. Thus a much later political view, from a different context, is illegitimately read back into *The Prelude* of 1805 (which critics of all persuasions agree to be superior to the reworking of the last year of Wordsworth's life). It is all the more misleading because Wordsworth's later dramatic heightening of the event of his visit to the Grande Chartreuse to coincide with a glimpse of 'Arms flashing and a military glare / Of riotous men commissioned to expel / The blameless inmates' (1850, ll. 424–6) is baseless: he visited in August 1790; the monks were not expelled until 1792. In any case, the expelling force, even had he seen one, was not, as de Man implies, the groups of revellers with whom Wordsworth and Jones celebrated the storming of the Bastille, 'that great federal day' (l. 346), as they travelled from Calais to Grenoble. It is hard to avoid the sense that de Man's hardening of Wordsworth's 'failure' into a specific political error (from a point of view adopted by Wordsworth only much later) relates to his own personal experience as an early supporter of National Socialism.

The recent 'new historicist' tactics, then, are an attempt to avoid de Man's egregious historical misreadings, and instead to charge Wordsworth with the offence of evading history altogether by his appeal to imagination. De Man's conclusion suggests this further possibility: 'For Wordsworth there is no historical eschatology, but rather only a never-ending reflection upon an eschatological moment that has failed through the excess of its interiority.'

Geoffrey Hartman, one of Wordsworth's best readers, was at pains to give a characteristically subtle and generous reading of the same passage in *The Prelude*.[46] This bears on our present subject, for it is noticeable that Hartman's defence of Wordsworth leans heavily on a rhetorical use of the concept of 'prophecy'. The outline of de Man's argument is still visible: nature leads the poet beyond nature through his experience of failures that have to be made good in other ways. But his failure to perceive the crossing is redeemed: 'his disappointment becomes retrospectively a prophetic instance of that blindness to the external world which is the tragic, pervasive, and necessary condition of the mature poet.'[47] That is, by placing a positive value on the imaginative vision, Hartman is able to convert Wordsworth's early 'failure' into an authentic prophecy of his later insight. Hartman, be it noted, does not equate the imaginative power with prophecy, but comes very close to it by implying that the growth of the true poet's mind towards this insight was inexorable and so the recognition of the imagination was not a later intrusion, imposition or reinterpretation with hindsight.

This use of the language of prophecy and prophet is not an isolated example; '*The Prelude*,' Hartman writes, 'foresees the time when "the Characters of the great Apocalypse" will be intuited without the medium of Nature.'[48] It is this rhetorical use of the terms of the period itself by modern critics to validate the poetry of Romanticism to which recent new-historicist critics, notably Jerome McGann in *The Romantic Ideology*, have objected. But I would argue rather that the borrowed language of prophecy does not represent the terms of the time: a new critical interpretation had intervened. The language of prophecy was already inauthentic. The language of apocalyptic is the true language of the time. Criticism may work in historical terms (strange new historicist who should think otherwise) but it must work in the terms that express the tenor, go with the grain of the times. But is this not fully visible also only with hindsight? Yes; we are all apocalyptics now.

In Wordsworth's progress across the Alps, I suggest, the would-be prophet puts off his assumed mantle; he comprehends his actual role as modern apocalyptic, who cannot envision the event, but only recreate it in words after the fact of which he was not aware. Far from evading reality – the political reality, the historical trauma of his time – he has lived it and understood it, and with it the limitations of his role. The very use of the words 'type' and 'symbol' bears the imprint of the long movement of critique stemming from the Deists: as Collins and Richard Carlile put it, the 'type' of the event is precisely not the event itself, and the recourse to 'type' is enforced on interpreters by the proven falseness of the predictions. The 'character of the great Apocalypse' is a sign of 'the end of the world', which idea is itself only the type of eternity. The sapping of the literal sense of prophecy is confirmed by the secular experience of event *manqué* in history, as internalized in the personal experience of the poet.

The poet is indeed an 'apocalyptic', a false prophet, who speaks after the fact, yet is still the preserver of the possibility of the millennium, and of the New Jerusalem, when history shows – as it always does – that the reality is less than the hope and the dream.

If the ambiguity of the Romantic apocalyptic poets' position has made them culpable in some eyes, it enabled them to survive the period of arrested apocalypse from 1789 to 1814 – and arrested apocalypse *is* the condition of being in history – with an apocalyptic hope still intact in the form of an imaginative utopia. As the old and the new hermeneutics has it, the true function and operation of apocalyptic is not the unveiling of secrets about God's plan for the Last Days but the release of hope. The apocalyptic hope, as we began by noting, is as much a hope for continuation as it is for an end. And this the Romantic apocalyptics of the poetic imagination succeeded in preserving.

But this hope is perhaps best expressed when all is said and done by a poet who still saw with a millennial eye closer to literal vision and expectation when in the pregnant moment of 1791 he wrote these lines on the New Jerusalem from 'Night' in the *Songs of Innocence*; for after all, 'one needs a proper end' (as was said approvingly about the Book of Revelation). This is one vatic voice that still rings true:[49]

And there the lion's ruddy eyes,
Shall flow with tears of gold.
And pitying the tender cries,
And walking round the fold.
Saying: wrath by his meekness
And by his health, sickness,
Is driven away,
From our immortal day.

And now beside thee bleating lamb,
I can lie down and sleep;
Or think on him who bore thy name
Graze after thee and weep.
For washed in life's river
My bright mane forever
Shall shine like the gold
As I guard o'er the fold.

NOTES

1 Christian Morgenstern, 'The End of the World', tr. by E. S. Shaffer, in *Comparative Criticism*, 6 (Cambridge, 1984), 268.

2 Norman Cohn, *The Pursuit of the Millennium* [1957] (London, 1970), 30–5.

3 John Donne, *The Divine Poems*, ed. Helen Gardner (Oxford, 1952).

4 Eric S. Rabkin, 'Introduction: Why Destroy the World?', *The End of the World*, eds. Rabkin, Martin H. Greenberg and Joseph D. Olander (Carbondale, Ill., 1983), p. ix.

5 Hermann Hofer, 'Apocalypse et fin-de-siècle: le cas de Barbey d'Aurevilly', in *Fins de siècle: Terme-évolution-révolution?* (Toulouse, 1989), 430.

6 Christopher Hill, 'A Nation of Prophets', in *The World Turned Upside Down: Radical Ideas During the English Revolution* [1972] (Harmondsworth, 1984); the evidence is given in his *Antichrist in Seventeenth-Century England*.

7 Franco Venturi. 'English Commonwealthmen', in *Utopia and Reform* (Cambridge, 1971), 66.

8 Reinhart Koselleck, *Critique and Crisis: Enlightenment and the Pathogenesis of Modern Society* (Cambridge, Mass., 1988), 98–126. First published as *Kritik und Krise: Eine Studie zur Pathogenese der bürglichen Welt* (Freiburg and Munich, 1959).

9 See E. S. Shaffer, 'Romantic Philosophy and the Organization of the Disciplines: The Founding of the Humboldt University of Berlin', in *Romanticism and the Sciences*, eds. Andrew Cunningham and Nicholas Jardine (Cambridge, 1990); and E. S. Shaffer, 'Politics and Letters: The Strife of the Faculties', *Comparative Criticism*, 11 (Cambridge, 1989).

10 Immanuel Kant, 'Das Ende aller Dinge', *Kant's Werke*, Bd. VIII (Berlin, 1912), 332.

11 Ibid., 334.

12 Robert Lowth, *Lectures on the Sacred Poetry of the Hebrews*, tr. G. Gregory (London, 1753), 50.

13 Michael A. Knibb, 'The Emergence of the Jewish Apocalypses', in *Israel's Prophetic Tradition: Essays in Honour of Peter Ackroyd*, eds Richard Coggins, Anthony Phillips and Michael Knibb (Cambridge, 1982), 152–80. The main apocalyptic writers are Daniel, Enoch, Ezra and Baruch.

14 Leslie Tannenbaum, *Biblical Tradition in Blake's Early Prophecies: The Great Code of Art* (Princeton, NJ, 1982), 142.

15 E. S. Shaffer, *'Kubla Khan' and The Fall of Jerusalem* (Cambridge, 1975), 82–5.

16   Paul Ricoeur, 'Towards a Hermeneutic of the Idea of Revelation' [1977], in *Essays on Biblical Interpretation*, ed. with an introduction by Lewis S. Mudge (London, 1981), 92–3.

17   Ibid., 111–12.

18   G. R. Balleine, *Past Finding Out: The Tragic Story of Joanna Southcott and her Successors* (London, 1956), 94.

19   Ibid., 13.

20   'Religious Musings', ll. 404–13, *Samuel Taylor Coleridge: Poems*, ed. John Beer (London, 1991), 75.

21   In Luther's Bible the coming of a champion or hero (*Held*) is suggested, although the name of Shiloh is not given. In Hebrew commentaries 'He' is often 'Judah': that is, the sceptre shall not pass until Judah come to Shiloh.

22   Balleine, *Past Finding Out*, 77.

23   Ibid., 84.

24   E. P. Thompson, *The Making of the English Working Class*, 2nd edn (Harmondsworth, 1968), 411.

25   Karl Mannheim, *Ideology and Utopia*, tr. L. Wirth and E. Shils (London, 1960), 192–6. Quoted in Thompson, p. 419.

26   Thompson, *The Making of the English Working Class*, 420.

27   Balleine, *Past Finding Out*, 94.

28   Friedrich Bleek, 'Beitrag zur Kritik und Deutung der Offenbarung Johannis; besonders mit Rücksicht auf Heinrichs Commentar und Vogels Programme über dieselbe', in *Theologische Zeitschrift*, hrsg. von Dr. Friedr. Schleiermacher, Dr. W. M. L. de Wette, and Dr. Friedr. Lücke. Heft 2 (Berlin, 1820), [pp. 240–315], 240.

29   *Theologische Zeitschrift*, Heft 2, 242–9.

30   Shaffer, *'Kubla Khan' and The Fall of Jerusalem*, 84–5.

31   *Theologische Zeitschrift*, Bd. 2, p. 248.

32   Ibid., 249.

33   Ibid., 251–2 n. 1.

34   Friedrich Bleek, *Lectures on the Apocalypse*, ed. L. T. Hossbach, English tr. ed. Samuel Davidson (London, 1875), p. vi.

35   Ibid., 135–7.

36   J. K. Hopkins, *A Woman to Deliver her People: Joanna Southcott and English Millenarianism in an Era of Revolution* (Austin, 1982), 162.

37   Coleridge, *Poems*, 163.

38   Marjorie Levinson, *Wordsworth's Great Period Poems: Four Essays* (Cambridge, 1986).

39   Alan Liu, *Wordsworth: The Sense of History* (Palo Alto, Calif., 1989), 13.

40   Ibid., 4.

41   Coleridge condemned those who 'frame oracles by private divination' as

'presumptuous fanatics'. Quoted in Shaffer, *'Kubla Khan' and The Fall of Jerusalem*, 323 n. 55.

42 Emile Benveniste, 'Les Relations de temps dans le verbe français', in *Problèmes du linguistique générale* (Paris, 1966), 237–50.

43 William Wordsworth, *The Prelude 1799, 1805, 1850*, eds. Jonathan Wordsworth, M. H. Abrams and Stephen Gill (New York and London, 1979), Book VI, ll. 519–20.

44 Paul de Man, 'Wordsworth and Hölderlin' [1956], tr. Timothy Bahti, in *The Rhetoric of Romanticism* (New York, 1984), 48.

45 Ibid., 58–9.

46 Geoffrey H. Hartman, 'A Poet's Progress: Wordsworth and the *Via Naturaliter Negativa*', *Modern Philology*, LIV (1962), 214–24.

47 Ibid., quoted in *The Prelude*, eds. Wordsworth, Abrams and Gill, 606.

48 Ibid., 610.

49 William Blake, *The Complete Writings*, ed. Geoffrey Keynes (Oxford, 1966). The lion and the lamb are drawn from Isaiah 11.6; 'life's river' from the description of the New Jerusalem in Rev. 22.1, 'a pure river of water of life'; and the contrast of 'Night' and 'immortal Day' from Rev. 21.25: 'And the gates of it shall not be shut at all by day: for there shall be no night there.'

8

Saint-Simonian Industrialism as the End of History: August Cieszkowski on the Teleology of Universal History

Laurence Dickey

The significance of Count August Cieszkowski's writings has tradition-ally been viewed as lying in two main areas.[1] On the one hand, Cieszkowski has been identified as an important figure in the emerg-ence of messianistic nationalism in Poland in the nineteenth century. In this connection, his reputation derives from a work published in 1848 entitled *Our Father*.[2] On the other hand, an earlier work by Cieszkowski, published in German in 1838, has been singled out as an important bridge-text in the development of Hegelianism into Marx-ism. And while some well-known scholars have commented on this book, entitled *Prolegomena to Historiosophie* (henceforth *Prolegomena*), it has been interpreted to this day as a text whose relevance lies in its contribution to the ideological origins of Marxism.[3]

In focusing this essay on the *Prolegomena*, I wish to place Cieszkowski's text in a different ideological context, one which gives a fuller account of the originality of Cieszkowski's thinking. In my view, the *Prolegomena* self-consciously presents itself as a "recapitula-tion" of about fifty years of German thinking on the purpose and direction of Western history.[4] And because Cieszkowski also thought German intellectual history during these years recapitulated in micro-cosm the macrocosmic history of the West, he organized his view of Western history around recent German interpretations of the teleology of what Schiller (and Kant shortly before him) called "world" or "universal history."[5]

Cieszkowki explained the *telos* of Western history in terms of the shifting significance of the beautiful, the true, and the good in Western consciousness.[6] For him, these shifts in consciousness – which registered themselves, successively, in art, science and philosophy, and action – constituted the three main stages in the unfolding of mankind's growing awareness of its *telos*.[7] What is more, Cieszkowski presented his views on the unfolding of man's teleological awareness and on the *telos* of Western history as part of a Providential plan for the religious redemption of humanity in and through history. In the *Prolegomena*, therefore, questions of teleology and of God's plan for the salvation of mankind are ideologically linked. Needless to say, this mixing of Providential and teleological considerations makes this text an extremely interesting document in the intellectual history of the "secularization" of European thought in the nineteenth century.[8]

In developing his views on man's telos and the telos of Western history,[9] Cieszkowski acknowledged many intellectual debts to German thinkers – Lessing, Herder, Kant, Schiller, Schelling, and Hegel.[10] Accordingly, the German sources of Cieszkowski's ideas are well documented and, under Cieszkowski's guiding hand, form themselves into an interpretation of the teleological development of recent German intellectual history itself. This is especially true in those parts of the *Prolegomena* in which Schiller and Hegel are discussed – two German thinkers who, not coincidentally, are represented in the *Prolegomena* as the respective spokesmen for the beautiful and the true in recent German thinking.[11]

When, however, Cieszkowski begins to situate himself in this sequence of German thinkers – so that Schiller stands to art as Hegel stands to philosophy as Cieszkowski stands to action and/or the good – his recapitulation of German intellectual history contains subtle shifts of emphasis which, in my view, subvert rather than sustain and extend the ideological dynamic formed by the Schiller–Hegel progression.

Indeed, the ideological moves Cieszkowski makes in the *Prolegomena* to work himself into the Schiller–Hegel sequence introduce profound changes into the German intellectual debate of the late 1830s. As we shall see, these changes allow Cieszkowski to read a plot structure into recent German and all of Western history which is designed to make it easier, in Cieszkowski's words, to grasp the "laws of [humanity's] development and progress" and, on the basis of that knowledge, to predict the course of future developments in history (Cieszkowski 1979, 49).[12]

In interpreting the *Prolegomena*, then, it is especially important to understand exactly how Cieszkowski's recapitulation argument works, for it is my contention that as Cieszkowski moves to place himself in continuity of development with Schiller and Hegel on one ideological level, he undermines his relationship with them on another. This rupture in the relationship between the three thinkers can be explained in terms of Cieszkowski's Catholicism and his affinity with post-1815 French thinking on social matters. In what follows, I propose to flesh out the historical and ideological contours of this rupture: (1) by locating Cieszkowski in terms of his time and place; and (2) by explaining the argument of the *Prolegomena* both as it unfolds internally in Cieszkowski's text and as it relates at strategic points to larger ideological debates in French and German thinking taking place outside of the text. In doing this, the essay will also touch on the conceptual issues of temporalization, historicization, and secularization as they figure in current discussions of nineteenth-century intellectual history.

I

Cieszkowski's Historicization of Hegel, I: "Knowing the Future"

August Cieszkowski (1812–1894) was born into a wealthy Polish family that had extensive landholdings in Central Poland. Cieszkowski's father apparently had close ties to the Catholic church, for sometime after August's birth, while residing in Italy and mourning his recently deceased wife, he received the title of count from the Pope.[13]

Before enrolling in a Warsaw gymnasium in 1829, young August was educated at home by tutors who taught him a variety of foreign languages – Latin, French, and German among them. In the fall of 1831 Cieszkowski left Warsaw for Cracow, where he enrolled as a student in the Jagiellonian university in February, 1832. After a period of study there, he shows up next in Berlin – in the Fall of 1833.[14]

Although Hegel had died almost two years earlier, Cieszkowski found the company and teachings of Berlin Hegelians most congenial. He appears, moreover, to have had a close student–teacher relationship with K. L. Michelet, an instrumental spokesman for Hegelianism in the 1830s, and with E. Gans, who not only influenced Marx in the late 1830s but also tried to assimilate French social and economic thinking to Hegelianism from the mid-1820s on.[15] At the same time as he was being introduced to German debates about the validity of Hegel's philosophy, Cieszkowski developed an interest in the so-called "social question." He may have been first introduced to questions of social and economic justice while attending Gans's lectures on *Rechtsphilosophie* after his arrival in Berlin.[16] Or he may have brought such concerns with him from Poland where Catholics had easy access to the emerging "social" concerns of their liberally-minded French counterparts.[17] Whatever the source of Cieszkowski's socio-economic perspective, his association with Hegelianism from 1833 on was always oriented more to practical than to theoretical considerations.

After studying at the University of Berlin for five semesters, the biographical particulars of Cieszkowski's life become more difficult to discern. Over the next few years, he seems to have traveled, and to have resided in Poland for a period while preparing the *Prolegomena* for publication. We know this because it was from Poland, beginning in June, 1836, that he started a correspondence with Michelet about the project. Two Cieszkowski scholars, Kühne and Liebich, have performed great scholarly services by drawing our attention to this correspondence and to the entries Cieszkowski made in diaries he kept during the years 1834–8.[18] Taken together, the Michelet correspondence (which continued for fifty more years) and the diaries illuminate how the *Prolegomena* took shape in Cieszkowski's mind before its publication in 1838.

Several things are noteworthy about the origins of the *Prolegomena* project during 1834–8. First, in three letters to Michelet – which cover the period June, 1836, to March, 1837 – Cieszkowski announces an intention to refigure the "categories" and "architectonic" of Hegel's logic (Liebich 1979a, 29). He told his teacher that he planned to focus on the "intrinsic process" by which "the idea" organically, objectively, and progressively reveals itself in "its totality" in history (Liebich 1979a, 30). By early 1837, Cieszkowski had become convinced that he could "seek [in the past and the present] the extrapolation of this progression and . . . [by so doing] discover . . . the future," a future, he said, that hitherto had "escaped" mankind's *intuitive* and *reflective* powers (Liebich 1979a, 30).[19]

This declaration is important because by late 1837, at the time he was actually preparing the *Prolegomena* for submission to Michelet for a reading, Cieszkowski's diary entries indicate that he was writing a book on "the determination of the future" (Liebich 1979a, 28). Since the *Prolegomena* begins with a discussion of the relationship between ways of "knowing the future" and the need for understanding the "organism of history" as an unfolding idea, it is easy to see the "germ" (*germe*) of the *Prolegomena* text in the reflections Cieszkowski recorded in his diary and articulated in his correspondence to Michelet.[20]

Second, if this body of evidence helps us understand how the idea of the "future" figured in Cieszkowski's project, it also suggests how that idea underpinned his critique of Hegel's logic and philosophy of history. For example, a diary entry from 1834 questioned Hegel's understanding of "progress" in history (Liebich 1979a, 28–9). Cieszkowski's complaint – and it was typical of contemporary criticisms of Hegel's (alleged) "panlogism"[21] – was that Hegel measured progress in history too narrowly, limiting it to "the progress of the history of philosophy as philosophy itself" (Liebich 1979a, 29). According to Cieszkowski, Hegel's philosophy, while carrying thought beyond the "subjective" position expressed in the simple intuitions of "art," never got beyond the stage of pure "philosophy" itself – that is, beyond the notion of philosophy as a "science" in which "the true" is realized theoretically and/or reflectively rather than practically (Liebich 1979a, 28–9). Hegel had elevated philosophy to the level of "self knowledge" in the *Phenomenology*; but given the restrictions history placed on Hegel's own philosophical perspective he could not foresee what the future held for philosophy. Or, as Cieszkowski put it in his diary, "absolute determination" of the "good" would be absent from Hegel's science of philosophy so long as Hegel refused to embrace the future as the sphere where thought would realize itself in action (Liebich 1979a, 29).

As is well known, and as Cieszkowski endlessly asserted, Hegel steadfastly refused to speculate on the future – which explains why after 1838 so many of Hegel's critics would characterize his philosophy as "stuck in theory".[22] In 1834, however, Cieszkowski probably sincerely believed – as had Feuerbach before him[23] – that he would do for

Hegelianism what Hegel had been unable (and unwilling) to do. Thus, Cieszkowski claimed that the practical task of his philosophy was to translate Hegel's theory into practice. For that, the future had to be opened up for the practical realization of the "truth" of Hegel's philosophy. Cieszkowski volunteered himself to be the agent of that realization.

On these grounds, it is easy to see how Cieszkowski's appeal to the future allowed him to "historicize" Hegel *as a thinker* while identifying himself as the agent whereby the truth of Hegel's philosophy would be realized in action. One of the consequences of this historicization of Hegel is that the latter's philosophy can be viewed as standing to that of Cieszkowski as Hegelianism in theory stands to Hegelianism in practice. Or to put it in terms we shall return to later, Hegel's philosophy stood to Cieszkowski's as a "figure" stands to its "fulfillment".

Finally, it is instructive that as early as 1834 Cieszkowski had conjectured in his diary that "Hegel's position in the history of philosophy is the position of the phenomenology in the *Encyclopedia*" (Liebich 1979a, 29). Clarifying that cryptic remark, Cieszkowski reflected that in order for the "idea of the good" to be realized in the sphere of action the scientific "truth" of Hegel's philosophy of absolute spirit must be grounded in the *praxis* of life (Liebich 1979a, 29).

Once again it is no coincidence that in the *Prolegomena* Cieszkowski associates realization of the good (in various spheres of life) with his own philosophy of action. On the surface, of course, such a formulation suggests that Cieszkowski saw himself as one of Hegel's epigones and his own philosophy as a development within Hegelianism. The figure/fulfillment relationship mentioned above supports this view. But just as we have learned to see how Paul distorted the meaning of Judaism as he Christianized the Old Testament with the figure/fulfillment strategy of interpretation, so we need to be careful about interpreting the Hegel–Cieszkowski connection in an uncritical way. For by late 1837 there is evidence in Cieszkowski's letters and diaries that he had been reading deeply in liberal Catholic and Saint-Simonian social theory and that he was of a mind to work much of what he found in that literature into his assessment and correction of Hegel's philosophy of history (Kühne 1938, 357–67; Liebich 1979a, 25–8).[24]

Caveats about how to interpret the Hegel–Cieszkowski relationship become all the more important when we recall how prevalent was discourse about "the future" in the social theory of French Catholic and Saint-Simonian thinkers from at least 1820 on. In his diaries, Cieszkowski pays tribute to many of these thinkers by name – Philippe Joseph Buchez among them (Liebich 1979a, 27). Buchez is known by scholars today either as an advocate of "social Catholicism" or as a Saint-Simonian – occasionally as both at once (Furet 1989, 910, quoting Enfantin). In fact, in a book Cieszkowski said influenced him greatly, *Introduction à la science de l'histoire* (1833), Buchez had offered many formulations that anticipated arguments found in the *Prolegomena* just five years later. For the most part, however, these anticipations go unacknowledged in the *Prolegomena*. What is more, Cieszkowski encourages his (mainly German) readers to think that his use of these arguments grew out of a philosophical process internal to Hegelianism itself.[25]

Liebich, however, has seen through this sleight of hand, remarking that "the fundamental inspiration of the *Prolegomena* belongs not to Hegel alone but perhaps almost equally to . . . Buchez" (Liebich 1979a, 47–8). That is a provocative statement; and in light of it we need to be open to two possibilities: (1) that, like H. Heine about this time, Cieszkowski's view of recent developments in German intellectual history had a French dimension; and (2) that Cieszkowski's text might have less to do with Hegelianizing Buchez (Liebich's view at one point, p. 48) than with expressing the socio-historical content of Buchez's outlook in Hegelian terminology (Liebich's view at another point, p. 128). If the former, we can confidently continue to approach Cieszkowski as Hegel's epigone; if the latter, there are solid reasons for thinking that rather than accepting his epigonic status Cieszkowski regarded himself – as Saint-Simon regarded himself – as the "apostle" of a new epoch of thought, an epoch in which thought would be de-philosophized as social *praxis* became the agent for the realization of the truth in action.[26]

II

Cieszkowski's Historicization of Hegel, II:
The *Telos* of Universal History and the Maturation of Human Consciousness

To resolve the matter of Cieszkowski's relationship to Hegel, we need only turn to the argument of the *Prolegomena* itself, for there

Cieszkowski makes it clear that his project entailed the historicization not only of Hegel but of the truth and meaning of Hegel's philosophy as well. Cieszkowski achieves this end by constructing a three-stage philosophy of history in which the third stage so radically transforms the content of the second stage – the one associated with Hegel – that it marks the beginning of a new epoch of history.

To make sense of this epochal breakthrough is a complex task which involves (at least) three levels of analysis. First, Cieszkowski uses the idea of the future so as to appear to be historicizing Hegel as a thinker without necessarily historicizing the meaning of Hegel's philosophy. Indeed, insofar as Cieszkowski equates Hegel's philosophy with the "truth," he is bound to become both the spokesman for it and the person responsible for translating it into a philosophy of action. Second, in keeping with the translation of truth into action, Cieszkowski must structure the *Prolegomena* so that his becomes the culminating voice of a development in German thinking that runs: Schiller, Hegel, Cieszkowski.[27] This sequence, as we shall see, represents the personification of two of Cieszkowski's other trinitarian sequences: art, philosophy, action; and the beautiful, the true, and the good. Third, and this is where his thinking begins radically to diverge from Hegel's, Cieszkowski wants to Catholicize the third term in each of the three sequences. Here Cieszkowski's organic conception of the unfolding of universal history begins to break down as his philosophy of history becomes increasingly anti-Protestant. As we explore the Catholic–Protestant tension in Cieszkowski's thinking, we will begin to appreciate the subtle way Cieszkowski distanced himself from Hegel and from German idealism as it had developed from 1780 onwards.

Let us now detail how each of the three levels of analysis manifests itself in the *Prolegomena*.

As was noted above, the *Prolegomena* originated in Cieszkowski's dissatisfaction with Hegel's refusal to assign the "future" a role in his philosophy of history. Cieszkowski's diaries, moreover, show that this had been his concern as early as 1834 – a full three years before Hegel's views on the philosophy of history became widely known through the publication of Gans's edition of Hegel's lectures on that subject.[28] It can hardly be surprising, therefore, that the *Prolegomena*'s opening chapter, entitled "The Organism of Universal History" (*Organismus der Weltgeschichte*), aims at proving that the future is knowable.

Cieszkowski begins by faulting Hegel for not including the future in the "organic course" of "history" as an unfolding "idea" (Cieszkowski 1979, 49). Without the future, and without knowledge of it, the laws of logic, which Hegel had tried to apply to the study of history, will not attain "the concept of the organic and ideal totality of history in its . . . architectonic perfection" (Cieszkowski 1979, 50, 52). Therefore, Cieszkowski declares: (1) that the establishment of knowledge of the future is an essential precondition for understanding the organic quality of history (Cieszkowski 1979, 52); (2) that "our first task [in the *Prolegomena*] is the cognition of the essence of the future through speculation" (Cieszkowski 1979, 51); and (3) that the "totality of universal history" – past, present, and future – can be "grasped integrally and absolutely as a speculative trichotomy" (Cieszkowski 1979, 51) in which, in the final stage, "all the members [of humanity] are mutually interdependent and [socially] condition each other" (Cieszkowski 1979, 53).

In advancing this declaration of principles, Cieszkowski is careful to pay "tribute to Hegel's genius" (Cieszkowski 1979, 51; cf. 59).[29] But, according to Cieszkowski, Hegel's open-mindedness did not extend to the philosophy of history. Here Hegel's stubborness, Cieszkowski contended, had "crippling effects," "robbing mankind" of the saving knowledge it required to make "progress," to achieve "architectonic perfection," and to realize its *telos* (Cieszkowski 1979, 51–2). Demonstrating the possibility of such knowledge, then, was Cieszkowski's first order of business.

Taking up this challenge, Cieszkowski asked: "how [can] consciousness come to appropriate [knowledge of the future] into itself?" (Cieszkowski 1979, 54) To answer this question, Cieszkowski divided all aspects of his inquiry into sets of threes. To that end, "the future can be determined" in three ways: "through feeling, through thought, and through the will" (Cieszkowski 1979, 54). With regard to these specific "mode[s] of determination," feeling operates naturally; thought through theory; and the will through practice (Cieszkowski 1979, 54). Cieszkowski designates the agents of these determinations "seers and prophets," "philosophers of history," and "executors of history," respectively (Cieszkowski 1979, 54). And over the next few pages, Cieszkowski strings together other sets of threes, all of which are meant to be homologous with each other. For example: "feeling, consciousness, and deed"; "thetic, . . . antithetic, and . . . synthetic";

"exteriority," "interiority," and "absolute teleology"; intuition, reflection, and deed; beauty, truth, and good; being, thinking, and doing; and so on (Cieszkowski 1979, 54–61).

As Cieszkowski develops the various linguistic aspects of this trichotomous semantic field, he "temporalizes" each of the three main divisions so that each becomes a stage of an unfolding historical sequence.[30] Cieszkowski's philosophy of history, therefore, unfolds in accordance with a movement that runs from "Antiquity," through Christianity (or the "Christian-Germanic world" of the present) into "the future" (Cieszkowski 1979, 54, 57, 59). And Cieszkowski ties these semantic strings of threes together when he attributes the genius of art and intuition to Antiquity; the genius of philosophy and reflection to Christianity; and the genius of execution of the will to the social *praxis* of the future (Cieszkowski 1979, 54–6). Cieszkowski's view of history becomes clearer still when he maintains that the three stages of history not only comprise the "organism of history" – in all of its parts – but also provide the "substantial categories of world [or universal] history" as a "teleological process" (Cieszkowski 1979, 56).

Beginning, then, with speculations about the three possible ways of knowing the future, Cieszkowski developed a "speculative trichotomy" that he proceeded to temporalize in the form of a three-stage view of history (Cieszkowski 1979, 59–60). He supported this teleological rendering of universal history with a collateral insistence that the stages of history were integral to mankind's "continuing self-formation" (*Sichgestaltens*) (Cieszkowski 1979, 53).[31] This claim allowed Cieszkowski to argue that "the true idea of humanity" revealed itself in history because each temporal advance in the three-stage sequence marked a growth in the "maturity [*der Reife*] of [mankind's] consciousness" (Cieszkowski 1979, 54–6).

For two reasons, this is a crucial ideological move for Cieszkowski. First, the maturation of consciousness theme permits Cieszkowski to hold that in the third and final age of history "mankind [could be said to have] attained the degree of maturity where its own decisions are completely identical with the divine plans of Providence" (Cieszkowski 1979, 56). On these terms, God's "will" can be done on earth as humanity acts freely, self-consciously, and collectively, to realize the Kingdom of God on earth (Cieszkowski 1979, 56).[32] Moreover, Cieszkowski implies that this "elevation of mankind to God" (Cieszkowski 1979, 65) is achieved in the third age of universal history under the dispensation of the Holy Spirit whose earthly mouthpiece, by implication, was Cieszkowski himself.[33] For Cieszkowski, therefore, entry into the third age marked not only mankind's arrival at maturity (or perfection) in a teleological sense but also the culmination of redemptive history in a Providential sense. This point is underlined when Cieszkowski maintains that the three ages in his historical scheme operate under the dispensations of the Father, the Son, and the Holy Spirit, respectively (Cieszkowski 1979, 65).[34]

Second, Cieszkowski argues throughout the *Prolegomena* that the first and second stages in his trichotomic division were "merely preparation and premises" (i.e., "figures") for the "universal synthesis" (i.e., the "fulfillment") attained in the third age (Cieszkowski 1979, 56–7; cf. 60). As was noted earlier, the figure-fulfillment typology has been essential to Christian theologies of history since the time of Paul and Irenaeus, who both employed the figure-fulfillment strategy to historicize the *Old Testament* and celebrate the *New Testament* as an advance in the religious consciousness of mankind.[35] But, as E. Auerbach has argued, Paul represents the relationship between the *Old Testament* and the *New Testament* as historically connected when, in fact, the connection is "figural" (Auerbach 1953, 73–4). The difference between an historical and a figural interpretation lies precisely in the lack of temporal or causal connection between the two testaments in the figural interpretation. So, even though Paul's figural representation of the relationship between the *Old* and *New Testaments* appears to be based on an earlier and later historical sequence, what actually allows Paul to bind the two books together is his claim to possession of a gift of insight into God's plan for the maturation of religious conscious among mankind (Auerbach 1953, 73).

I mention this because much of what Auerbach tells us about the dynamics of figural interpretation applies to Cieszkowski's trichotomous scheme of universal history and to his understanding of his relationship with Hegel. Clearly, Cieszkowski has organized important parts of his work around an interpretive typology of anticipation and fulfillment in which transformations of religious consciousness in an intramundane sense become reference points for measuring the maturation or perfection of humanity in a teleological sense. Moreover, in chapter 2 of the *Prolegomena*, entitled "The Categories of Universal History" ("*Kategorien der Weltgeschichte*"), Cieszkowski relates the intramundane and teleological processes not only to the unfolding of "universal history" but also to "the penetration of ['rational providence'] into history" through the agency of revelations (Cieszkowski 1979, 61, 65). As the argument at the end of chapter 2 demonstrates, Cieszkowski sees universal history simultaneously as a macrocosm for mankind and as a microcosm relative to God's plan for mankind's salvation. In that respect, Cieszkowski has no qualms about associating himself with Augustine and Bossuet, whose work, Cieszkowski maintained, had confirmed that "divine rule [was] . . . the principle of universal history" (Cieszkowski 1979, 64).

Now, in the 1820s and 1830s, it was common for French and German thinkers to talk about history this way.[36] Earlier, of course, Lessing, Kant, Schiller, Schelling, and Hegel, to name just the notables, had turned German Protestant thinking about history in the direction of what I have called elsewhere the theology of the divine economy in history (Dickey 1987a). And because of their success in this endeavor, we tend to trace later manifestations of this kind of thinking to German Protestant sources, especially to the main philosophers of German idealism.

But in the 1820s and 1830s many Catholic thinkers in Germany as well as in France were using the tripartite periodization of history to prod the Catholic church to respond to the "social question." In that connection, it is important to understand that many Catholic renderings of the three-stage view of history associated the third stage of universal history with a distinctively *social* outlook that had an economic as well as an anti-Protestant dimension. Given Cieszkowski's Catholic background and ready acknowledgment of his indebtedness to French Catholic social theory, the question arises as to which tradition of three-stage discourse is deployed in the *Prolegomena*. Or, to put it another way, is there evidence in the *Prolegomena* of anti-Protestantism?

III

The Displacement and Transformation of Hegel's Concept of *Sittlichkeit*[37]

The answer to these questions can be found in chapter 3 of the *Prolegomena*. This chapter bears the title "The Teleology of Universal

History" (*Teleologie der Weltgeschichte*) and constitutes half of Cieszkowski's book.[38] Coming after a rather wide-ranging discussion of the relationship between God and the development of human consciousness in history, chapter 3 begins in a carefully focused way – with a specific examination of the relationship between art and philosophy in recent German thinking.

In the midst of this discussion, Cieszkowski introduces Schiller and Hegel. Having reminded us that "it is the essence of the idea [of absolute spirit] to establish the [particular] idea of the beautiful as the first stage of the teleological process of world history" (Cieszkowski 1983, 58; cf. 62), Cieszkowski asserts that, among the Germans, Schiller had carried this aesthetic idea to a point of historical perfection.[39] And when Cieszkowski relates the Schillerian perspective on art to the previous aesthetic achievements of the "Grecian spirit" (Cieszkowski 1983, 59), we can see how the first stage of universal history in Cieszkowski's speculative trichotomy has been personified in Schiller's conception of beauty. Hegel enters chapter 3 the same way – as a personification of a truly "philosophical" standpoint that corresponds to the Christian era of universal history (Cieszkowski 1983, 62). Thus, the movement in German intellectual history from Schiller to Hegel, from art to philosophy, recapitulates in microcosm the macrocosmic movement from the Ancient to the Christian period of universal history.[40] Slightly altering the terms of the sequence, Cieszkowski elaborated by saying that "[b]eauty is carried over into truth" as we move from Schiller's *Aesthetic Education* to Hegel's *Philosophy of History* (Cieszkowski 1983, 60–2).

According to Cieszkowski, "the present" is completely and scientifically conceptualized in Hegel's philosophy of "absolute idealism" (Cieszkowski 1983, 62–3). It goes without saying, moreover, that Cieszkowski wished to represent himself as the personification of the third and culminating stage of history.[41] For that reason, he dwells on his own relationship to Hegel, in order to explain the transition from the latter to himself in terms consistent with his own claims about the organic and teleological aspects of universal history. So, after Hegel's philosophy reproduces in thought the feelings and intuitions first registered among the Germans in Schiller's aesthetics (Cieszkowski 1983, 72), Cieszkowski proposes, through an act of will informed by *Historiosophie*, to "translate" Hegel's philosophy into the social "*praxis*" of a new epoch of world history (Cieszkowski 1983, 70, 72).

But if Cieszkowski meant to imply that his philosophy of social action is the culminating moment in the *telos* of universal history – the moment when mankind becomes fully mature (Cieszkowski 1983, 77) – it is not exactly clear what he thinks is being concretely realized either in his own philosophy or in the third age of history.[42] Is the Christian-Hegelian philosophical content of the second age being made actual in the social life of the third? Is Cieszkowski, as he sometimes says, simply grounding in the "concrete reality" of social life teleological insights Hegel had conceptualized in terms of the categories of the "logical idea" (Cieszkowski 1983, 70)? Is this "transition" from logical thought to social action the "world-historical turning point" that ushers in the third age of universal history (Cieszkowski 1983, 64, 65, 70)? Indeed, is this when "philosophy," descending from "the height of theory to the plane of *praxis*," becomes "practical" and "positive" (Cieszkowski 1983, 77, 83, 85–6)? If so, there is little to separate Cieszkowski's position from that of a group of thinkers that I have identified elsewhere as "Old-Left Hegelians" (Dickey 1993). On those terms, Cieszkowski's philosophy of action is hardly different from the kind of Protestant collectivism that came to be associated with Hegel's philosophy of *Sittlichkeit* in the 1820s and 1830s.[43]

However, a careful look at chapter 3 makes it clear that Cieszkowski was not writing in the Old-Left Hegelian tradition of discourse. There, in a thirty-page stretch of text, Cieszkowski's language suggests a radical departure from that tradition. His aim is to explain how his philosophy of "the deed and social activity" surpasses the "true philosophy" of Hegel (Cieszkowski 1983, 77). As he counts the ways, the same words and phrases appear again and again. Some of the linguistic descriptions he applies to Hegel had been used earlier in the *Prolegomena* to characterize the Christian era of universal history. So much the better, then, to tie Hegel and Christianity together in one *ensemble* of meaning. Accordingly, Hegel's philosophy has many Christian features, for it is: abstract; inward; private; modern; theoretical; an expression of "abstract ego"; interior; one-sided; filled with "empty abstractions"; oriented towards the "abstract man"; "esoteric"; and "not yet mature" (Cieszkowski 1983, 65–75, 78, 87).[44]

The questions we need to ask now are these: what kind of language is this? And who talked like this in 1830s? It is certainly not a language Hegel had ever used to represent himself. Quite the opposite: throughout the 1820s Hegel had used this language to criticize the one-sidedness and anti-social character of many aspects of Protestant orthodoxy from Luther on.[45] At the same time, Hegel offered his own philosophy of *Sittlichkeit* as the key to developing a more responsible and socially engaged Protestantism – the kind of "improved" or "re-conditioned" Protestantism that anti-Protestant groups in France ridiculed throughout the 1820s.[46] Nor is the language Cieszkowski uses that of the Old-Left Hegelians. In fact, Michelet reminded Cieszkowski of that upon reading the *Prolegomena* in 1838 (at the time, Michelet even alluded to the *Prolegomena*'s Saint-Simonian quality).[47] Does this mean that in the *Prolegomena* Cieszkowski de-legitimized Hegel with the very language Hegel had previously used to criticize the narrowness of Lutheran orthodoxy? Is that one of the ways Hegel became the philosopher of Protestant orthodoxy? Or is there something still more complicated going on here?

I think the latter for the following reasons. To begin with, there are clear indications that one of Cieszkowski's main concerns in the *Prolegomena* was to show that the particular forms in which God's spirit reveals itself in universal history unfold in accordance with an outside–inside–outside pattern of sequential development (Cieszkowski 1983, 76; cf. Cieszkowski 1979, 54).[48] In this, Cieszkowski assigns Hegel's philosophy the premier position in the second – the interior or Christian-Germanic – period of universal history.

This placement is highly revealing for several reasons. First, the outside–inside–outside scheme allows Cieszkowski to position himself relative to Hegel in terms analogous to those Hegel had used in the *Philosophy of History* to position himself relative to Luther. Second, the placement of Hegel in an age marked by interiority and inwardness (*Innerlichkeit*) obliterates the differences between Luther's and Hegel's understandings of Protestantism (Cieszkowski 1983, 61, 65, 73, 75–7). A telling third point follows from this, for according to the logic of Cieszkowski's sequences of threes both Protestantism (as a religious tendency in Christianity) and Hegelianism (as the philosophy of Protestantism and Christianity) are superseded in the third age of history – which means that the move from the second to the third age of history entails a corresponding movement from interiority to exteriority.

Finally, when Cieszkowski says that he has explained the "transition" from the second to the third age of history "in Hegel's own terms," he has to qualify this by adding that while doing so he had "only altered the results thereof" (Cieszkowski 1983, 77). What

Cieszkowski means, of course, is that his explanation of the transition involved a transformation and a displacement of Hegel's philosophical principles: a displacement because Cieszkowski appropriated for himself the philosophical synthesis Hegel had organized around the idea of *Sittlichkeit*; and a transformation because – as we shall see in more detail in a moment – Cieszkowski gave the idea of *Sittlichkeit* an economic twist that was quite foreign to anything either Hegel or the Old-Left Hegelians would have countenanced. As we further explore exactly how Cieszkowski managed this translation/transformation, the question of what kind of language Cieszkowski used to de-legitimize Hegel will be answered.

IV

Anti-Protestantism and the Three-Stage View of History

Although the strategy whereby Cieszkowski simultaneously displaces and transforms the principles of Hegel's philosophy is presented by him in the form of the figure-fulfillment typology, there is another way of viewing how Cieszkowski places himself relative to Hegel in the *Prolegomena*.

What I have in mind becomes clear when we recall Cieszkowski's Catholicism and his extensive knowledge of French social thinking – Catholic and otherwise. For example, the outside–inside–outside pattern of teleological development he advances within the framework of his "innocent" correction of Hegel's philosophy of history is a well-established trope in the intellectual history of early modern Europe. Most often associated with German romantic and idealistic modes of thinking, it had long been, as M. H. Abrams notes, an important trope in Christian theologies of history. And as Reeves and Gould have recently shown, aspects of the outside–inside–outside movement are prevalent in the various three-stage views of history that dominated French thinking after 1815, much of it Catholic (Reeves and Gould 1987).

As was noted previously, French renderings of the three-stage view tended to be anti-Protestant. It is ironic, moreover, that among liberal Catholic thinkers in Germany, and especially among those who had taken so much of their thinking about history and the history of Christianity from Schelling and Hegel, the anti-Protestant bias of the three-stage view was just as pronounced (Reardon 1985; Dietrich 1979). To be more precise, in French and German Catholic interpretations of the three stages of history the inside stage of the outside–inside–outside pattern is equated with a set of values which are invariably linked to Protestantism as an antisocial mode of *philosophical* (not necessarily Christian) discourse. In light of this, we need to ask again whether there is evidence of anti-Protestantism in the *Prolegomena*? For if there is, it will help to show from where Cieszkowski derived the language he used to represent Hegel as a philosopher of interiority.

On this score, Cieszkowski does not disappoint, for the *Prolegomena* actually closes with a ten-page section in which Cieszkowski's neo-Catholic or social Catholic or liberal Catholic or Saint-Simonian religio-economic biases against Protestantism emerge full blown. Cieszkowski says that in Christian and Protestant thinking "freedom" is conceptualized "abstractly" rather than "concretely" (Cieszkowski 1983, 82).[49] As such, Cieszkowski reasons, in Christian, Protestant, and Hegelian thought "only the abstract man [*abstracte Mensch*] is acknowledged as free" (Cieszkowski 1983, 82). Cieszkowski then calls this view of freedom "merely ideal" and relates it to a form of "subjectivity" that "has been driven to its highest point . . . [in] Protestantism in the sphere of religion and liberalism in the sphere of politics" (Cieszkowski 1983, 82).

From here, Cieszkowski proceeds to say that in order to become real this "abstract man" must become "concrete" (Cieszkowski 1983, 83). Fittingly, he becomes concrete "through the process of action," but in a particularly Cieszkowskian sense, for according to Cieszkowski man becomes "positively concrete" in an "organic" sense only when he becomes "a proprietor" (*Eigenthumer*) in an economic sense (Cieszkowski 1983, 83, 86). And to set-off this "real man" from the "abstract man" of Christianity, Protestantism, and Hegelian philosophy, Cieszkowski insists on designating proprietorship as a better social measure of "moral" selfhood than the property rights sanctioned by the "legal" abstractions of liberalism and natural law (Cieszkowski 1983, 83, 86).[50] Cieszkowski (p. 87) underlines this point later by calling the former a "social individual *par excellence*" (*socialem Individuum*) and the latter a "naked I" (*nackte Ich*).

In this context, Cieszkowski's translation of Hegel's philosophical principles into a philosophy of *praxis* and of Hegel's abstractions into concreteness involves three radical transformations of Hegel's thinking, each of which illuminates the ideological magnitude of Cieszkowski's fiddling with the "results" of Hegel's principles.

First, in Cieszkowski's account of the process whereby abstractions become concrete the subjectivity of abstract man is "recollected" (*erinnerte* in a double sense) and objectively reconstituted in comprehensive social terms (Cieszkowski 1983, 76, 85). With this, Cieszkowski tells us, "an important step has been made towards the development of organic truth in reality" (Cieszkowski 1983, 84). More specifically, Cieszkowski adds that as this occurs a social system that previously had been organized around "private relations" becomes "positive," "organic," and truly "social" (Cieszkowski 1983, 83–7). And it is hardly a linguistic accident that Cieszkowski associates this organic development with the full maturation of human consciousness in history (Cieszkowski 1983, 84). In this respect, Cieszkowski's translation contains a transformation whereby subjectivity is, in Cieszkowski's word, "recollected" into a "social" whole – "a church in its highest sense" (Cieszkowski 1983, 87).[51]

A second transformation in Cieszkowski's translation of Hegel's principles involves the "economization" of what Cieszkowski calls the "organic condition" (Cieszkowski 1983, 86). In Cieszkowski's terminology, this condition is "social" and entails the redemption of "humanity" from the antisocial implications of Christianity's, Protestantism's, and Hegel's conception of abstract freedom.[52] But as he brings the *Prolegomena* to a close, Cieszkowski resorts repeatedly to language which unmistakably derives from French sources. This language, moreover, is meant to add substance to the idea of proprietorship, for it is socioeconomic in nature and is explicitly related to Fourier, and Saint-Simonian social theory. Indeed, it would not be too much to say that Cieszkowski's aim in this section of the *Prolegomena* was to ident-ify private property as pivotal to the sustaining of the abstract conception of freedom that he categorized as "the real social original sin" (Cieszkowski 1983, 82–3, 86–7). Given that perspective, it was natural for Cieszkowski to argue that establishment of "organic truth in reality" required the institutionalization of an economic scheme in which an expanded notion of proprietorship would become the main moral measure of justice in society (before him, Buchez had done just that in the opening chapter of the *Introduction*).[53]

Finally, and this theme too is easily related to Saint-Simonian discourse in the 1820s and 1830s, Cieszkowski claims that as subjectivity is recollected in a social system of socioeconomic justice the distinction between "state" and "civil society" would vanish (Cieszkowski 1983, 87). Perhaps thinking of events in Belgium, France, and Poland in 1830, Cieszkowski held that in the third age of universal history "the state" would abandon its "abstract separateness" and "one-sidedness" and become, thereby, "a member of humanity and . . . [part of a completely inclusive] social state" in which government's task would be to minister to, and ameliorate the needs of society's least-advantaged groups (Cieszkowski 1983, 87).[54] Thus, like many French thinkers after 1825 (and many German ones after 1842), Cieszkowski sought a "social" rather than a "political" solution to the Social Question.[55] At the same time, the depoliticized nature of Cieszkowski's social philosophy was a sharp departure from Hegel's (and later Ruge's) more politically focused endeavors to deal with the social question.

V

The Economization of Protestantism and of *Sittlichkeit*

In light of these three transformations and the fundamental restructuring of Hegel's thinking that follows from them, we can now ask about Cieszkowski's French sources – at least about the possibility of Cieszkowski having inserted French categories of social thought into Hegel's philosophy of history. To simplify our task, we can ask: (1) in which French discourses is Protestantism both described in negative terms and assigned a position in the second age of a three-stage scheme of history? and (2) in which French discourses are organic, positive, and truly social values to be realized in the third and culminating age of history? Here Saint-Simonian discourse (broadly understood to include the writings of Saint-Simon and the Saint-Simonians as well as those of Comte in the early 1820s) becomes relevant to an understanding of Cieszkowski in general and of his relationship to Hegel in particular. And as we begin to take heed of the possibility of a shaping

Saint-Simonian influence on Cieszkowski's correction of Hegel's philosophy of history, the view of Cieszkowski the epigone – simply
translating Hegel's thought into action – becomes quite problematic,
even untenable.

I cannot, of course, go into detail on this issue here. Suffice it to say
that the famous Saint-Simonian rendering of history into an organic–
critical–organic trichotomy goes a long way towards explaining the
way in which Christianity, Protestantism, and Hegel are represented in
the *Prolegomena*.[56] Indeed, countless examples of negative representations of Protestantism and of what Saint-Simon called the Protestant
"metaphysics" of the "philosophers" in "the north of Germany"
(Saint-Simon 1952, 107) can be found in the writings of Saint-Simon,
Comte, and the Saint-Simonians from at least 1820 on. All the representations, moreover, derive their explanatory power from a philosophy of history in which Protestantism and philosophical idealism are
assigned prominent places in a "critical" era of history that is an
ensemble of antisocial values – in religion, philosophy, literature, politics, and economics.[57]

Given this ideological background, the semantic field Cieszkowski
employs in the *Prolegomena* to set-off his views from Hegel's has a
French aspect about it. Of special interest in this regard are remarks
Bazard and Enfantin, the two principal leaders of the Saint-Simonian
movement around 1830, made about the role Protestant values played
in the critical era of history. As is well known, all the Saint-Simonians
dated the beginning of the critical era from the Reformation. From
that point in time, Bazard and Enfantin argue, European values became
increasingly egoistical and antisocial. To substantiate that claim, they
identified Protestantism in religion; romanticism and idealism in literature and philosophy; liberalism in politics; and *laissez-faire* in economics
as parts of one internally consistent value *ensemble*.[58] Granted, the two
Saint-Simonians did not create this *ensemble* themselves. In 1829, after
all, B. Constant had offered a picture of himself in terms of just such
an *ensemble* of values, writing that,

> For forty years I have defended the same principle, liberty in everything,
> in philosophy, in literature, in industry, in politics: and by liberty I mean
> the triumph of individuality [*individualité*].[59]

But Bazard and Enfantin did cast the *ensemble* in a negative light that
was reinforced by its depiction as the overarching value system of the

critical era of history, an era that had all the features of the "inside" era of universal history we discussed earlier.

In the *Prolegomena*, Cieszkowski seems to follow the Saint-Simonians in viewing the religious, political, and economic values of the second age of history as components of a single *ensemble* of anti-social values. That is very clear from his remarks – noted earlier – that Protestantism in religion, liberalism in politics, and individualism in economics provided the core values of the second age of universal history (Cieszkowski 1983, 82–3). It is worth observing, moreover, that within five years of the publication of the *Prolegomena*, F. Engels chose to illustrate the "bourgeois" essence of this *ensemble* of antisocial values by asserting that Adam Smith is "the economic Luther" (Engels 1983, 282).[60]

But Cieszkowski did not need to wait for Engels to set the terms of this religio-economic alignment. Buchez had done that quite well in the opening chapter of the *Introduction* when he explained "egoism" as a joint deduction from the religious and economic values of liberalism and traced egoism's origins to a system of "physical organization" (civil society in the key of liberal political economy) in which antisocial values had institutional supports (Buchez 1842, vol. 1: pp. 3, 38–40).

That Cieszkowski's contemporaries discussed Christianity, Protestantism, and German idealism in terms that charged them with responsibility for the propagation of antisocial values can be explained in terms of the ideological connection Saint-Simon, Comte, and the Saint-Simonians posited between liberty of conscience and the rights of private property.[61] This connection, which emerged in Saint-Simon's writings around 1817, provided socialist discourse in the 1820s and 1830s with much of its power. But the ideological device that makes this religio-economic alignment possible – makes it possible to say that Smith is the economic Luther – is a three-stage view of history in which the meaning of Protestantism and liberal political economy are jointly deduced from their assignment to the critical/second/inside age of universal history. And however much the Saint-Simonians may have acquiesced in the historical necessity of the so-called "destructive" work undertaken by the ideological agents of the critical age,[62] the support those agents ultimately gave to antisocial values in the spheres of religion, politics, and economics is invariably used by the Saint-Simonians to delegitimize them and the *ensemble* of values to which they gave expression.

If we return now to Cieszkowski with the economization of both Protestantism and *Sittlichkeit* in mind, we see that the teleological movement in his philosophy of history operates on converging religious and economic levels. On the one hand, there is the religious movement that unfolds in history, moving from Antiquity, through Christianity, and on into the future. This movement culminates in a moment when humanity in its collective capacity elevates itself to – perhaps even becomes – God. On the other hand, there is an economic movement in Cieszkowski's historico-teleological scheme, one which involves a major shift in the "index symbols" that Cieszkowski uses to register the change in the teleological progression from the second to the third age of universal history.

E. Cassirer has told us what to be alert to when index symbols change in eighteenth- and early nineteenth-century philosophies of history (Cassirer 1951, 158–9). He argues that during this period philosophies of history, despite their apparent theological form,

> no longer look to the concept of God for their justification. . . . The relations between the concept of God and the concepts of truth, morality, and law are by no means abandoned, but the direction changes. An exchange of index symbols takes place, as it were. That which formerly had established other concepts [i.e., God], now moves into the position of that which is to be established [the Kingdom of God and/or the Golden Age in the future], and that which hitherto had justified other concepts now finds itself in the position of a concept which requires justification.[63]

With regard to the *Prolegomena*, Cassirer's insight cues us to the twofold "secularization" of the index symbols Cieszkowski uses to delineate the teleological unfolding of universal history. On the religious level, as Cieszkowski says, men become "conscious artisans" rather than "blind instruments" of their own salvation in the third age (Cieszkowski 1979, 56). On the economic level, realization of the Kingdom of God on earth hinges on a socio-economic imperative. For in the latter the ethical life of community (i.e., *Sittlichkeit* in its conventional sense) has been economized through the agency of an expanded conception of proprietorship. Indeed, according to the logic of recollectivization that governs "work" and "social life" in the third age (Cieszkowski 1983, 80), the antisocial implications of private property are eliminated once property is put at the service of *Sittlichkeit* rather than the interest of the individual.

Admittedly, the *Prolegomena* does not provide detailed plans for the economic reorganization of society. In 1839, however, in a lengthy essay on "Credit," Cieszkowski is much more expansive, both as to why he thinks "laissez-faire" economics has been historically superseded and as to what role organic institutions will play in the new economic system (Cieszkowski 1979, 88).[64] And yet, there is a reference in the *Prolegomena* which I think tells us much about Cieszkowski's economic intentions (Cieszkowski 1983, 65–6 n. 14).[65] It comes in a footnote to a passage where the subject under discussion is the transition in German thinking from art (in Schiller) to philosophy (in Hegel). No doubt thinking of himself, Cieszkowski conjectures that philosophy is about to be superseded by what he calls "another [rising] star" (Cieszkowski 1983, 66). In the note, Cieszkowski tries to clarify what he means by "another star."

He begins by insisting on separating Hegel's achievements in the field of philosophy from religion proper. Cieszkowski then says that a truly "religious" perspective must encompass "the whole absolute sphere of the spirit in which art, philosophy, etc. [*u. s. w.*] are only particular stages" (Cieszkowski 1983, 66 n. 14). For Cieszkowski, therefore, religion has historically realized itself "as art" (in Antiquity) and "as philosophy" (in the Christian era). By the same token, religion will reveal itself in the third age of universal history "as etc.," a strange formulation that on the surface has no obvious economic content. So, religion as "etc." could stand for just about anything in Cieszkowski's mind – action, deed, good, *praxis*, church, the social future, etc.[66]

Two points about Cieszkowski's use of etc. are in order here. First, the etc. stage is clearly meant to be a cipher for the third age of universal history. Second, we find the same odd "art, philosophy, etc." phrase in Buchez's *Introduction* (Buchez 1842, vol. 1, pp. 320, 346), a book we noted earlier expressed views on history similar to those found in the *Prolegomena*.[67]

Now, the context in which the "etc." phrase is used by Buchez helps illuminate Cieszkowski's economic intentions in the *Prolegomena*. That is because in the *Introduction* Buchez discusses "art," "science [philosophy]," and "etc." as social forces the realization of which successively and progressively register humanity's religious achievements in history. In his own clarification of "etc.," Buchez specifically associates the term with "practice" (*pratique*); with "work" (*travail*); and with what the Saint-Simonians called the "industrial" character of the third, organic age of history (Buchez 1842, vol. 1, p. 474). Buchez underlines the social character of these terms by offering them as correctives to the antisocial tendencies of *laissez-faire* economics and "egoistic" social behavior (pp. 481, 486)

It is well known, of course, that the basic thrust of Buchez's work in 1833 was Saint-Simonian in a socioeconomic sense and Catholic in a religious sense. For that reason, his outlook has been often labeled "social Catholicism" (Furet 1989). Can we apply that label to Cieszkowski, who shares so many of Buchez's basic views? After all, Buchez talked, as Cieszkowski would after him, about ways of knowing the future; of "executors" of history whose task it was to oversee the institutionalization of "industrialism" in the third and final age of history; and much more (Buchez 1842, vol. 1, pp. 54–8, 251–6). And if we recall: (1) how Bazard and E. Rodrigues, following Saint-Simon's *New Christianity*, constructed views of the third age of history around various sets of linguistic homologies: art, science, and industry; beauty, truth, and utility; organic, critical, and organic;[68] (2) how in 1825 the sequence "art–science–industry" appeared in the title of the Saint-Simonians' first journal, *Le Producteur*;[69] and (3) how the Saint-Simonians declared in 1829 that "Catholicism" was simply "Christianity" in its capacity as a "social institution";[70] then the Saint-Simonian character of Cieszkowski's formulations stands out all the more. There are, in other words, reasons for thinking that the "etc." phrase is a linguistic code for the religio-economic industrial doctrine of Saint-Simonianism.

VI

Infiguration, Linguistic Secularization, and the Plot Structure of European History, 1688–1838[71]

Thus far we have observed Cieszkowski recapitulating aspects of universal history on two levels and in two time frames, each comprised of three stages. There was the three-stage scheme which began in Antiquity, ran through Christianity, and carried over into the future. And there was the scheme that ran Schiller–Hegel–Cieszkowski. What tied these two schemes together, moreover, were the constantly reiterated sequences: the beautiful, the true, and the good; and art, philosophy, and action.

In bringing this essay to a close, I wish to focus on a problem in the history of ideas that arises once we realize how essential was the organic–critical–organic sequence to Cieszkowski's restructuring of Hegel's philosophy of history. That sequence, after all, allowed Cieszkowski to represent Hegel as the philosopher both of Christianity and of Protestantism and as an inward-oriented thinker whose thought, because it was allegedly antisocial, needed to be superseded if the "social future" were to be realized in action. Here the twin-ideas of "interiority" and "egoism," key terms in the Saint-Simonian critique of liberalism in the 1820s, permitted Cieszkowski to place Christianity, Protestantism, and Hegelian philosophy in the same *ensemble* of antisocial values.[72]

In his appropriation of the organic–critical–organic scheme, however, Cieszkowski took over a philosophy of history which contained within it yet another recapitulation of European history – one which was sandwiched between the larger Western and shorter German schemes. In the *Prolegomena*, this third recapitulation is very hard to detect, but it is there, and its presence requires us to reflect again on the Catholic nature of Cieszkowski's thinking.

To sketch the main features of this recapitulation, it is useful to begin with the thesis of M. H. Abrams's *Natural Supernaturalism*. In his brilliant study of European romanticism in the late eighteenth and early nineteenth centuries, Abrams showed how, in his words, German romantics "recast, into terms appropriate to the historical and intellectual circumstances of their age" (Abrams 1971, 29; cf. 237), the "Christian" story of the "creation, fall, and redemption" of man (p. 188; cf. 245).[73] As Abrams convincingly explains, this perennial Christian "plot" structure manifests itself in countless works of romantic literature and philosophy in which the story revolves around metaphysical questions of consciousness – of its unity, division, and reachievement of unity on a self-conscious level (Abrams 1971, 245–6, 260). The rich detail Abrams provides to sustain his thesis about how "supernatural" Christian categories were "displaced" by the German romantics to "natural" frames of reference (Abrams 1971, 13, 65), reminds us how persistent Christian themes were in much that passed for "secular" literature in the nineteenth century. One could indeed say that, while "outwardly" eliminated – "demythologized" is Abrams's word (Abrams 1971, 91) – the Christian plot structure of creation, fall, and redemption continued to be "inwardly present" in European thinking until well into the nineteenth century (following F. Cornford, I shall conceptually refer to the process by which something becomes outwardly absent but inwardly present as "infiguration").[74]

Now, Abrams's great work encourages us both to think of German idealism as the philosophy of romanticism and to conceptualize both "isms" as contributions to the process whereby Christianity was "secularized" in the nineteenth century (Abrams 1971, 91–2). At the same time, Abrams suggests that one of the reasons Marxism is viewed as a "secular theodicy" is because it takes over so much of this plot structure from Christianity through its ideological connections with romanticism and idealism (Abrams 1971, 315–16).

However intriguing are the ideological connections drawn in Abrams's book, it is nonetheless true that *Natural Supernaturalism* pays no attention whatsoever to the different uses Catholics and Protestants made of this Christian plot structure. As we have seen, the plot structure of organic–critical–organic, which F.-A. Isambert has shown conforms to the unity–division–unity pattern of consciousness's development (Isambert 1959), was virulently anti-Protestant. In France, it was employed on the left and right to counter a liberal-Protestant agenda promoted by Villers, de Staël, Constant, Cousin, and Guizot.[75] In Germany, Novalis and A. Müller used it for similar purposes in the 1790s and early nineteenth century respectively. With all due respect to Abrams, then, we need to probe more deeply into the anti-Protestant character of such usage, for as we have seen that usage constitutes one of the primary ideological features of the *Prolegomena*.

The need for developing this focus of analysis was appreciated by K. Mannheim who, as long ago as 1927, wished to determine how "right-wing" Catholic motifs came to figure so conspicuously in "left-wing" philosophies of history after 1815 in Europe (Mannheim 1971, 148–9; cf. 163, 215 n. 1). Reflecting on this question, Mannheim suggests that Novalis and Müller were key figures on the German side of the issue (pp. 188–9, 215). If, for example, we peruse Müller's work between, say, 1808 and 1816, we can see what Mannheim means.

During these years, Müller inveighed against Protestantism and political economy (Luther and Smith by name) for inaugurating processes that led to the "privatization" (*Privatisieren*) of modern life in general

(Müller 1922, 298–9) and to the "egoistic" and "antisocial spirit" (*antisozialen Geistes*) of modern life more particularly (Müller 1921, 21; and Müller 1923, 78–80).[76] In language that anticipates Cieszkowski almost exactly, Müller assigned key roles to Protestantism, natural law, and liberal political economy in the process of privatization. Protestantism, he said, promoted "private religion"; natural law, in turn, provided the impetus for a "rights"-based orientation in politics; and liberal economics constituted the driving force behind private property rights and the rise of the competitive market (Müller 1922, 298–9). Müller, does this, moreover, while drawing direct connections between the religious anarchy of the Reformation, the political anarchy of the French Revolution, and the economic anarchy of the modern market system (Müller 1922, 267–99).

In most modern scholarships, Müller is discussed as a (notorious) "political romantic." But as Mannheim observed, Müller's writings express "Catholic" concerns that had been articulated earlier by Novalis (Mannheim 1971, 188, 215). Although Novalis's famous essay of 1799, "Christendom or Europe," was not published until 1826, its content is organized around a view of European history in which Protestantism is blamed for the religious, philosophical, and political turmoil Europe had experienced since the Reformation (Novalis 1955). Anyone who reads Novalis's essay with an eye to its language cannot help but see a parallel between his three-stage periodization of European history, which culminated in an "age of resurrection" and regeneration of the "organic" ties of community, and the organic–critical–organic periodization used later in France by the Saint-Simonians (Novalis 1955, esp. 132–7). And lest we mistakenly think Novalis's essay represents an early organic version of a romantic philosophy of history rather than a Catholic one, we need only note the parallel representations of European history in "Christendom or Europe" and the mid-1790s writings of Bonald and Maistre – the two great Catholic theocrats.

Turning to France, we discern a strong Catholic influence exerting itself on Saint-Simon and Comte from 1820 on as well as on main figures in the Saint-Simonian movement from 1825 on.[77] The key documents here are an essay jointly written by Saint-Simon and Comte in 1820 entitled "A Brief Appraisal of Modern History," and Comte's own path-breaking "Plan of the Scientific Operations Necessary for Reorganizing Society" of 1822/4.[78] There, among many other important ideological formulations, we find the following: (1) an early attempt to render European history in terms of the organic–critical–organic periodization; (2) a wholesale assault on Protestantism as the religious source of a doctrine of "independence" and "free inquiry" that, in the long run, spread to philosophy and politics and, in the process, undermined authority everywhere in Europe;[79] (3) an attempt to characterize the "critical era" of history as essentially Protestant;[80] and (4) a program for re-establishing organic unity in the "social future" through a process of recollectivization.

For our purposes, however, the most telling aspect of these essays is Saint-Simon's and Comte's frank acknowledgment of their debts to the theocrats, Bonald and Maistre, for showing them how European history unfolded from the Middle Ages on.[81] In this, both plainly reveal the Catholic origins of the anti-Protestant bias we have detected in French Catholic and so much Saint-Simonian social thought after 1817. Their acknowledged borrowings also draw attention to one of the strategic ideological cross-over points whereby "right-wing" theocratic conceptions of history were appropriated by the self-proclaimed "apostles" of the "left."

Aside from the ideological cross-over we observe here, what is crucial for us to grasp is the pivotal role the depiction of Protestantism plays in left and right (or antiliberal) interpretations of European history. As was previously noted, it was common for socialists and Catholics in the 1820s and 1830s to link their critiques of liberalism to the antisocial implications of Protestantism. In this, we suggested that, while Protestantism was economized by its linkage with the individualism associated with *laissez-faire* economics, acquisitive economic behavior was increasingly viewed as an antisocial, even a sinful form of behavior – the sort of behavior to which the antisocial term "enthusiast" could be attached.[82] In addition, we noted how the direction of the index symbols in these formulations gradually shifted away from overt religious and toward economic references.

In the works of Bonald and Maistre in the mid-1790s, we observe the development of a negative *ensemble* of religious, political, and economic values without the shift in index symbols – which is to say, God and Providence remain the driving forces behind Bonald's and Maistre's explanations of the course of European history from the Middle Ages on. So, for example, the plot structure in Maistre's conception of history traces the atheism, anarchy, and egoism of modern life to the antisocial consequences of Protestantism's doctrine of liberty of conscience (Maistre 1974, esp. 88–9, 143–5; Maistre 1884).

In the context of the political upheavals of the 1790s, it is easy to see how in Maistre's thinking Catholicism stood to Protestantism as religion stood to irreligion and as order stood to disorder. But there is more, because behind the plot structure used by the theocrats to map the contours of European history from, say, the Reformation on, there is the figure of Bossuet whose famous diatribe against Protestantism, *History of the Variations of the Protestant Churches* (1688), set the terms for this plot structure in some very revealing ways (Bossuet 1836).

H. Heine understood Bossuet's influence on modern conceptions of Protestantism very well, noting in *Concerning Religion and Philosophy in Germany* (1835) that the argument of the *Variations* was still strong in the 1830s (Heine 1985, 147; Bossuet's argument had recently been reinforced by Lamennais, the so-called "second Bossuet," in volume 1 of his *Essai sur L'Indifférence* [1817]. As is also well known, Lamennais greatly influenced the thinking of Comte and the Saint-Simonian contributors to *Le Producteur* in the mid-1820s). As Heine explains, Bossuet had convinced generations of Catholics that the Reformation set the pattern for a series of disastrous events in European history, all of which had anarchy at their core. More specifically, Bossuet succeeded in persuading Catholics that a "specter of anarchy" would hang over Europe so long as Protestantism thrived – as atheism and perpetual heresy in religion; as anarchy and permanent revolution in political life; and as egoism and avarice in economic life.[83]

Among the key terms Bossuet uses to characterize what Protestantism entails as a religious outlook is "self-love" (*amour-propre*). According to Bossuet, *amour-propre* is a sinful disposition that, under the guise of nurturing "independence" and the exercise of "private judgment" in religious matters, actually entailed putting love of self before love of God (Bossuet 1836, esp. 25–9; also see Bossuet 1816, vol. 10, pp. 343–446, esp. 379–87). The so-called two-loves argument that Bossuet resorts to here is an old Christian adage.[84] In Bossuet's hands, though, the argument is *temporalized*, for the Reformation is represented in Bossuet's thinking as the historical moment when *amour-propre* threatened through the agency of Protestantism to become permanently institutionalized as a way of living among European nations.

Writing at the end of the seventeenth century, Bossuet could see that Protestantism had become more a "philosophy" than a religion (Bossuet 1836, 196) – a philosophy of atheism, anarchy, and *amour-propre*, he said time and again. Given this language, it is easy to see how the French theocrats as well as Novalis and Müller could interpret the historical sequence Reformation–Enlightenment–Revolution with the language they did. For each of these events was interpreted as a prime manifestation of Protestant disorder the corrective of which lay in the regeneration of Catholic values.

Two points need to be borne in mind here. First, for many nine-teenth-century Catholic thinkers the period of European history since the Reformation was equated with man's theological fall from grace into sin. As such, Protestant individualism – in whatever form – had an aspect of sin about it. Second, over the course of the three hundred years from the Reformation, *amour-propre* came to be associated as much with avarice in a materialistic sense as with pride in a psychologi-cal sense. As this shift of emphasis gradually took place, the meaning of *amour-propre* as an index symbol changed. So, when Cieszkowski joined French socialists in equating egoism, subjectivity, abstract free-dom, and private property with original sin, we can see how depen-dent was his and their discourse for its coherence on Catholic meanings – specifically on an anti-Protestant Catholic plot structure which, despite changes in the index symbols governing it, was absent, but present – infigured – in their discourse even when its subject matter was economic rather than religious in nature. What has happened here, in short, is a secularization of language without any corresponding change in the grammar – the plot structure – governing the meaning of the language.[85] Accordingly, we can only begin to grasp the mean-ing of the *Prolegomena* after thinking through the conceptual impli-cations of infiguration and linguistic secularization in the left's appropriation of the right's interpretive categories.

Turning still more directly to Cieszkowski, we can see how a third recapitulation of European history operates in the *Prolegomena*. This particular recapitulation would seem to start with Bossuet and culmi-nate, say, with Bonald and Maistre in the 1790s and later in Lamennais' writings from 1809 on. All three of these thinkers exercised shaping influences on the thought of Saint-Simon, Comte, and the Saint-Simonians in the 1820s and 1830s. Indeed, it is from these famous French Catholic thinkers that the latter derived the plot structure

around which they organized their organic–critical–organic conceptions of history and their views on how an "industrial" third age of
history would supersede a "liberal" second one. That is why, despite
their frequent economic contrast of liberalism and industrialism, the
Saint-Simonians concluded their first year of public lectures in 1829
with a statement about how humanity, under the auspices of Saint-
Simon's "religion of the future," would evolve away from an "inner
[*intérieur*] and purely individual" value system and toward a "collective" one.[86] In either the religious or economic cases, in other words,
"egoism" would be overcome as a system of social organization.[87]

For a variety of reasons, then, it seems to me most inappropriate to
interpret Cieszkowski's *Prolegomena* as a document in the intellectual
history of Hegelianism. If, however, we shift the ideological context
of the *Prolegomena* from Germany to France, then many of the ideological formulations in Cieszkowski's essay make more sense. That does
not make it easier to decide whether Cieszkowski's text is best
contextualized in terms of French socialism; or social Catholicism; or
some version of a religion of the future that is Christian without being
either Catholic or Protestant; or a post-Christian religion of humanity.
But at least we will know what questions need to be asked in order to
give this important nineteenth-century thinker his due.[88] Beyond that,
we can begin to conjure with the wider issue of Catholic infiguration
in nineteenth-century socialist philosophies of history.

NOTES

1 For an overview of the literature on Cieszkowski, see A. Liebich
   (1979b), 156–65.
2 An extensive discussion of this book and its publishing history can be
   found in W. Kühne (1938), and in Liebich (1979b), 159–60.
3 In no particular order: G. Lukács (1971), 6–8; N. Lobkowicz (1967),
   193ff; L. Kolakowski (1978), vol. 1, pp. 85–8; J. Toews (1980), 235–42;
   K. Löwith (1967), 141–2; and, especially for our purposes here, A.
   Walicki (1975). The latter has taken Cieszkowski studies to a new level
   with his refusal to interpret Cieszkowski in an exclusively German
   ideological context.
4 I am using this term in its formal theological sense. R. A. Markus (1954)
   explains its early function in the writings of Irenaeus, a Christian thinker
   who resolved problems of continuity and change in Christian views of

history with a strategy not unlike that used by Cieszkowski to explain his relationship with Hegel in the 1830s.

5 Schiller (1972), 331; Kant (1963), 23–6.

6 A very old philosophical distinction indeed, but one that was being re-figured by French and German thinkers from 1815 on. Among the Germans, Hegel's student F. W. Carové, a Catholic with ties to the Saint-Simonians in the 1820s, developed a view of the beauty, truth, good sequence that is remarkably similar to that which we find in the *Prolegomena* (see Toews 1980, 139, particularly). In France, Cousin and Jouffroy (among the liberals) used the distinction frequently in their work when discussing the evolution of human consciousness in history. Representative statements from both thinkers can be found in Ripley (1838), vol. 1, pp. 96, 308–18; and vol. 2, p. 182. One Polish critic of the *Prolegomena* accused Cieszkowski of borrowing his historical scheme from Cousin (Liebich 1979a, 62).

7 The translation of the beautiful, true, and good sequence into an art, science–philosophy, action sequence is most prominent among Saint-Simonian thinkers of the 1820s. On this, their so-called "social trinity," see Manuel (1962), 165ff.

8 I address this theme in section VI below.

9 For a discussion of the differences between the two teleological concep-tions, see the remarks on "self-realizing" teleology in Dickey (1987a), index entry.

10 Kühne (1938), 134–5, lists Cieszkowski's German references.

11 In keeping with n. 7 above, Cieszkowski also equates Schiller's and Hegel's writings with artistic and philosophical consciousness, respect-ively. Here, I think, is where Cieszkowski begins to structure his discus-sion of German intellectual history in accordance with French categories of historical thinking. For example, his rendering of logical progression in history is very similar to Buchez's understanding (1842, vol. 1, pp. 321–54, esp. 339–40) of "the logical ages" of universal history.

12 Unless otherwise indicated, all references to Cieszkowski's writings refer to translations that can be found in Cieszkowski (1979) and (1983). I have checked all translations against the Kraus reprint (1976) of the 1838 Berlin original.

13 For biographical information on Cieszkowski's life, I have depended on Kühne (1938) and Liebich (1979a).

14 Liebich (1979a), 15, argues for 1833; Kühne (1938), 11, 55, relies on Cieszkowski's son's dating of 1832. Stepelevich (1974), offers 1831 without any explanation.

15 For Gans and Michelet, see Toews (1980). N. Waszek (1987) discusses Gans's French interests. D. Kelley (1978) examines the Gans–Marx

relationship in the late 1830s.

16 See Cieszkowski's *curriculum vitae* in Kühne (1938), 426.

17 Conversely, Lamennais and Montalembert followed Polish developments closely, especially after 1830 (Liebich 1979a, 215–16). Both, for example, promoted Mickiewicz as a writer, a thinker whom Cieszkowski revered in the 1820s.

18 Kühne (1938), 357ff, has published the correspondence. The relevant diary entries are discussed in Liebich (1979a), chs 1 and 2.

19 My emphasis, because of the relevance of these two terms to the art/philosophy and beauty/truth linguistic sequences Cieszkowski will later develop in the *Prolegomena*.

20 In Cieszkowski's correspondence with Michelet (all of it in French), the word *germe* appears often. The Saint-Simonians frequently used this term in discussions of the philosophy of history. Before them, Lessing and Kant, two favorite writers of the Saint-Simonians in the 1820s, had used the term in their own theologies/philosophies of history. E. Rodrigues (1831), 163, translates Lessing's German (passage no. 46 in *The Education of the Human Race*) with *germe*. That passage is revealing in the context of the *Prolegomena* and Cieszkowski's *Our Father*. On Lessing's influence on the latter, see Kühne (1938), 267.

21 See Dickey (1993), 315ff, for Hegel and panlogism.

22 Ruge, e.g., in Stepelevich (1983), 256.

23 See Dickey (1993) for the Hegel–Feuerbach relationship in 1828.

24 Liebich (1979a), 332 nn. 59 and 61, follows Lobkowicz (1967) and Walicki (1975) in stressing the French connection here.

25 Kühne (1938), passim, and esp. p. 46, never questions the connection between Hegel and Cieszkowski, arguing that Cieszkowski's concept of action follows naturally from developments internal to German philosophical thinking. Walicki (1975), 199–200, offers a corrective.

26 See Liebich (1979a), 16, 19, where he contrasts the consciousness of epigones and that of more apocalyptically oriented thinkers.

27 In a letter to Michelet (Kühne 1938, 362), Cieszkowski speaks of "l'économie" of the chapters of his book. The usage suggests an argument consistent with what I call elsewhere (Dickey 1987a) the theology of the divine economy. Cieszkowski's *Our Father* unfolds according to the same economy as well.

28 Kühne (1938), 22, and Liebich (1979a), 23, speak of Gans's edn as a catalyst for the *Prolegomena*. In light of Cieszkowski's belated reading of the edition, and of the trajectory of his thinking from 1834 on, this seems misleading.

29 See Dickey (1993) for specifics.

30 Although the concept of temporalization has been used by H. Arendt

(1954, 76–9) to explain the politics of philosophies of history after 1789, there is, as C. Meier (1990, 158, 167, 179) has appreciated, much useful discussion of the temporalization process in studies of Greek political thinking in the 5th century BC. See, e.g., E. Voegelin (1957), 167, 267, 355; and Cornford (1907).

31 As Cieszkowski's diary entries indicate, he often talked about self-forma-tion in terms of *Bildung*. As such, much that Abrams (1971) says about the role of *Bildung* in German philosophies of history is relevant to Cieszkowski.

32 For similar language, see M. Hess, quoted from 1841 in Avineri (1985), 71–2.

33 There is evidence in the *Prolegomena* that Cieszkowski used the personi-fication strategy deliberately. Jouffroy theorized about the strategy of personification in the 1820s. See his views in Ripley (1838), vol. 2, p. 140.

34 Consult K. Löwith (1949), 208ff, for Schelling's variation on this in the 1830s. As Reeves and Gould (1987), 52, 90, and Reardon (1975), 83 n. 78, have observed, French thinkers employed this scheme, too. The latter provides a quote from Lamennais that is most illuminating for Cieszkowski.

35 Auerbach (1953) and Markus (1954).

36 According to E. Halévy and C. Bouglé (1924), 499–501 n. 361, the three-age view of history was "in the air" in the 1820s and 1830s.

37 See Toews (1980), 239, for a particularly acute conceptualization of the theme I pursue in this section.

38 In his correspondence (Kühne 1938, 362, 365), Cieszkowski termed this part of his work the "most original." He also once (Kühne 1938, 367) characterized his historical efforts as a *romans pseudohistoriques*. Kant (1963, 24, 53) used a similar formulation in two of his famous essays on the philosophy of history in the 1780s.

39 C. Villers (1807), 227–32, had made the point earlier. I mention Villers because it is apparent to me that many aspects of the French Catholic opposition to Protestant-inspired liberalism in France after the Revol-ution can be understood against the background arguments and language of this book.

40 In this scheme, in other words, Hegel's philosophy represents the "sec-ond standpoint of the teleology of history" (Cieszkowski 1983, 62).

41 Accordingly, two of Cieszkowski's sequences would run: romanticism, idealism, and the true idea of humanity; legal, moral, and the absolutely practical/social.

42 Cieszkowski (1979), 53, says his notion of the future encompasses es-sences not necessarily particulars.

43 A hint that Cieszkowski is not thinking this way is signaled by his reference (Cieszkowski 1983, 76) to the "rehabilitation of matter," a Saint-Simonian conception that alludes to economic justice as the measure of a society's moral well-being. On the theme, see Manuel (1962), 151ff.

44 Kühne (1938), 429–30, produces a Cieszkowski fragment entitled "Über die Deutsche," in which the Germans are represented as a one-sided, abstract-oriented people. Cieszkowski's emphasis here fits in nicely with the New-Left Hegelian critique of German philosophy as abstract and dualistic (e.g., in M. Hess). But it also coincides with the Saint-Simonian critique of Christian-Germanic thinking as dualistic and transitional in its historical character as well as with Schelling's emerging views in the 1830s. On the latter, see Breckman (1993), 114ff.

45 See, e.g., Hegel (1984), 493, and Hegel (1956), 416ff.

46 B. Constant (1838), 311, used the phrase "improved Protestantism" in 1826 to show how Protestant conceptions of liberty had evolved with recent changes in European history. In this, he uses the phrase to summarize an argument (297–302) that mirrors exactly the defence of Protestantism found in the closing chapter of Hegel's *Philosophy of History*. From the Catholic side, Baron Eckstein contested Constant's claim in *Le Catholique* (see Reardon 1975, 15). In the *New Christianity*, Saint-Simon explicitly separated "New Christianity" from "improved Protestantism" (Saint-Simon 1952, 108).

47 See Michelet's letter (Kühne 1938, 370) and Liebich's statement (1979a, 31). For Michelet's experience with the Saint-Simonians, see Kühne's comments, p. 376 n. 8. More recently, Breckman (1993, 244ff) has made some important points with regard to the possibility of a Saint-Simonian influence on Feuerbach, and especially with reference to the latter's negative views of Protestantism.

48 Cieszkowski's exact terms are *Aeusserlichkeit* and *Innerlichkeit*.

49 Since Villers (1807) and de Staël in the early 1800s, there had been a tendency among French thinkers to depict German philosophers as one-sidedly theoretical and introspective in character (see, e.g., de Staël [1987], 182–3, and [1813], 278–81; also see Jouffroy [Ripley 1838], vol. 2, pp. 122, 129). In the 1830s, in the hands of Catholic thinkers such as L. Bautain, these qualities became associated with "egoism" and in a manner similar to the way Saint-Simonians associated liberalism with egoism in their writings. On Bautain, see Reardon (1975), 113ff, esp. 128–9. In Germany in the 1830s, Schelling's work, which had become increasingly congenial to Catholics, moved in a similar direction (Breckman 1993, 114–24).

50 In the text, Cieszkowski exploits the difference in German between

Moralität and *Sittlichkeit* to imply that Hegel is the philosopher of the former not the latter.

51 Cieszkowski's aim here is to de-couple Catholicism from the institution and dogmas of the church and to put Catholicism in the vanguard of the emerging social forces of the period. Statements to this effect among the Saint-Simonians can be found in Halévy (1924), 346, and in Manuel (1962), 147–8, quoting E. Rodrigues from 1829.

52 At one point, Cieszkowski calls this "supersensible interiority" (1983, 61; cf. 80).

53 The stunning point that Buchez develops here is that egoism emerges as a social rather than individual force as economic processes become increasingly geared to the competitive market. Aspects of this insight can also be found in Lamennais (1859, vol. 1, pp. 259–316) as early as 1817.

54 In the language of the Saint-Simonians, politics becomes administration.

55 The shift from the "political" to the "social" has been much discussed by students of the intellectual history of the period.

56 For details on the origins of this scheme, see Isambert (1959), and Manuel (1963), 219–36.

57 Appreciated long ago by Halévy (1924), 122 n. 2, and more recently by Gruner (1973), 140–1, 147.

58 Two quotations from Enfantin – one from 1829, the other from 1830 – are apt here. See Halévy (1924), 195–6 n. 83, and Gruner (1968), 467. In the latter, Enfantin – in a truly extraordinary statement – says of the "critical" era of history that it is represented "in religion by Protestantism, in politics by liberalism, in industry by competition, in morality by self-interest . . . , and in literature by romanticism" (my tr.). For Basard, see *The Doctrine of Saint-Simon*, more generally, esp. lectures 1–3 (Iggers 1958).

59 Constant (1980), p. 519. Ten years earlier, another liberal, Daunou, said similar things. See Daunou, quoted in Halévy (1924), p. 130 n. 14.

60 The connection between "egoism" and the "bourgeoisie" was also made by the Saint-Simonians. See Halévy (1924), 415, and the accompanying note.

61 See Spitzer (1987), ch. 6, for how the Saint-Simonians developed this connection in their journal, *Le Producteur*, in 1825 and 1826.

62 The notion that the Enlightenment and the Revolution worked together to destroy Old Regime values and institutions without replacing them with new ones is already evident in Maistre's writings in the 1790s. The same notion appears in Saint-Simon's writings before 1814, although never in systematic form. But the main proponents of this view in the late 1810s and early 1820s were French liberals in the circle of Cousin (e.g., Jouffroy) who found the philosophy of eighteenth-century liberal-

ism wanting in constructive, though not destructive energy. G. Kelly (1992, 76, 90) and Spitzer (1987, 90–2, 113ff) have fleshed this out for us. Kelly suggests, moreover, that this new group of liberals wished to respiritualize liberalism in order to meet the objections of detractors who criticized liberalism for its materialism. While French liberals, in Jouffroy's words (Ripley 1838, vol. 2, p. 101), no longer swore by "Condillac" in the 1820s, liberal French Catholics, following Ballanche (who like Jouffroy had ties to Cousin), began to employ the same scheme to discredit the Enlightenment. See Reardon (1975), 54–5, for Ballanche.

63   Cassirer (1951), 159. My insertion of the "Golden Age" reference is meant to remind that the motto of the Saint-Simonians in the 1820s held that the Golden Age was, in their words, "not behind us but in front of us." See Hayek (1952), 231, for a discussion. Cassirer's idea of index symbols can easily be related to the work of H. Blumenberg (1983). The latter, while discussing the twentieth-century debate about "secularization," argues that interpretations of secularization turn on whether we interpret such index changes – especially those registered in language – as "transformations" or "alienations" of religious substance. From that perspective, Blumenberg's "linguistic-secularization" argument and Cassirer's index-symbol argument are quite similar.

64   Liebich (1979a), ch. 6, examines the piece in detail.

65   Lobkowicz (1967), 199, draws attention to the importance of this note.

66   Liebich (1979a), 62–3, notes Polish criticism of Cieszkowski's vagueness on this point.

67   Book III of Buchez's *Introduction*, vol. 1, elaborates the meaning of this phrase.

68   Note Halévy's (1924) comments on Basard, pp. 161 n. 47, 321 n. 200. For Rodrigues, see E. Rodrigues (1831), 27–31.

69   Spitzer (1987), ch. 6, on *Le Producteur* in general.

70   Halévy (1924), 346.

71   Blumenberg's (1983) argument about "inner secularization" is close to what I mean by infiguration; and both relate to what he calls "linguistic secularization" (see n. 63 above).

72   If we recall that Protestant apologists in France from Villers and de Staël on held positive views of interiority and reflectiveness, then this is an excellent example of linguistic appropriation for the purpose of de-legitimizing an opponent.

73   Blumenberg (1983), 27, argues the same point, but draws different conclusions.

74   Cornford (1907), 132.

75   Very clear in the case of Lamennais' attacks on Villers from 1809 on.

76　Müller's 1810–11 critiques in the *Berliner Abendblätter* of Kraus's favorable views of the economic teachings of Adam Smith fit in here, too.

77　Pickering (1993), 164ff, has recently added considerably to our knowledge of the Saint-Simon/Comte relationship between 1817 and 1824. For all that, though, her analysis of the two texts discussed below is questionable.

78　I have used the translations in Fletcher (1974). It is worth noting that the latter essay was given to Hegel in Berlin by d'Eichthal in 1824. See Hayek (1952) and Pickering (1993) for details.

79　As is the case with the idea of interiority (n. 72 above), these are code words in Protestant and Catholic polemics of the period. In England, dissenters such as R. Price and M. Wollstonecraft used them positively as did Villers (1807) in France in his apology for the Reformation. Conversely, Maistre and Lamennais attached negative meaning to them as well as to other related terms. What is more, Villers (1807), 227–32, presents the "scrutinizing disposition" and "free examination" as character traits of the "Germanic race" in general and of "Protestant nations" in particular. Cieszkowski's piece, "Über die Deutsche" (n. 44 above), is part of this ideological tradition. It should be noted, moreover, that in Bossuet and Lamennais "curiosity" is at once a Protestant and critical philosophical category. Villers (1807) develops a positive perspective on this, claiming Protestant origins for the impetus behind much of modern scientific thinking. In light of this, Blumenberg's (1983) attempt to ground "curiosity" in the ideological context of Renaissance science rather than Reformation theology has deeper roots than his readers might otherwise appreciate.

80　See Halévy's comments (1924), 146 n. 30, 157 n. 39, 195–6 n. 83, 410 n. 80, as well as the Saint-Simonian argument itself, pp. 179–201.

81　This is reasonably well known: See e.g. Baker (1975), ch. 6, esp. pp. 371–82. Pickering (1993), 265ff, 354ff, shows how Lamennais fits into the picture quite well.

82　There are aspects of this in Burke's writings. See Pocock (1989).

83　Baker (1990), 207–9, discusses the Protestant/anarchy connection in French thinking from Bossuet on. In 1817, Lamennais (1859, 274ff) rehearsed Bossuet's points and called the whole ensemble of destructive values "liberal" (285).

84　Lamennais (1859), 395, after quoting Bossuet, employs the two-loves scheme to explain the connection between Protestantism, egoism, and materialism.

85　The process I am describing here seems to support what K. Löwith means by "secularization." The alternative view developed by

Blumenberg (1983), however, needs to be considered carefully. For comments on some of the issues Blumenberg raises, see Dickey (1987b).

86 Halévy (1924), 487.
87 Halévy (1924), 500.
88 Walicki's excellent point (1975), 204.

REFERENCES

Abrams, M. H. (1971): *Natural Supernaturalism*. New York.

Arendt, H. (1954): *Between Past and Future*. New York.

Auerbach, E. (1953): *Mimesis*. Princeton.

Avineri, S. (1985): *Moses Hess: Prophet of Communism and Zionism*. New York.

Baker, K. (1975): *Condorcet*. Chicago.

Baker, K. (1990): *Inventing the French Revolution*. New York.

Blumenberg, H. (1983): *The Legitimacy of the Modern Age*, tr. R. Wallace. Cambridge, Mass.

Bossuet, J. (1816): *Oeuvres de Bossuet*, vol. 10. Versailles.

Bossuet, J. (1836): *The History of the Variations of the Protestant Churches*, 2nd edn, vol. 1. Dublin.

Breckman, W. (1993): *Dethroning the Self: The Young Hegelians and the Political Theory of Restoration*, Ph.D. Thesis, History Department, University of California, Berkeley.

Buchez, P. (1842): *Introduction à la science de l'histoire*, 2nd edn, vol. 1. Paris:

Cassirer, E. (1951): *The Philosophy of the Enlightenment*. Boston.

Cieszkowski, A. (1979): *Selected Writings of August Cieszkowski*, ed. and tr. A. Liebich. New York.

Cieszkowski, A. (1983): *Prolegomena to Historiosophie*, in *The Young Hegelians*, ed. L. Stepelevich. New York, 55–89.

Constant, B. (1838): "The Progressive Development of Religious Ideas," in *Specimens of Foreign Standards of Literature*, ed. G. Ripley, vol. 2. Boston, 292–319.

Constant, B. (1980): *De la Liberté chez les modernes*, ed. M. Gauchet. Paris.

Cornford, F. (1907): *Thucydides Mythistoricus*. London.

Dickey, L. (1987a): *Hegel: Religion, Economics and the Politics of Spirit, 1770–1807*. New York.

Dickey, L. (1987b): "Blumenberg and Secularization: 'Self-Assertion' and the Problem of Self-Realising Teleology in History," *The New German Critique*, 41, 151–63.

Dickey, L. (1993): "Hegel on Religion and Philosophy," in *The Cambridge Companion to Hegel*, ed. F. Beiser. New York, 301–47.

Dietrich, D. (1979): *The Goethezeit and the Metamorphosis of Catholic Theology in the Age of German Idealism*. Bern.

Engels, F. (1983): "Outlines of a Critique of Political Economy," in *The Young Hegelians*, ed. L. Stepelevich. New York, 278–302.

Fletcher, R. (1974): *The Crisis of Industrial Society*, ed. R. Fletcher. London.

Furet, F. (1989): "Buchez," in *A Critical Dictionary of the French Revolution*, ed. F. Furet and M. Ozouf, tr. A. Goldhammer, London, 908–15.

Gruner, S. (1968): "The Revolution of July 1830 and the Expression 'Bourgeoisie' ". *Historical Journal*, 11, 462–71.

Gruner, S. (1973): *Economic Materialism and Social Moralism*. Paris.

Hayek, F. (1952): *The Counter-Revolution of Science*. Glencoe, Ill.

Halévy, E. and Bouglé, C. (1924): *Doctrine de Saint-Simon*, eds E. Halévy and C. Bouglé. Paris.

Hegel, G. (1956): *The Philosophy of History*, tr. J. Sibree. New York.

Hegel, G. (1984): *Hegel: The Letters*, tr. C. Butler and C. Seiler. Bloomington, Ind.

Heine, H. (1985): *The Romantic School and Other Essays*, eds J. Hermand and R. Holub. New York.

Iggers, G. (1958): *The Doctrine of Saint-Simon*, ed. G. Iggers. New York.

Isambert, F. (1959): "Époques critiques et Époques organiques," *Cahiers internationaux de sociologie*, 27, 131–52.

Jouffroy, T. (1838): "How Dogmas Come into Existence," in *Specimens of Foreign Standards of Literature*, ed. G. Ripley, vol. 2. Boston, 122–42.

Kant, I. (1963): *On History*, ed. L. Beck. Indianapolis, Ind.

Kelley, D. (1978): "The Metaphysics of Law," *American Historical Review*, 83, 350–67.

Kelly, G. (1992): *The Human Comedy: Constant, Tocqueville and French Liberalism*. New York.

Kolakowski, L. (1978): *Main Currents of Marxism*, tr. P. Falla, vol. 1. Oxford.

Kühne, W. (1938): *Graf August Cieszkowski*. Leipzig.

Lamennais, F. (1836–7): *Oeuvres Complètes de F. de la Mennais*, vol. 6. Paris.

Lamennais, F. (1859): *Oeuvres de F. de Lamennais*, vol. 1. Paris.

Liebich, A. (1979a): *Between Ideology and Utopia*. Dordrecht.

Liebich, A. (1979b): *Selected Writings of August Cieszkowski*, ed. A. Liebich. New York.

Lobkowicz, N. (1967): *Theory and Practice*. London.

Löwith, K. (1949): *Meaning in History*. Chicago.

Löwith, K. (1967): *From Hegel to Nietzsche*, tr. D. Green. New York.

Lukács, G. (1971): "Moses Hess and the Problem of the Idealist Dialectic," *Telos*, 10, 3–34.

Maistre, J. (1884): "Réflexions sur le Protestantisme," in *Oeuvres Complètes*, vol. 8, 63–97. Lyon.

Maistre, J. (1974): *Considerations on France*, tr. R. Lebrun. London.

Mannheim, K. (1971): *From Karl Mannheim*, ed. K. Wolff. New York.

Manuel, F. (1962): *The Prophets of Paris*. Cambridge, Mass.

Manuel. F. (1963): *The New World of Henri Saint-Simon*. Notre Dame.

Markus, R. (1954): 'Pleroma and Fulfillment,' *Vigiliae Christiana*, 8, 193–224.

Meier, C. (1990): *The Greek Discovery of Politics*, tr. D. McLintock. Cambridge, Mass.

Müller, A. (1921): *Ausgewählte Abhandlungen*, ed. J. Baxa. Jena.

Müller, A. (1922): *Die Elemente der Staatskunst*, ed. J. Baxa, vol. 1. Jena.

Müller, A. (1923): *Schriften zur Staatsphilosphie*, ed. R. Kohler. München.

Novalis (1955): "Christendom or Europe," in *The Political Thought of the German Romantics*, ed. H. Reiss. Oxford, 126–41.

Pickering, M. (1993): *Auguste, Comte*. New York.

Pocock, J. (1989): "Edmund Burke and the Redefinition of Enthusiasm: The Context as Counter-Revolution," in *The French Revolution and the Creation of Modern Political Culture*, vol. 3. Oxford, 19–43.

Reardon, B. (1975): *Liberalism and Tradition*. New York.

Reardon, B. (1985): *Religion in the Age of Romanticism*. New York.

Reeves, M. and Gould, W. (1987): *Joachim of Fiore and the Myth of the Eternal Evangel in the Nineteenth Century*. Oxford.

Ripley, G. (1838): *Specimens of Foreign Standards of Literature*, ed. G. Ripley, 2 vols. Boston.

Rodrigues, E. (1831): *Lettres sur la Religion et la Politique, 1829*. Paris.

Ruge, A. (1983): "A Self-Critique of Liberalism," in *The Young Hegelians*, ed. L. Stepelevich. New York, 237–59.

Saint-Simon, H. (1952): "New Christianity," in *Social Organization, The Science of Man and Other Writings*, ed. F. Markham. New York, 81–116.

Schiller, F. (1972): "The Nature and Value of Universal History: An Inaugural Lecture," *History and Theory*, 11, 322–34.

Spitzer, A. (1987): *The French Generation of 1820*. Princeton.

Staël, Madame de (1813): *Germany*, vol. 3. London.

Staël, Madame de (1987): *Major Writings of Germaine de Staël*, tr. V. Folkenflik. New York.

Stepelevich, L. (1974): "August Cieszkowski: From Theory to Praxis," *History and Theory*, 13, 39–52.

Toews, J. (1980): *Hegelianism*. New York.

Villers, C. (1807): *An Essay on the Spirit and Influence of the Reformation by Luther*, tr. B. Lambert. Dover, NH.

Voegelin, E. (1957): *The World of the Polis*. Baton Rouge, La.

Walicki, A. (1975): "August Cieszkowski's Works of 1838–1842 Within the Intellectual Context of Their Times," *Dialectics and Humanism*, 3, 197–209.

Waszek, N. (1987): "Eduard Gans on Poverty: Between Hegel and Saint-Simon," *Owl of Minerva*, 18, 167–78.

9

Apocalypse, Millennium and Utopia Today

Krishan Kumar

'Could this world really end? If it did, what would it mean?'
Will This World Survive? (Watchtower Bible and
Tract Society, Pennsylvania, 1992)

The Year 1000: Endings and Beginnings

It has always been something of a disappointment to me that the year
1000 AD – the natural and, in a certain sense, the only point of
comparison for our thinking about the impending year 2000 – was
attended by such relatively modest millennial hopes and strivings. Even
more disappointing is to find how little fear there was. I had always
imagined – inspired, I expect, by some vaguely remembered bits of
popular history – that there was great apprehension as the year 1000
approached, and that the year itself was marked by expressions of
great terror. After all, what could be more terrifying than the imminent end of the world? Was that not what was expected in the year
1000?[1]

It turns out that the legend of the terrors of the year 1000 was
fabricated towards the end of the fifteenth century. What Georges
Duby calls *'ce mirage historique'* was the work of humanists intent on
highlighting the darkness of the barbaric Middle Ages, by comparison
with the enlightenment of the age of classical antiquity that preceded
it, and which they sought to restore in their own time. 'At the centre
of medieval darkness, the Year One Thousand, antithesis of the Renaissance, presented the spectacle of death and abject submission.'[2]

And yet this myth is not the whole story of the year 1000, especially if we regard that millennial year as part of a whole climate of expectation covering the tenth and eleventh centuries. There was, it seems, considerable tension and terror in the middle of the tenth century, and at somewhat earlier and later times – though not, it appears, in the year 1000 itself.[3] And there was good warrant for these fears, and accompanying hopes. There was the authority of Augustine himself, who had declared that the world was now in its sixth and final age. Augustine refused to speculate on its precise duration, in earthly time. But several medieval writers, not to mention many popular prophets, did try to work out the duration of the sixth and last period. If, as Augustine had said, the millennium began with the birth of Christ, then it must end a thousand years after his birth, in the year 1000. The Venerable Bede therefore announced that the end of the world would come in the year 1000, and was followed in this by other thinkers in the centuries leading up to the tenth century. *Mundus senescit* – 'the world grows old'. This sentiment of a Merovingian chronicler of the seventh century was widely shared, and the phrase is repeated at regular intervals in the succeeding centuries. It occurs along with other expressions of unease and unrest, usually couched in apocalyptic tones, both before and after the year 1000.[4]

Indeed, in one of those repeated examples of the consequences of 'the failure of prophecy', expectations of the end of the world intensified and multiplied after the year 1000. Nor was this only the belief of the millenarians, those who, like the followers of Joachim of Fiore, looked forward to a new Golden Age on earth, a thousand-year period of peace and joy under the rule of a returned Christ. Belief in the end of the world – the apocalyptic belief, in the conventional use of that term – is not simply logically distinguishable from the belief in the earthly millennium but was so distinguished by many Christian thinkers of the Middle Ages. While millenarianism had been proclaimed a heresy as early as AD 431 (at the Council of Ephesus), the medieval church continued to express its belief in the end of the world, though constantly revising and proroguing the time of the expected end. The Universal Church, and the Universal Holy Roman Empire that was its secular arm, were in fact seen as the preparation for the end of earthly existence. That was their essential task.

The Reformation, as is well known, far from breaking with this tradition of belief reinvigorated it with its own brand of apocalyptic

fervour. The constant revisions of the Roman Church, the constant
postponement of the end of the world to an indefinite future, were
seen as the clear signs that the Antichrist ruled in Rome. For Luther
and his disciples, the evidence pointed unmistakably to the conclusion
that the end of the world was imminent. The struggle against the
'whore of Babylon', the appearance in Europe of the Turks, seen as
the unchained people of Gog, showed that the drama of the Book of
Revelation was being played out before their eyes, in their own time.
'The Reformation as a movement of religious renewal carried with it
all the signs of the End of the World.'[5]

Here is an important theme: the link between the end of the world
and its renewal. The message of the Reformation was that the very
troubles of the time were the signs of hope. Henri Pirenne makes a
similar point about the tenth century:

> The famous legend of the terrors of the year 1000 is not devoid . . .
> of symbolic significance. It is doubtless untrue that men expected the
> end of the world in the year 1000. Yet the century which came in at
> that date is characterized, in contrast with the preceding one, by a
> recrudescence of activity so marked that it could pass for the vigorous
> and joyful awakening of a society long oppressed by a nightmare of
> anguish.[6]

Out of the turmoil of the tenth century came the economic and
cultural renaissance of the eleventh and twelfth centuries. Out of the
violence and destruction of the apocalypse, comes the millennium. The
Church, in its concern to discourage social radicalism, might try to
keep apart ends and new beginnings, destruction and creation, death
and renewal. The one was a matter of earthly, the other of heavenly
life. Both before and after the Reformation this separation was widely
challenged. Christian millenarianism kept alive the hope that the end
of the world, which was foreordained and certain, would also be the
beginning of a new life – and a life which for a period at least would
be on this earth. The apocalyptic myth holds, in an uneasy but dynamic tension, the elements of both terror and hope. The apocalyptic
ending will also signal the millennial beginning. However frightful the
contemplation of the end, there is no need to despair: a new world will
be born.

The Year 2000: Endings Without Beginnings?

As we approach the end of our own millennium, who can fail to sympathize with our present-day apocalypticists? The signs betokening the end seem only too clear. The world appears more unstable and dangerous than at any time in the past half century; deeper-lying problems, the result of centuries of development, also seem to be coming to a head.

A new 'world disorder' is upon us. The Cold War may have been a 'balance of terror', but it preserved the peace. The ending of the Cold War has unleashed demons of all kinds. Eastern Europe – the former Soviet empire – is a battleground of warring groups and nations, against a background of economic collapse. The huge nuclear arsenal is portioned out, thus increasing the risk of nuclear war probably to a greater extent than in the age of the Cold War. With the break-up of Czechoslovakia, and the renewal of age-old hostilities between ethnic groups in the region, Central Europe too sits on shifting sands. Most horrifically, the Balkans have reverted to their traditional posture of internecine strife. The scenes from Bosnia alone, relayed nightly to the television screens of the world, have conjured up with grim faithfulness the images of the Apocalypse.

Moving westwards, the picture is not much more cheering. A trade war between Europe and América looms. The European Community is heading towards greater disintegration than integration. A massive and apparently intractable recession grips the economies of the West, pushing unemployment up beyond fifteen per cent of the population and paralysing the world economy as a whole. Homelessness and crime reach record levels. So too does lack of trust in the good faith and competence of governments.

Expand the picture, and the gloom deepens. In Africa the much-acclaimed move to democracy has led, by a further step, downwards to endemic civil war and economic chaos. In the Middle East a resurgent Islam threatens a new and ferocious *jihad* against the secular West and its supporters. In India persistent communal violence between Hindus and Muslims is undermining the integrity of the state; in China all political development seems frozen, promising many bloody Tiananmen Squares in the future. Elsewhere in the former Third

World crippling indebtedness has virtually halted economic development and in many cases pushed it back.

At a deeper level, and affecting every part of the world, is the spectre
of ecological devastation, compounded by what many see as the moral
devastation of Aids. In a valedictory piece in *The Independent* at the end
of 1992 – in which he seemed to be bidding farewell to more than a
customary task – the columnist William Rees-Mogg wrote:

> If we are lucky, mankind as it is has about 50 years left. Most of the
> graphs of human development, population, ecology, technology, nu-
> clear proliferation and the spread of disease are on an explosive curve.
> The lines shoot off the graph somewhere in the middle of the next
> century.[7]

Anyone can draw up their own list of impending terrors. Rees-
Mogg's oracular pronouncement has much in common with all the
preceding paragraphs of this section. For they are of course the common coin of apocalyptic journalism. We have been here many times
before: for instance in the 1920s and 1930s, when Oswald Spengler's
Decline of the West chimed in so well with the *Weltschmerz* of European
intellectuals; and again in the 1970s, after the first oil shock of 1973
and the realization that the dizzying economic growth of the post-war
period might not be forever. Why take current prophecies of doom
more to heart? What is so different, so novel, now? Doomsayers can be
found at any time and place. It is an amusing intellectual game to place
earlier prophecies of the end of the world against any current crop of
expectations. They can generally be made to sound uncannily apt.
Here for instance is Augustine, in the fifth century:

> As the end of the world approaches, errors increase, terrors multiply,
> iniquity increases, infidelity increases; the light, in short . . . is very often
> extinguished; this darkness of enmity between brethren increases, daily
> increases, and Jesus is not yet come.[8]

The millennial hint at the end of this passage points to an important
difference between past and present doomsayers. Earlier ones, however
scathing their denunciation or profound their anguish, generally retained something of the messianic or millennial hope that out of the
ruins would come regeneration. This was true even of the extravagant
fantasies of destruction of the *fin-de-siècle* decadents of the last century.[9]

Still, we might expect our current Jeremiahs, lacking even the residual religious faith of their predecessors, to be predominantly gloomy. And, who knows, they may even turn out to be right. What interests me however is something different, something, to my mind, more novel. And that is that even those pronouncements that seem to be about hopeful developments in the world are strangely muted. It is not that their authors doubt the truth of their assertions; it is that these do not seem to bring them much cheer. Their statements are marked by a distinct melancholy. We expect this of our doomsters, but it is surprising to find it in those who think we live in the best of all possible worlds. Dr Pangloss should not be so miserable. Whence those tears?

We should note that this is an unusual state of affairs. Previously good and bad, optimism and pessimism, fed off each other. The imagination of disaster, the apocalyptical imagination, usually carried with it, as I have said, a sense of hope, of something constructive emerging from the ruins. Similarly millennial hopes, or the utopian imagination, were commonly coupled with the belief that a great disaster – what H. G. Wells called 'a cleansing disillusionment' – must precede the emergence of the millennial kingdom or the good society. That is indeed perhaps why Wells, who combined images of apocalyptic destruction with glowing pictures of utopia, had such a wide appeal. The general point is well put by Hans Magnus Enzensberger:

> The idea of the apocalypse has accompanied utopian thought since its first beginnings, pursuing it like a shadow, like a reverse side that cannot be left behind: without catastrophe, no millennium, without apocalypse, no paradise. The idea of the end of the world is simply a negative utopia.[10]

What we seem to have today is the apocalyptic imagination without hope but also, more strikingly, a kind of millennial belief almost entirely emptied of the conflict and dynamism that generally belong to it. It is a millennial belief without a sense of the future. We have, it seems, at the end of the second millennium achieved *the* millennium, the hoped-for state of peace and plenty. But it brings no pleasure, and promises no happiness. In this sense it seems not to make much difference whether we look with foreboding to a dismal future, or proclaim our good luck at the way things have turned out. Neither brings any comfort.

I am thinking in particular of the announcement of 'the end of history', especially as it has been formulated by the American political thinker Francis Fukuyama. This has clearly struck a chord, if one takes as evidence the public discussion it has generated in so many different countries. The break-up of communism in Eastern Europe is the main development underlying the claim; but there are other political changes – in southern Europe, South America, and south Asia – that together add up to what appears to be a world-wide movement towards democratic or liberal forms of government. This leads Fukuyama to argue that there is no longer any basic ideological conflict in the world. Liberal democracy, underpinned by a market economy, is the clear choice of the vast majority of the nations of the world. It is in that sense that history has ended.

Fukuyama rejoices in this fact (if it is a fact); but it is a curious kind of rejoicing. There would seem to be some cause for satisfaction if, as Fukuyama thinks, we are at the end of a 200-year period of ideological strife that has caused bloody wars and countless revolutions – including the revolutions of Nazism and Stalinism. And there are indeed some people in the West who have indulged in an orgy of triumphalism. But the more reflective responses, including Fukuyama's, are sober to the point of depression. Fukuyama is concerned at the selfishness and excessive individualism of liberal societies, their relentless erosion of all forms of community and social morality. To function properly, liberal societies depend upon non-liberal or pre-liberal cultural traditions, especially those stemming from religion. It is precisely these traditions that liberalism undermines. If the whole world is becoming liberal, the whole world is also becoming amoral.

There is a further, more serious, problem. Liberal democracy, says Fukuyama, 'constitutes the best possible solution to the human problem'. But its world-wide achievement is evidently a cause for despondency as much as for celebration. For it seems to drive out of human life much that made that life worthwhile. It inaugurates nothing new, no new era of creativity or constructive growth. In a melancholy echo of the medieval chroniclers, Fukuyama observes that 'we . . . live in the old age of mankind'. The prospect for the 'Last Man' is of 'centuries of boredom' as he quietly lives out his final years.

> The end of history will be a very sad time. The struggle for recognition, the willingness to risk one's life for a purely abstract goal, the worldwide

ideological struggle that called forth daring, courage, imagination, and idealism, will be replaced by economic calculation, the endless solving of technical problems, environmental concerns, and the satisfaction of sophisticated consumer demands. In the post-historical period there will be neither art nor philosophy, just the perpetual caretaking of the museum of human history.[11]

'Postmodernity' is another kind of ending that does not sound very exciting. Here too we are told of 'the death of grand narratives', an end to any possible belief in Truth, History, Progress, Reason or Revolution (still less Revelation). That sounds final enough. And, in its way, it is meant to be liberating. But again there is no sense of a new departure, a new freedom now that the scales of illusion have fallen from our eyes. Instead we are invited to take a purely pragmatic or ironic stance towards the world, to avoid public commitment and devote ourselves to the pursuit of private purposes and private life.[12]

Again, the point is not so much whether or not we agree with the analysis as the mood in which it is conducted. It is a mood of quiet resignation, almost of weariness, spiced with a certain malicious glee at the collapse of long-standing certainties. Martin Jay has observed that the postmodernist school exhibits many of the qualities discussed by Freud in his essay, 'Mourning and Melancholia' (1917). There is the same alternation of moods of melancholy and mania that Freud discerned in the phenomenon of chronic or abnormal mourning (melancholia). One might say, as it was once said by a leading postmodernist, Jean-François Lyotard, that postmodernism expresses 'a kind of grieving or melancholy with respect to the ideas of the modern era, a sense of disarray'. If so, it might explain why the postmodern apocalypse comes not with a bang but a whimper. It is a version of the apocalypse that dwells obsessively on the end, without any expectation of a new beginning. It is, Jacques Derrida has said approvingly, 'an apocalypse without vision', without redemptive hope; it is 'an end without an end'.[13]

We might observe that this sense of endings without new beginnings has been more or less constant throughout the twentieth century. There were certainly 'utopists' such as H. G. Wells who fought against this. But, in spite of his international fame, Wells was swimming against the tide. By the end of his life, in 1946, even he came to acknowledge this. Wells was the one who had called the First World

War 'the war that will end war'. He had joined with J. B. S. Haldane, J. D. Bernal and other scientists in looking to science for the salvation of society. Now, faced with a second world war, and the failure of science and scientists to direct the course of social development, he announced that man was 'at the close of his specific existence . . . *Homo sapiens*, as he has been pleased to call himself, is in his present form played out.'[14]

Wells here echoed, at almost mid-century, D. H. Lawrence's lament at the time of the First World War. For Lawrence, as for so many European intellectuals, the horrific nature of the war had killed off irredeemably all the hopes that had sustained the nineteenth-century belief in progress. 'In 1915 the old world ended,' he wrote in *Kangaroo* (1923). But, as he expressed it in a letter of that very year, 1915, unlike Wells he saw no prospect of a new world arising from the ashes of the old.

> I am so sad for my country, for this great wave of civilization, 2000 years, which is now collapsing, that it is hard to live. So much beauty and pathos of old things passing away and no new things coming . . . the winter stretches ahead, where all vision is lost and all memory dies out.[15]

There have been repeated claims throughout the century, by artists, scientists and social activists, that things have not come to an end, that a new birth is at hand. All seem to have ended, as with Wells, in disillusion and recantation, or with repudiation by their listeners. Modernist art and literature pictured themselves, in apocalyptic terms, as marking a total rupture with the past, and a leap into a new future.[16] Postmodernism, with the cordial concurrence of the bulk of ordinary people, dismissed this as arrogance and elitism. Scientists – who, Sir Charles Snow told us, 'had the future in their bones' – promised that their knowledge would free the world of war and want. Baron Frankenstein rather than Francis Bacon seems, in the event, to have been their mentor. The Bolsheviks, in their revolution of 1917, aspired to offer the world the model of a new society, free from exploitation. Seventy years later, amidst a crumbling economy and an embittered population, the experiment was pronounced a failure – not just for Russia, it seemed, but for the whole world.

But could hope reside in another quarter? Was the alternative to Bolshevism any more reassuring or inspiring? That alternative has focused primarily on America. The United States has been, with the USSR, one of the two utopian exemplars of modern times. In the 1950s its culture and civilization were proclaimed the destiny of the world. The USA represented industrial civilization and, declared a group of prominent American social scientists in a famous book of the time, American-style industrial society had become 'the goal of mankind and the essence of national aspiration'.[17]

It is America that, once more, is the model underlying the announcement of 'the end of history' today. This time, however, it is not American technology but the American ideology – individualism, capitalism, consumerism – that is seen as the all-conquering force. And there's the rub. For as we have seen, that ideology no longer has the power to inspire utopian hopes. Even in its early heroic days, in the writings of Adam Smith and others, the claims made on its behalf were severely qualified. It was accepted as much for negative reasons – for its unwarlike qualities – as for its contribution to economic and social wellbeing.[18] During its heyday as *laissez-faire* liberalism it had to contend with the alternative utopia of socialism, which at the very least deflated its pretensions. Now the socialist utopia has lost its appeal. But, with the exception of certain sections of East European opinion, the capitalist utopia is likewise tarnished. Capitalism unleashed is seen to threaten the life-support systems of the planet. Left unchecked it bids fair to turn the world into a moral and material wasteland. Alternatives to capitalism, in the sense of whole new systems, are not currently on offer. But that still leaves capitalism as no more than the least worst rather than the best or even the good society.[19] This is hardly the stuff of utopia.

It has often been said that the most creative thought of the twentieth century has been in the direction of what one might call 'radical conservatism', rather than in the tradition of nineteenth-century progressivism. Certainly this has been true of much of the best literature of our time, as in the writing of Yeats, Pound, Eliot and Lawrence. What this suggests is the inability of twentieth-century industrial society to produce persuasive or lasting images of itself as the form of the future. Thinkers have turned back, to the past, for the values and visions that sustain them. Technocratic utopias of various kinds have had their moments – in the 1930s and 1950s especially – but they have failed to take a hold on the contemporary imagination for more than a brief period. The sheer facts of twentieth-century history – world war, the Holocaust, nuclear weapons, environmental destruction – have again and again told against them. It has been impossible to sustain for long the faith that the world is getting better and that, with the help of some more science and technology, it will get better still. The images of the future that have stamped themselves on popular consciousness remain those of *Brave New World* and *Nineteen Eighty-Four*, rather than the hopeful technological utopias of H. G. Wells or B. F. Skinner.

Modernity is characterized in principle by an openness to the future that has generally been hostile to utopian 'closure'. All utopias seem to represent obstacles to the change and novelty on which modernity thrives. Nineteenth-century utopianism nevertheless adapted to this requirement with considerable success. It replaced the static schemes that had been the staple of utopia since Thomas More with the more open, experimental and dynamic schemes of Robert Owen, Saint-Simon, Fourier, Marx and Wells. Change and development were, with varying degrees of persuasiveness, built into their utopias. The very popularity of these schemes showed that, whatever the difficulties faced by utopia in the modern epoch, the need for utopia remained strong.

In our time, modernity's progressiveness has been called severely into question. Its dynamism and open-endedness, its lack of an overarching system of values, now seem more of a threat than a promise. The postmodernist retreat is one response. Postmodernity flattens time; it solves the problem of the future by simply denying the relevance of the concepts of 'past', 'present' and 'future'. It denounces modernity's belief in progress and attacks its faith in science and technology. To that extent it echoes the cultural conservatism of the earlier part of the century. But, unlike that, it refuses to replace modernity with anything; this denial of an alternative is indeed its principle characteristic.

Utopia too has retreated in the face of this faltering of confidence in the future. Its coexistence with modernity depended on the belief that the future could be shaped, and to an extent discerned, by reason. It was one of the most persuasive features of the anti-utopia of the twentieth century to point to this belief as a dangerous illusion. Even more damagingly, it was part of the argument of anti-utopians such as Evgeny Zamyatin and Aldous Huxley that in so far as reason *was* being realized in the modern world, the results were disastrous. If the modern utopia took its stand on reason and science, then it too was condemned by the kind of civilization that reason and science had brought into being.[20]

The anti-utopia, whose popularity in our century has far exceeded that of the utopia, like the poets and writers turned its back on the present. It buried modern civilization in the name of values and practices that, it was generally prepared to admit, had disappeared beyond the possibility of revival. It contemplated the end of the modern world, whether in a blaze of apocalyptic violence or by a slow decline through boredom, without the hope that death would mean, as so often in the past, rebirth. The law of entropy, which announced the ultimate running-down of the universe, seemed finally to have extended its sphere of operation to human society.

Millennium and Utopia

I suppose it is inevitable that our apocalypses should be low-keyed – especially once the idea of a nuclear apocalypse has moved to the background. 'Apocalypse', as Anthony Giddens has said, 'has become banal.' Secular apocalypses tend to be statistical – the extrapolation of long-term trends, or the calculation of 'statistical risk parameters' threatening human existence.[21] The end will come as the result of a steady increase in population, or a slow poisoning of the planet. Catastrophe will be expressed in lines on a graph rather than in the imagery of the Book of Revelation.

Moreover, there is no intrinsic reason why end-of-the-century, or even end-of-the-millennium speculations should be linked to millennial expectations. Only in the first millennium could the two really be expected to coincide. Once the first millennium had passed without the world's coming to an end, prophecies of the Second Coming and a new millennium could in principle fix on practically any date.

But calendrical endings, centennial and millennial, did prove enticing. Melancthon, in the sixteenth century, put the waning of the final epoch of man after the passing of two thousand years from the birth of Christ; and Newton, calculating after his own fashion, prophesied around 1700 that papal rule would end in the year 2000. Frank Kermode has said that 'it is a peculiarity of the imagination that it is always at the end of an era', and that 'our sense of epoch is gratified

above all by the ends of centuries'.[22] So it is certainly not surprising
to find in our own time, at the end not just of a century but a
millennium, a strong sense of finality, of a story told and done with.[23]

But still the question remains: why, unlike earlier centuries, is our
sense of an ending so flat, so lacking in *élan*? Why have we truncated
the apocalyptic vision, so that we see endings without new beginnings?

We seem to be in the presence here of a debased millenarianism,
without a compensating utopian vision. Now, although millenarianism
and utopianism are fed by different sources and different traditions –
the one mainly Christian, the other mainly classical – they have for
most of their history to a good extent overlapped. Some people have
even argued that utopia is mainly a secularized millennialism. I do not
myself think that – I think they have largely independent histories –
but I don't doubt that for much of the time they complemented each
other. Millennialism supplied the dynamism, the heightened sense of
expectation of a coming crisis out of which would rise a new world.
Utopia provided the picture of the new world, painted in such colours
as to make us want to live in it.[24]

We need both millennium and utopia. We need, first, something
that lends urgency and the sense of a forward movement. The idea of
the millennium sees the whole of human history from the viewpoint of
the future. Unlike the cyclical conceptions of antiquity, which saw
only eternal return to the starting point, the Christian millennium sees
the breakthrough to something radically new. Even if we do not know
when we will get there, even if we never get there, the millennium
beckons, like a beacon, and draws us on. It is the Faustian spirit in
history, preventing us from spending too long in one way of life, or
lapsing into a complacent admiration of the present. The millennium is
a constant check to a tendency of self-satisfaction. It represents what
the Marxist philosopher Ernst Bloch called the principle of *noch nicht*:
which means not only 'not yet' but also 'still not'. It thus carries the
sense both of what is expected, what will be in the future, and what
is lacking in the present, what should impel us to change our condition. Together they add up to a dynamic process of becoming whose
motivating force is an ever-present future.[25]

The millennium contributes the element of hope – 'the unfinished
forward dream', to quote Bloch again, the '*docta spes*', which we might
translate as 'knowing hope', hope based on an anticipated future. But
it is a future which is typically sketched out only in the vaguest terms,

as in the Book of Revelation. All the emphasis is on the movement towards the goal, the time of waiting and preparation. The end is more or less preordained – this could lead, in some varieties of millenarianism, to a passive waiting for the end. But when it will be, what form the future dispensation will take, are obscure matters largely out of control of believers. For the believer, what matters is to get into the right state of readiness, to be in the right frame of mind as well as body. The world will surely end and the millennium come; there will be 'a new heaven and a new earth'; we can live our lives in the expectation of the end; but of the world to come we have only the merest glimpses.[26]

If the millennium supplies the means or the movement towards the end, utopia is concerned with the ends themselves. But how it does so is not as straightforward as is generally thought. Utopia is certainly about presenting pictures of the ideal society. Unlike millennialism, it is relatively indifferent as to the means of achieving that ideal. Typically in the utopia, voyagers come upon utopia because their ship was blown off course; or they stumble upon it in some remote mountain valley; or someone sleeps or dreams his or her way into some future utopia. The means are downplayed; all the concentration is on the nature of the end, on what happens when you arrive in the good society.

But the more interesting utopias are not simply blueprints or designs for the good society (the exception here is principally the architectural or urban utopia, which however has its own specific purpose).[27] They are not usually detailed descriptions of political or economic institutions. More typically they are concerned with the feel of the good society, the texture of life there. The skill of the good utopist is in the imagination of what it would be like to live in a utopia. Utopia is the imaginative recreation of the good life. Its way of focusing upon ends is by making us long for them.

William Morris's utopia, *News from Nowhere* (1890), is one of the finest examples of this (Thomas More's *Utopia*, I would argue, is another). It is notoriously lacking in detail as to the workings of the future (communist) society it portrays. But it is shot through with what one might call the expressive or emotional structures of utopia. Its high point is an idyllic journey up the Thames, by rowing boat, culminating in the arrival at a beautiful house near the source of the Thames (quite evidently Morris's own house, Kelmscott Manor). Morris wants us to share in that experience, to live it with such intensity that we long for the kind of society in which such joyful experiences are not the exception but the norm.

Writing about *News from Nowhere*, the French sociologist Miguel Abensour has said that it is about 'the education of desire'.[28] Morris is not trying to persuade us to construct a communist society in the manner of those 'scientific socialists', Marx and Engels, nor in the way, a few years earlier, the American socialist Edward Bellamy had painstakingly tried to do in his utopia, *Looking Backward* (1888). Morris largely takes for granted the superior efficiency and humanity of communism. What he wants to do is to reshape our feelings – to do, in other words, what a work of art does. He wants us, in effect, to fall in love with the good society, so that we will do everything in our power to attain it.

So if the millennium supplies the element of hope, utopia supplies the element of desire. The one tells us that change is possible, the other why we need to make the change, what we might gain if we do so. But I don't want to exaggerate the difference of function. As I have said, millennialism and utopianism have accompanied and reinforced each other throughout their history. Millennial hopes, it has been suggested, underlay even that most secular of utopias, the rationalist utopia of the eighteenth-century Enlightenment.[29] They were prominent in the Enlightenment's offspring, the French Revolution, and the whole mythology of revolution that sprang from it. In the nineteenth century, one might even say that the millennial aspect was uppermost. This is especially true of Marxism, which was largely concerned with the dynamics of change and notoriously reluctant to give much idea of the future communist society ('I do not write recipes for the cookshops of the future', was Marx's biting riposte to the requests for such a sketch). But it is only in the twentieth century that the two – millennium and utopia – have seriously parted company from each other.

The Need for Utopia

I have said that the current pronouncements of 'the end of history', and the like, are a form of debased millenarianism. They are millenarian because the people who make them see a process of development, a kind of social evolution, that has finally delivered humanity from historic conflicts. Humanity has made many false turns, taken many false trails, on the way. But here at last, at the end of the second millennium, *is* the millennium, the consummation of mankind's development.

This kind of millenarianism has in fact been quite common in the twentieth century. It is there in communism and Fascism, and in many varieties of messianic nationalism in the Third World.[30] But at least these movements had the courage of their convictions. They believed, stridently, fervently, fanatically, that the millennium *had* arrived, and that the world would from now on be a place of plenty and joy. The vision of the millennium was positive, however unattractive it might appear to some of us.

I call the present vision a debased millenarianism because it is lacking in that positive quality. It sees an end without a new beginning. It has no conviction that the world that is emerging at the end of the second millennium has any new principle of development. It is glad that democracy has won, and the enemy defeated. It is pleased to deflate what it sees as the hubris of thinking that we understand or could understand the laws of history, or that there can be grand rational schemes for solving the world's problems. But neither post-historicists nor postmodernists seem very happy at these developments. There is no millenarian joy. The post-historicists are anxious, almost resigned. The postmodernists take refuge in irony and a sort of juvenile frivolity, when they do not simply express boredom with the world. The mood is in both cases profoundly negative. The story has ended; there is nothing more to be said.

This negative note seems to me to reflect the weakness of utopia in our time. As compared with millenarianism, utopia has received a great battering in the twentieth century. It has been on the defensive since the beginning of the century. From the First World War to the Second and beyond, it has been assailed by the likes of Yevgeny Zamyatin, Nicholas Berdyaev, Aldous Huxley, Arthur Koestler, George Orwell, Karl Popper and Leszek Kolakowski. It has been charged with leading to tyranny and totalitarianism. The collapse of communism in Eastern Europe has been seen – not least in Eastern Europe itself – as the final vindication of this anti-utopianism.[31]

Much of this, in addition to being excessively pessimistic and even misanthropic, seems also to fall within a familiar vein of ethnocentrism.

Because Europeans, or at least European intellectuals, are disappointed with the fruits of the Enlightenment; because the Enlightenment's greatest utopia, the utopia of socialism, has apparently been a spectacular failure; so, it is claimed, the world must renounce utopia. European thought and European experience are visited upon the whole of the contemporary world. The disillusionment of the European intelligentsia must be the starting point for serious reflection anywhere and everywhere.

We should note that, even in Western societies, the pessimism of the intelligentsia has not been whole-heartedly endorsed by the mass of the population. A species of 'popular utopianism' thrives in the spaces of popular culture. Pop songs, Hollywood movies, and television soap operas are replete with utopian imagery.[32] True, this is often nostalgic or escapist. The world of Australian soaps such as *Neighbours* and *Home and Away*, and even of more realistic English varieties such as *Coronation Street* and *East Enders*, is a fantasy world of community and neighbourly intimacy; while the glamorous and glossy setting of *Dallas* and *Dynasty* evoke images of wealth and power such as can satisfy the wildest desires. This is the 'poor man's utopia', the utopianism that is fed by the fantasies of the Land of Cockaygne. But it is none the less powerful for that; and it shows that, whatever jaded intellectuals might feel, images of the good life continue to appeal to a wide section of the population of Western industrial societies.

And not just to the masses. Certain specific groups in Western societies have in recent years turned to utopia as the most suitable vehicle for their aspirations. Feminists have been among the most active and creative in this. Lacking, as they see it, a past in which women have led free and fulfilling lives, they have turned to the future, to science fiction and utopia, to explore the forms and conditions of women's emancipation. In works such as Marge Piercy's *Woman on the Edge of Time* (1976), Ursula Le Guin's *The Dispossessed* (1974) and Sally Gearhart's *The Wanderground* (1980), they have sketched utopian (and dystopian) pictures of possible futures for women.[33] Utopia has appealed as a challenge to the imagination. It has expressed not simply the confidence of feminists in the rightness and feasibility of their aims, but the acceptance that these aims are varied and to some extent competing. Utopia has been the form through which they can conduct 'thought experiments' about alternative futures; it enables them to debate the future.

Ecologists have, regrettably, so far largely eschewed utopian fiction. But they are another group who have found the utopian way of thinking powerfully conducive to their purposes. Ecologists conceive of the problems of the planet on the grandest scale. They are forced to think holistically, to see the world as a system in which everything is related to everything else. The damage done to the polar ice-cap is traced to the energy requirements of industrial capitalism; global warming to our everyday reliance on fossil fuels and consumer durables.

Utopia too has always thought holistically. It seizes the world according to some central principle of functioning. In addition it is concerned not just with how things work but how they should work. What better form for showing the ecologically sound and ecologically sustainable world in a vivid and persuasive way? With the exception of such works as Ernest Callenbach's *Ecotopia* (1975) the ecological utopia has, as I have said, not been much expressed in the formal literary utopia. But with the examples of William Morris's *News from Nowhere* and Aldous Huxley's *Island* (1962) – both 'ecotopias' before the name – behind them, it should not be long before someone sees the potentiality and, indeed, the necessity for putting ecological ideas into a fully developed utopia. Meanwhile there are some attractive ecological works strongly marked by the utopian imagination, such as Robert Van de Weyer's *Wickwyn* (1986) and André Gorz's *Paths to Paradise* (1985).[34]

The feminist and the ecological utopias suffer from being restricted to particular constituencies. On the whole it is feminists who read feminist utopias and ecologists who read ecological utopias. The debates take place within confined circles; only rarely, as at the time of some particular environmental disaster, do they affect the wider consciousness of society. It is this that lends force to the view that, despite the persistence of popular utopianism and the appeal of utopia to particular groups, utopia is generally a spent force in the West. But that only serves to underline the possibility that, whatever might be the case in Western Europe and North America, things may look very different in the wider world.

And indeed if we look beyond the confines of the West we may be inclined to think that utopia is, if anything, too resurgent, too rampant. We are not, of course, referring here to the formal utopia which has been written in the West since the time of Thomas More (and which,

I think, is essentially a Western or European thing). But if utopia embraces, as it so often has in its history, schemes of total reconstruction or regeneration, then the evidence of its continued vitality is only too clear.

Even in parts of Europe, in its central and eastern regions, utopian forms appear to be flourishing. The ex-communist world has been the loudest in proclaiming the 'death of utopia'; at the same time it has been rapidly re-inventing it. Central European intellectuals such as Milan Kundera and Georgy Konrad have revived the dream of *Mitteleuropa* – seen not, as in some of its earlier expressions, as the theatre of German ambitions but as a civilization and a way of life different and more attractive than that of either West or East. This they would like to see as the future destiny of Central Europe, now that it has thrown off the shackles of Soviet rule.[35] Central Europeans like to stress their tradition of scepticism and irony, their suspicion of all utopian thinking. It is no denial of this to say that, as is common with other fervent anti-utopians, they have elevated the anti-utopian qualities of Central European culture to utopian status.

For their part their erstwhile master, the Russians, have of late been elaborating their own utopias to replace the defunct utopia of communism. These take a variety of forms, but most of them draw upon the tradition of thought that stresses Russia's uniqueness, its distinctive history as compared with the West. They range from Alexander Solzhenitsyn's call to return to the institutions and practices of late-nineteenth-century Russia, through various revivals of Populist and Slavophil ideologies, to full-blooded nationalist demands for a regeneration of Russia along the lines of Orthodoxy and Empire. More concretely there have been movements based upon the idealization of especially valued or symbolically important groups and practices, as in popular support for the revival of the Cossack culture of southern Russia.[36]

Elsewhere in the former Soviet Empire there has been an explosion of one of the most powerful forms of contemporary utopianism: messianic nationalism. This is frequently combined with the other world-wide contemporary manifestation of utopianism, religious fundamentalism. In both these cases utopianism is fed, as often in the past, by millennialism. The nationalist and the religious fundamentalist alike claim that the success of their aims will lead to the total liberation and regeneration of their societies. Resurgent Islam as much as fanatical

Hinduism see in the return to religion the solution to all the ills that afflict their people. In the Balkans, the Middle East, southern Africa, nationalism offers a similar vision of a people culturally purified and freed of age-old domination.

Nationalism and religious fundamentalism have their expression in the contemporary West, too. But they have not so far convulsed entire societies, as they have elsewhere and as they did in the West's own past. Here too the present Western disenchantment with utopia reveals itself. Western populations are generally distrustful of schemes promising total solutions. The experience of nationalist and fundamentalist movements suggests that this is no bad thing.

But this should not blind us to the source of the appeal of these movements. In however dangerous a form, they express that longing for a vision that has been a prime characteristic of practically all human societies up to the present time. It is Western society, not the rest of the world, that is the aberrant case. The hostility to utopia in the twentieth century has made it almost impossible to offer, at the highest levels of the culture, visions of the good society and the good life. It is not just that to write a utopia today is to invite amusement or mockery. More importantly, all that is strongest and best in contemporary Western culture works against it.

I don't wish to defend everything that has been done in the name of utopia. But I think that many of the attacks misconceive its nature and function. As I have tried to suggest, utopia is not mainly about providing detailed blueprints for social reconstruction. Its concern with ends is about making us think about possible worlds. It is about inventing and imagining worlds for our contemplation and delight. It opens up our minds to the possibilities of the human condition.

It is this that we most seem to need at the present time. There are doomsters enough – though they have their part to play, like the prophets of old, warning and admonishing. There are also our latter-day millenarians, somewhat jaded in their outlook on the world, and rather prepared to settle for a quiet life and the idle ticking-over of the engine of history. Without wishing to bang the inspirational drum too loudly, this hardly seems enough.

When the exiled Polish poet, Czeslaw Milosz, contemplated the ruins of communism at the end of 1989 he felt some satisfaction. But though he had an habitual distrust of utopias, he did not join with his compatriots in Eastern Europe in celebrating the 'death of utopia'. 'I hope,' he wrote, 'that the turmoil in these countries has not been a temporary phase, a passage to an ordinary society of earners and consumers, but rather the birth of a new form of human inter-action . . . The failure of Marx's vision has created the need for another vision, not for a rejection of all visions.'[37] With the characteristic wariness of a bruised East European intellectual, he hoped this would be a vision in a 'non-utopian style'. We should respect this response to a bitter experience. But let us not quarrel about words. The need for a vision is the thing. I would call this an appeal for the renewal of utopia, the constant searching for alternative ways of life. As the second millennium ends, in a state of confusion and uncertainty, this is surely the time to be thinking about how we are to live in the third millennium.

NOTES

1 'Un peuple terrorisé par l'imminence de la fin du monde: dans l'esprit de bien des hommes de culture, cette image de l'An Mil demeure encore vivante ajourd'hui', Georges Duby, *L'An Mil* (Paris, 1980), 9.

2 Duby, *L'An Mil*, 9 (my tr.).

3 The evidence is surveyed in Henri Focillon, *The Year 1000*, tr. from the French by F. D. Wieck (New York, 1969), 39–72. Focillon thus sums up the position: 'We are faced with a paradoxical situation: for the middle of the tenth century and all through the eleventh, we possess either compelling proof, or else significant traces, of the belief in the world's end; for the years immediately before the year 1000 and for that year itself, we no longer have any. The decisive moment, it would seem, left men indifferent.' Ibid., p. 62.

4 See A. J. Gurevich, *Categories of Medieval Culture*, tr. from the Russian by G. L. Campbell (London, 1985), 113–22; also Focillon, *The Year 1000*, 53–9.

A fruitful source of dispute was whether the millennium referred to by Augustine was to be dated from the birth of Christ or his death. The first put the end of the world in the year 1000, the second in the year 1033. This partly accounts for the excitement surrounding the otherwise innocent-sounding year 1033, the thousandth anniversary of Christ's Passion. The excitement was increased by the great famine of that year; the Burgundian monk Glaber reported on this that 'men believed that the orderly procession of the seasons and the laws of nature, which until then had ruled the world, had relapsed into the eternal chaos; and they feared that mankind would end.' Focillon, *The Year 1000*, 67–8; see also

Duby, *L'An Mil*, 33–40.

5   Reinhart Koselleck, *Futures Past: On the Semantics of Historical Time*, tr.
    from the German by K. Tribe (Cambridge, Mass., 1985), 6.

6   Henri Pirenne, *Medieval Cities*, tr. from the French by D. Halsey (New
    York, 1956), 56.

7   William Rees-Mogg, 'Is This the End of Life as I Know It?', *The
    Independent*, 21 December 1992, 17. This prediction is very close to that
    of the famous Club of Rome report of 1972, which concluded: 'If the
    present growth trends in world population, industrialization, pollution,
    food production, and resource depletion continue unchanged, the limits
    to growth on this planet will be reached sometime within the next one
    hundred years.' Donella H. Meadows, and others, *The Limits to Growth*
    (London, 1972), 23.

    For further examples of current apocalyptic thinking, see Charles
    Krauthammer, 'The End of the World', *The New Republic*, 28 March
    1983, 12–15; Joe Bailley, *Pessimism* (London and New York, 1988); Paul
    Boyer, *When Time Shall Be No More* (Cambridge, Mass., 1991); Martin
    Jay, 'Apocalypse and the Inability to Mourn', in *Force Fields: Between
    Intellectual History and Cultural Criticism* (London, 1992). For a grim
    scenario of the future following upon the collapse of communism, see
    Ken Jowitt, *New World Disorder: The Leninist Extinction* (Berkeley, Calif.,
    1992).

8   Quoted in Herbert A. Deane, *The Political and Social Ideas of Augustine*
    (New York, 1963), 71.

9   Martin Jay, 'Fin-de-siècle Socialism', in *Fin-de Siècle Socialism, and Other
    Essays* (New York and London, 1988), 12. The cultural despair, amount-
    ing to a cult, of the writers and artists was in any case only one side of
    the coin of *fin-de-siècle* civilization. The other side was astonishing econ-
    omic and technological progress, and a general increase in the quality of
    life for the mass of the population. See Eugen Weber, *France, Fin de Siècle*
    (Cambridge, Mass., 1986); Mikulas Teich and Roy Porter, eds, *Fin de
    Siècle and Its Legacy* (Cambridge, UK, 1990). That the disintegration of
    liberal society at the end of the nineteenth century was at the same time
    the occasion of a singular burst of cultural creativity is also the theme of
    Carl E. Schorske, *Fin-de-Siècle Vienna: Politics and Culture* (New York,
    1980).

10 Hans Magnus Enzensberger, 'Two Notes on the End of the World', *New
    Left Review*, 110 (July–Aug. 1978), 74; cf. also the further comment:

    > The pictures of the future that humanity draws for itself, both positive and
    > negative utopias, have never been unambiguous. The idea of the millen-
    > nium, the sunshine state, was not the pallid dream of a land of milk and

honey; it always had its elements of fear, panic, terror and destruction. And
the apocalyptic fantasy, conversely, produces more than just pictures of
decadence and despair; it also contains, inescapably bound up with the
terror, the demand for vengeance, for justice, impulses of relief and hope.'
(p. 79)

For the 'dual structure' of the Apocalyptic paradigm, see also Vita
Fortunati, 'The Metamorphosis of the Apocalyptic Myth: From Utopia
to Science Fiction', in K. Kumar and Stephen Bann, eds, *Utopias and the
Millennium* (London, 1993), 81–9.

11   Francis Fukuyama, 'The End of History?', *The National Interest*, Summer
     1989, 18; Fukuyama, *The End of History and the Last Man* (London,
     1992), 334, 338. For the criticism of liberal-market society as amoral see
     also the powerful earlier statement by Fred Hirsch, *Social Limits to Growth*
     (London, 1977).
          Most commentators on Fukuyama appear to know no more than the
     title of his book. For one of the few serious discussions of his argument,
     see Perry Anderson, 'The Ends of History', in *A Zone of Engagement*
     (London/New York, 1992), 279–375. For earlier versions of 'the end of
     history' idea, see Lutz Niethammer, *Post histoire: Has History Come to an
     End?* (London, 1993).

12   See, e.g., Richard Rorty, *Contingency, Irony and Solidarity* (Cambridge,
     UK, 1989).

13   See Jay, 'Apocalypse and the Inability to Mourn', 7–21. The same
     combination of melancholy and mania, 'anxiety and uneasiness' coupled
     with the cult of 'play, impulse, and fun', is noted by Stjepan G.
     Mestrovic, who links it to the *fin-de-siècle* mood of the last century. 'The
     threat of apocalypse is converted into entertainment.' *The Coming Fin de
     Siècle: An Application of Durkheim's Sociology to Modernity and Postmodernism*
     (London and New York, 1992), pp. ix–x, 1–8.

14   H. G. Wells, *Mind at the End of its Tether* (London, 1945), 18.

15   D. H. Lawrence, letter to Lady Cynthia Asquith, November 1915, in
     The Collected Letters of D. H. Lawrence, ed. Harry Moore (London, 1962),
     vol. 1, p. 378.

16   See Malcolm Bradbury and James McFarlane, eds, *Modernism 1890–1930*
     (London, 1976), 19–55; Francis Haskell, 'Art and the Apocalypse', *The
     New York Review of Books*, 15 July 1993, 25–9.

17   Clark Kerr, and others, *Industrialism and Industrial Man* (1960; 2nd edn,
     Harmondsworth, 1976), 265. This was the book that, among others of
     the period, announced 'the end of ideology' in the world: science and
     technology would, irrespective of political ideologies, deliver up indus-
     trial civilization to those willing and able to harness their force to social

purposes.

18 See Albert O. Hirschman, *The Passions and the Interests: Political Arguments for Capitalism Before Its Triumph* (Princeton, 1977).

19 See further on this Krishan Kumar, 'The Limits and Capacities of Industrial Capitalism', in *The Rise of Modern Society* (Oxford, 1988), 100–28.

20 See K. Kumar, *Utopia and Anti-Utopia in Modern Times* (Oxford, 1987), 224–87.

21 Anthony Giddens, *Modernity and Self-Identity* (Cambridge, UK, 1991), 183. On the risks facing the world, see Ulrich Beck, *Risk Society: Towards a New Modernity*, tr. from the German by Martin Ritter (London, 1992). Cf. also Enzensberger: 'The doom we picture for ourselves is insidious and torturingly slow in its approach, the apocalypse in slow motion.' 'Two Notes on the End of the World', 75. Some secular apocalypses, such as Marxism, escape this fate by drawing upon the messianic tradition.

   For the end of the world as seen through twentieth-century literature, see W. Warren Wagar, *Terminal Visions* (Bloomington, Ind., 1982).

22 Frank Kermode, *The Sense of an Ending: Studies in the Theory of Fiction* (London, 1968), 96. See also Hillel Schwartz, *Century's End: A Cultural History of the Fin-de-Siècle from the 990s to the 1990s* (New York, 1990).

23 Nor of course that publicists of all kinds will seize on the occasion to advance their cause irrespective of its relevance to millennial speculation – for example, the BBC TV series, *Millennium*, broadcast on BBC2, Feb.–Mar. 1993, whose subject was 'tribal wisdom and the modern world'.

24 For these traditions, and the differences between them, see Kumar, *Utopia and Anti-Utopia*, 2–19; Kumar, *Utopianism* (Milton Keynes, 1991), 3–19. See also Ernest Lee Tuveson, *Millennium and Utopia: A Study in the Background of the Idea of Progress* (New York, 1964); T. Olson, *Millennialism Utopianism and Progress* (Toronto, 1982).

25 See Ernst Bloch, *The Principle of Hope*, 3 vols (Oxford, 1986); see also Ruth Levitas, *The Concept of Utopia* (London, 1990), 83–105.

   For Bloch the principle of *noch nicht* was part of the utopian impulse; I have interpreted it as part of millennialism since I think Bloch's 'philosophy of hope' is largely inspired by Judaeo-Christian messianism rather than the utopian tradition. See Michael Löwy, *Jewish Libertarian Thought in Central Europe: A Study in Elective Affinity* (London, 1992).

26 Something of this characterization of the millennium as opposed to utopia, can be found in J. C. Davis, 'Formal Utopia/Informal Millennium: The Struggle between Form and Substance as a Context for Seventeenth-century Utopianism', in Kumar and Bann, eds, *Utopias and the Millennium*, 17–32.

27 See Helen Rosenau, *The Ideal City: Its Architectural Evolution in Europe* (London, 1983); Robert Fishman, *Urban Utopias of the Twentieth Century: Ebenezer Howard, Frank Lloyd Wright and Le Corbusier* (New York, 1977).

28 See the discussion of Abensour in E. P. Thompson, *William Morris: Romantic to Revolutionary*, rev. edn (London, 1977), 786–94; see also Kumar, 'News from Nowhere and the Renewal of Utopia', *History of Political Thought*, 14 (Spring, 1993), 133–43.

29 The classic statement of this, still to me persuasive, is Carl Becker, *The Heavenly City of the Eighteenth-Century Philosophers* (New Haven, 1932).

30 Hegel, an acknowledged influence in Fukuyama's case, is the figure that links some of the later and earlier forms of twentieth-century millenarianism (or historicism, as Karl Popper calls it). For the earlier examples, concentrating mainly on Fascism and communism, see Norman Cohn, *The Pursuit of the Millennium* (London, 1962).

31 For a discussion of twentieth-century anti-utopianism West and East, see Kumar, 'The End of Socialism? The End of Utopia? The End of History?', in Kumar and Bann, eds, *Utopias and the Millennium*, 63–80.

32 On utopianism in popular culture see Richard Dyer, 'Entertainment and Utopia', in S. During, ed., *The Cultural Studies Reader* (London, 1993), 271–83; Fred Inglis, *Popular Culture and Political Power* (Hemel Hempstead, 1988), 104–22.

33 For the feminist utopia, see Tom Moylan, *Demand the Impossible: Science Fiction and the Utopian Imagination* (New York and London, 1986); Jan Relf, 'Utopia the Good Breast: Coming Home to Mother', in Kumar and Bann, eds, *Utopias and the Millennium*, 107–28.

34 Currently the best places to look for ecotopia are the pages of the ecological magazines such as *The Ecologist*, *Resurgence* and *The Co-Evolution Quarterly*.

35 See Timothy Garton Ash, 'Does Central Europe Exist?', in *The Uses of Adversity* (Cambridge, UK, 1989), 161–91; Kumar, 'The 1989 Revolutions and the Idea of Europe', *Political Studies*, 40 (1992), 439–61.

36 See, e.g., Alexander Solzhenitsyn, *Rebuilding Russia*, tr. from the Russian by Alexis Klimoff (London, 1991). For some recent ideas and movements, see Anna Moltchanova, 'The Re-evaluation of Western Values in Post-Socialist Russia', M.A. Sociology dissertation, Central European University, Prague, 1993.

37 Czeslaw Milosz, 'The State of Europe: Christmas Eve 1989', *Granta 30: New Europe* (Cambridge, UK, 1990), 164–5.

PART III

10

Versions of Apocalypse: Kant, Derrida, Foucault

Christopher Norris

Apocalyptic pronouncements are common enough in the writing of recent *avant-garde* French intellectuals. They go along with that strain of theoretical anti-humanism which heralds an end to all traditional (anthropocentric) philosophies of language and interpretation. Thus Foucault has a much-quoted passage in *Les Mots et les choses*, describing 'man' – or the imagined autonomous subject of humanist discourse – as a figure drawn in sand at the ocean's edge, soon to be erased by the incoming tide.[1] This is seen as the upshot of a widespread cultural mutation whereby the human sciences have come to recognize that 'man' is nothing more than a figure composed by certain (mainly nineteenth-century) discourses of knowledge. Such illusions are no longer tenable for an age that has witnessed – among other things – the rise of structural anthropology, the 'linguistic turn' across manifold disciplines, and the loss of any comforting faith in *history* as the universal ground and telos of human knowledge. Nietzsche and Saussure are the joint inspiration of this movement 'beyond' the metaphysical certitudes of nineteenth-century thought. Saussure points the way toward an all-embracing theory of language and discursive formations that would leave no room for the individual subject as origin or locus of meaning. Nietzsche sets the terms for a sceptical critique of those philosophies, from Socrates to Hegel, which identify *truth* with the bringing-to-light of a distinctively human self-understanding.

The effect of this upheaval in modern discourse is to bring about a radical 'decentring' of the subject in relation to language and experience. No longer can it appear self-evident that certain human faculties ('reason' or 'intuition') give access to truths whose *a priori* character transcends all mere relativities of time and place. This presumption was defended by philosophers like Kant, who sought a universal grounding for reason and morality in the laws laid down by the autonomous subject for its own 'free' choice of rational ends. Gilles Deleuze has provided perhaps the best account of how the various faculties are organized by Kant into a system of hierarchical relations where ultimate authority is involved in a relay of perpetually delegated functions.[2] Only under the moral law, as established by 'practical reason' in the Kantian sense, can existence take on the intelligible aspect of a freely-willed autonomous choice of principle. It is in the interests of 'speculative reason' that thinking goes beyond the realm of phenomenal cognition and proposes for itself an existence in accord with the maxims of moral law. Kant can thus explain how the sovereign principles of ethical conduct take rise from a condition of 'free causality' wherein the subject both enacts and obeys laws of its own (freely chosen) imposition.

Kant's overriding concern in all this is to establish a public sphere of agreed-upon principles and values, such that the individual subject rejoices to concur in laws laid down for the communal good. By this means he hopes to transcend the kind of drastic Hobbesian antinomy that treats social existence as a mere aggregate of isolated wills pursuing their own self-interest at the others' expense and only held in check by the authority vested in a sovereign power. Kant's response to this depressing picture is to set out the terms of what amounts to a charter for the liberal-humanist consensus view of moral and political good. The individual is a freely choosing rational agent whose liberty consists precisely in acknowledging the limits placed upon naked self-interest by the duty of consulting larger issues of shared moral concern. Hence Kant's insistence that ethical judgement is exercised in the *interest* of a rational being whose choices are dictated by its own 'intelligible' nature, and not by some external (heteronomous) source of compulsion. In Deleuze's words: 'when reason legislates in the practical interest, it legislates over free and rational beings, over their intelligible existence, independent of every sensible condition. It is thus the rational being that gives itself a law by means of its reason.'[3] The converse of this is the Kantian argument that to act *against* the dictates of practical reason is to cut oneself off from the rational community, or ethical 'kingdom of ends', which alone provides ultimate justification for human actions and motives. When we choose against the law,

Deleuze writes, 'we do not cease to have an intelligible existence, we merely lose the condition under which this existence forms part of a nature and composes, with the others, a systematic whole. We cease to be subjects, but primarily because we cease to be legislators.'[4] And this because the individual, in thus choosing, surrenders his or her moral autonomy and consents to take a law from the determining conditions of narrow or material self-interest.

Deleuze is by no means an uncritical exponent of Kant's doctrines. He rehearses them in detail, but mainly with a view to bringing out the various conflicts that develop as Kant tries to adjudicate the rival claims of the various faculties (and delegated functions) that enact this imaginary courtroom scene. There appears to operate a system of rotating chairmanship, established in order to prevent authority from exerting some coercive law-giving power, and hence undermining the sovereign integrity of individual conscience. Deleuze offers a sharply diagnostic reading of the strains and the tactical evasions thus imposed upon Kant's ethical system. But his account remains within the public sphere envisaged by the discourse of Kantian critical reason. That is to say, it mounts an immanent critique of the concepts and categories in question, pursuing their logic to the point of exposing the residual antinomies that Kant is only able to surmount by circuitous detours of argument.

Deleuze published his book on Kant as early as 1963. It thus predates by a good decade those later writings like the *Anti-Oedipus* (co-authored with Félix Guattari) where Deleuze broke altogether with the paradigms of Enlightenment critical reason and took the post-structuralist turn toward a style of apocalyptic discourse.[5] To put it like this is of course to ignore some significant differences of view. Deleuze was no more a typecast 'post-structuralist' than he had been an ortho-dox Kantian in the earlier book. The *Anti-Oedipus* adopts an embattled stance against just about every variety of present-day 'advanced' critical thought, including – most importantly – Lacanian psychoanalysis. It treats them as mere reinforcements of a repressive social order which they tend to perpetuate even when supplying the concepts and theories by which to contest it. Thus psychoanalysis props up the institutions of social and familial power precisely in so far as it accords a privileged explanatory role to notions like that of the Oedipus Complex. Such theories are devoid of radical force because (as Deleuze and Guattari argue) their analyses are fatally complicit with the very forms of societal repression whose workings they claim to expose. It is to forestall such recuperative after-effects that the *Anti-Oedipus* adopts a style of resolutely *post*-theoretical discourse, a rhetoric of schizoid (polymorphous) desire supposedly beyond all reach of explanatory concepts. It thus takes a stand squarely opposed to Lacan's insistence on the socializing agency of language, the induction of the subject into an order of instituted power and authority by way of 'successfully' passing through the Oedipal phase.

All the same it is clear that Deleuze and Guattari represent a dissident fraction *within* the post-structuralist enterprise, rather than occupying ground altogether outside its conceptual reach. Their rhetoric of polymorphous 'schizo-desire' envisages a breakdown in the order of self-possesed 'rational' subjectivity which in turn promises an end to the regime of repressive social law. In his study of Kant, Deleuze could still expound the antinomies of pure and practical reason in a style that sought to make rational sense of them, even while revealing their inbuilt aporias. The concept of the *subject* is the point upon which all these conflicts and antinomies converge. As we have seen, it is required to serve *both* as the source of an autonomous, self-acting moral will *and* as the subject of universal laws whose validity is confirmed precisely by its own (rational and willing) state of subjection. Deleuze spells out this paradoxical condition in a faithfully Kantian gloss. 'This is what "subject" means in the case of practical reason: the same beings are subjects and legislators, so that the legislator is here part of the nature over which he legislates.'[6] At least for the purposes of cogent exposition Deleuze can follow Kant to the point of concluding: 'we belong to a suprasensible nature, but in the capacity of legislative members.' It is the abandonment of this Kantian position – and, along with it, the associated burden of conflicts and antinomies – that most clearly marks the emergence of post-structuralist theory. On the one hand this involves that 'decentring' of the subject in relation to language that follows from a thoroughgoing sceptical critique of humanist values and beliefs. On the other it signals a decisive break with the kinds of problem typically thrown up by the Kantian discourse of enlightened liberal reason. These problems are henceforth regarded, *not* as crucial issues in the working-out of a coherent ethical or political creed, but as symptoms of a merely local and transitory stage of discursive relations. They are taken to belong to that episode of thought which produced 'man' – the universal subject – as a figment of his own discursive imaginary. Thus the Kantian antinomies amount to nothing more than a momentary fold in the fabric of human knowledge, a product of the ruling presuppositions that characterized this episode of thought. That the raising of such problems might once have possessed a genuinely *critical* or emancipatory force is an idea no longer available on the terms laid down by post-structuralist theory.[7]

Hence – as I have suggested – the apocalyptic tone which often goes along with current assertions of an end to humanist ideology. What is envisaged 'beyond' this radical turn is a strictly inconceivable new dispensation where the laws of reason would cease to apply in anything like their presently constituted form. Such is the condition darkly hinted at in the closing sentences of Derrida's essay 'Structure, Sign and Play in the Discourse of the Human Sciences'. It is a passage often cited by those who would willingly identify deconstruction as the present-day descendant of a Nietzschean irrationalism pushed to the giddy extreme. We are faced, Derrida writes, with the 'as yet unnameable' emergence of a new kind of discourse, one whose outlines we can barely glimpse and whose birth can be proclaimed 'only under the species of the nonspecies, in the formless, mute, infant, and terrifying form of monstrosity'.[8] Such rhetoric no doubt signals a desire to shake up the conventions of academic discourse. But it also conveys – as with similar passages from Foucault – the sense of an impending mutation of discourse perceived both as promise and threat, revelation and catastrophe.

And yet, as Derrida has often declared, there is no getting 'beyond' logocentrism or the Western 'metaphysics of presence' unless by abandoning every attempt to think or communicate. Deconstruction works best – indeed, can only work at all – by a patient attention to those symptoms of textual strain and contradiction that mark the limits of traditional discourse. So we need to look elsewhere for some idea of what is at stake in the tonings of apocalypse frequently encountered in Derrida's prose.

II

An answer begins to take shape if we turn to some of his more recent writings, where Derrida shows an increasing concern with the larger (political and institutional) bearings of deconstructive thought. These texts are all concerned with the 'principle of reason', or the history and consequences of a tradition of thought whose present-day manifestations arguably include technology, the arms race, mass communication and the modern (technocratic) university. They are all strongly marked by that apocalyptic tone which Derrida adopts in the full knowledge of its dubious antecedents and its constant liability to be misconstrued as a species of irrationalist doomsday-talk. What Derrida is broaching in these essays is a deconstruction of the principle of reason precisely in so far as it works to *exclude* all forms of apocalyptic thinking from the discourse of philosophy and science at large. But at the same time he is anxious to maintain his distance from the kind of mystified Heideggerian harking-back to origins that rejects modern reason and all its works in the quest for some long-lost authentic realm of primordial Being. If Derrida is alert to the repressive effects of an instrumental reason identified with science and technology, he is equally aware of the dangerous seductions exerted by an ersatz 'jargon of authenticity'. Like Adorno, Derrida has to tread a path between opposed temptations: on the one hand the modern 'dialectic of enlightenment', on the other a strain of illuminist or mystagogic thought whose irrational tendencies he also needs to resist.

These issues are addressed most directly in an essay whose title Derrida adapts from Kant: 'Of an Apocalyptic Tone Recently Adopted in Philosophy'.[9] What Kant set out to do in this polemical address was to heap scorn on those charlatan 'philosophers' who pretended to arrive at ultimate truths by pure, unaided *intuition*, thus avoiding all commerce with the Kantian 'tribunal' of intersubjective rational judgement. These mystagogues and voices of apocalyptic wisdom are denounced by Kant for a whole variety of reasons. One is the old Socratic charge against the poets and rhetoricians: that they use language to immensely persuasive effect without the least evidence that they actually *know* what they are talking about. Then there is the equally disturbing possibility that a 'tone' may be mimicked, feigned or deployed out of context, a trick whereby the 'upstart' or parvenu philosopher can put himself on a level with the true practitioners. But worst of all, from Kant's point of view, is the confusion thus brought about between truths accessible to reasoned enquiry and truths of revealed moral law. The mystagogues offend against reason, morality and religion alike when they collapse the terms of this crucial (Kantian) distinction. As Derrida puts it, summarizing Kant: 'they do not distinguish between pure speculative reason and pure practical reason; they believe they *know* what is solely *thinkable* and reach through feeling alone the universal laws of practical reason' (AT, 12). For Kant, as we have seen, the dictates of morality issue from a source of universal law, but a source whose absolute binding power is established through a rational community of ends and endorsed by the individual conscience. The real complaint is that these false *illuminati* set up as purveyors of a truth vouchsafed to them alone, and denied to the genuine philosophers whose task it is to determine the proper (communal) limits and capacities of human reason.

Thus Kant's mistrust of the 'apocalyptic tone' goes along with his liberal-humanist desire to place philosophy on a democratic footing of open participant debate. It is a project with strong institutional links, as Derrida remarks in connection with another of Kant's 'marginal' productions, his essay 'The Conflict of the Faculties'.[10] This takes the form of a proposal for the setting up of a consultative body to decide the various issues of priority arising between university departments. Philosophy is ranked among the 'lower' faculties, those whose proper function is to arbitrate in matters of a strictly *formal* concern. Other questions – 'the most serious for existence' – are reserved by Kant for those higher faculties whose authority derives from their directly representing the voice of moral or political power. Theology, medicine and law are among the subject-disciplines that Kant assigns to this superior realm. Meanwhile philosophy, as a member of the 'parliament of knowledge', can best exert a regulative influence by not overstepping the limits laid down for critical discourse. Philosophy, in Derrida's words, 'has the right to inspect everything touching on the truth of theoretical (constative) propositions but no power to give any orders' (AT, 11). Hence Kant's attack on those deluded mystagogues who think to pronounce oracular truths without first submitting their claims to the tribunal of theory or enlightened critique. Their fault is in some sense *political*, a matter of 'playing the overlord', arrogating powers that properly belong to the higher (legislative) bodies. In thus 'raising the tone' of philosophic discourse they seek (and again I quote Derrida's commentary) to 'hoist themselves above their colleagues or fellows and wrong them in their right to freedom and equality regarding everything touching on reason alone' (AT, 11).

At one level Derrida's text may be said to identify with the mystagogues and the spokesmen of 'apocalyptic' wisdom, as against the

Kantian tribunal of enlightened critical reason. There is always, he writes, a police-force in waiting, a regime of juridico-discursive power set to restrain the unruly elements that give themselves this 'lordly' tone. And the veto extends to those (like Derrida) who would challenge the rigid demarcation between *philosophy* on the one hand and *rhetoric* on the other. For Kant, 'all philosophy is indeed prosaic', and any suggestion that thinking should revert to its 'poetical' (pre-Socratic) origins is a mere affront to rational dignity and truth. The zealots of unaided intuition reveal their hand most clearly in resorting to metaphor as a substitute for reasoned debate. 'This cryptopolitics is also a cryptopoetics, a poetic perversion of philosophy' (AT, 14). And this because metaphor – or 'poetic' language in general – claims access to a realm of transcendent vision unaccountable to plain prose reason. What Kant so dislikes about the poet-philosophers is their habit of indulging a rhapsodic style which avoids the honest labour of rational thought. 'This leap toward the imminence of a vision without concept, this impatience turned toward the most crypted secret sets free a poetico-metaphorical abundance' (p. 12). And of course the modern parallels are not far to seek when analytical philosophers (for instance, John Searle) accuse Derrida of working his sophistical arts to pervert and obscure the content of what he reads.[11]

So there is clearly a sense in which Derrida sides with those thinkers who refuse the restricted economy of language and thought handed down by Kantian tradition. This sympathy is further evidenced by the 'apocalyptic' strain in Derrida's text, the rhetoric of which – especially in its closing pages – evokes all manner of prophetic and chiliastic overtones, from Christian and Jewish sources alike. More specifically, it involves rhetorical figures (like prosopopeia) which insist that they belong to an order of discourse beyond all reduction to 'constative' – theoretical – language. Thus Derrida singles out the injunction 'Come!' (the climactic moment of many apocalyptic texts) as an instance of the *tonal* modulation that cannot be captured by any analysis on standard rhetorical or logico-grammatical lines. Such discourse, he writes, 'tolerates no metalinguistic citation' and eludes the subtlest efforts of a classifying system based on the idea of language as a straightforward communicative medium. At this point Derrida takes up a number of connected themes from his earlier text *La Carte postale*.[12] These centre on the metaphor of the postal system as a regulative framework controlling the flow of information and ensuring that messages promptly arrive at their proper destination. This system is complicit with the classical economy of discourse, that which determines the limits of communicable sense within the shared rationality of knowledge. It operates to marginalize or exclude any message that threatens to disrupt the system by ignoring its rules of address.

Such are the effects of apocalyptic language as Derrida here describes them. In transgressing the limits of straightforward communicative utterance they likewise transgress those laws laid down for the conduct of rational debate. Once again it is the Kantian 'parliament' of faculties – the discourse of free and equal voices under the law of reason – which shows itself quick to register this threat.

> By its very tone, the mixing of voices, genres and codes, apocalyptic discourse can also, in dislocating destinations, dismantle the dominant contract or concordat. It is a challenge to the established receivability of messages and to the policing of destinations, in short to the postal police or monopoly of posts. (AT, 11)

Its effect, in short, is to open up that series of detours, relays and extravagant swerves from destination whose impact on the regulative system of exchange Derrida sets out to explore in *La Carte postale*. The postcard is an emblem of everything haphazard or marginal to the process of 'proper', controlled communication. It is a message casually inscribed on the reverse of some more or less significant image or scene whose import may complicate the message beyond all hope of assured understanding. The particular postcard that so caught Derrida's fancy was one that he discovered in the Bodleian Library. It was taken from the frontispiece of a fifteenth-century fortune-telling book and depicted a scene with Plato (apparently) standing to dictate his thoughts to a seated Socrates who obediently writes them down. Thus the postcard encapsulates the deconstructive strategy of reversing that age-old logocentric prejudice that equates Socratic wisdom with the authority of voice and origins, and writing with all that threatens or subverts that authority. To imagine a Socrates who *writes* is to think a way beyond the logocentric order to a different epoch – that of postcards, grammatology, telecommunication – where writing would at last come into its own.

So there is, one could say, an elective affinity between the project of deconstruction and the 'apocalyptic tone' whose effect is likewise to suspend or problematize everything pertaining to the ground-rules of

communicative reason. But simply to equate them – or to read
Derrida's text as itself a species of apocalyptic utterance – is to ignore
the many signs of a complicating logic at work. It involves, for one
thing, a drastic misconstrual of the role played by metaphors of
voice, presence and origins in Derrida's writing. The apocalyptic tone
can scarcely be described without resorting to such metaphors. It
operates – according to the Kantian charge-sheet – by 'perverting the
voice of reason, by mixing the two voices of the other in us, the voice
of reason and the voice of the oracle' (AT, 11). The mystagogues
disdain the whole business of rational debate, believing that it suffices
to 'lend an ear to the oracle within oneself'. Now it will hardly be
supposed – by anyone familiar with Derrida's writings – that such
claims are to be taken at anything like face value. What his texts most
consistently seek to demonstrate is the way that such appeals to the
self-present (logocentric) 'voice' of inward truth run into all manner of
unlooked-for complications as soon as one examines their textual
strategies of argument. In his essays on Rousseau, Husserl and Saussure
(among others) Derrida sets out to establish (1) that philosophy has
very often been wedded to this deep-laid 'metaphysics of presence'; (2)
that the result has been a systematic bias in favour of *speech* above
writing; and (3) that to deconstruct the texts of this tradition is to bring
out their radical incapacity to hold that opposition in place.[13] An entire
metaphorics of truth and authority rests on precisely this delusive
indentification between voice, self-presence and authentic knowledge.
Deconstruction seeks to unsettle that identity, to reveal the workings
of a discrepant ('supplementary') logic which cannot be thus called to
order.

It would therefore be a naïve reading that interpreted Derrida's
'apocalyptic tone' as a harking-back to some mystique of primordial
Being and truth untouched by the latter-day discourse of philosophic
reason. He may provisionally side with those intuitive adepts who at
least have the virtue of creating problems for that juridico-discursive
'police-force' devoted to maintaining the enlightenment status quo.
But deconstruction itself involves a labour of thought – an effort of
rigorous demystification – which in many ways aligns it more closely
with the Kantians than with their high-toned opponents. There is,
Derrida writes, no escaping the 'law and destiny' of present-day enlightened thought. This law takes the form of a 'desire for vigilance, for
the lucid vigil, for elucidation, for critique and truth' (AT, 22). To this

extent it may be hard to distinguish the Kantian imperatives of rational critique from the deconstructive drive to dismantle or subvert the 'logocentric' ruses of language. These projects converge at numerous points since they both take aim at a certain kind of mystical-intuitive 'truth' devoid of critical warrant. Thus when Derrida summarizes Kant's main grounds for mistrusting the apocalyptic tone, it is by no means simply in order to expose the Kantian insecurity or lack of resource in face of these 'lordly' mystagogues. The purveyors of apocalypse 'scoff at work, the concept, schooling . . . to what is given they believe they have access effortlessly, gracefully, intuitively or through genius, outside of school' (AT, 7). If such pretensions are anathema to the partisans of enlightenment, they are equally subject to the sceptical rigours of a deconstructionist reading.

This text therefore helps us to define more precisely what is entailed by Derrida's ambivalent espousal of the so-called 'apocalyptic tone'. It is *not* (as his commentators often mistakenly imply) just one more instance of that fashionable rhetoric of crisis adopted by thinkers who imagine that they have come out on the far side of humanist or anthropocentric tradition. That all such pronouncements are inherently premature and self-deceiving is the burden of Derrida's essay 'The Ends of Man'. Here he makes the point – with particular regard to Heidegger, Sartre and Foucault – that philosophies attempting to situate themselves 'beyond' the so-called humanist epoch always fall prey to unexamined motifs or logics which subvert or compromise that claim. This applies not only to Heidegger and Sartre but also to those later movements of thought that strove to purge themselves of all such 'anthropocentric' residues. Despite the 'alleged neutralization of metaphysical principles', it remains the case – so Derrida argues – that 'the unity of man is never examined in and of itself'.[14] A certain anthropologism continues to haunt the discourses of structuralist and post-structuralist theory, no matter how stridently they assert the claims of a rigorous theoretical anti-humanism. 'The thinking of the end of man . . . is always already prescribed in metaphysics, in the thinking of the truth of man.'[15] Deconstruction is itself caught up in this predicament, since it can no more break altogether with humanist assumptions than escape once and for all the 'metaphysics of presence' vested in natural language. What it *can* do most effectively is alert us to the hidden teleologies and motives which continue to organize these various, more or less 'apocalyptic' gospels of the end of man. From which it must appear – as Derrida argues – that 'the critique of empirical anthropologism is only the affirmation of a transcendental humanism'.[16]

Equally premature are claims to transcend that other component of enlightened modernity, the Leibnizian principle of reason. The crucial text here is Derrida's 'Cogito and the History of Madness', a detailed critique of Foucault's *Madness and Civilization*.[17] What chiefly engages his attention is Foucault's claim to have written, not a 'history of psychiatry' (that is, an account from *within* the regime of 'rational' psychiatric discourse), but 'a history of madness itself, in its most vibrant state, before being captured by knowledge'.[18] Derrida's response is to show (via a reading of Foucault on Descartes) that thought is self-deluding if it claims to have achieved a standpoint 'outside' or 'beyond' the very discourse of philosophic reason. Foucault's aim is to think back to that inaugural moment when Descartes deployed his 'hyperbolical doubt' to demarcate the henceforth separate realms of reason and madness. The correlative in socio-practical terms is that progressive isolation (or internment) of unreason whose history Foucault reads in the various institutions set up to contain and to study its effects. Madness is defined precisely on the terms laid down by an increasingly self-confident reason. It is the dark side of a thoroughly 'enlightened' tradition that none the less needs to confirm its own normality by constantly rehearsing such rituals of exclusion. Thus Descartes figures as the intellectual founder of a discourse that issues in the modern regime of institutionalized psychiatric practice.

Derrida's reading takes issue with Foucault on three main counts. Firstly, there is no such clear demarcation in Descartes' text between the discourse of reason and the hyperbolic doubt that threatens (*genuinely* threatens) the philosopher's enterprise. The 'mad audacity' by which Descartes conjures up his malign demon is perhaps not perceived because we are nowadays 'too well assured of ourselves and too well accustomed to the framework of the Cogito, rather than to the critical experience of it'.[19] This experience goes well beyond the limits assigned to it by Foucault's (distinctively modern) reading. Hence Derrida's second objection: that Foucault is reading the Cartesian text in terms of a modern (post-Kantian) economy of discourse whose grounding assumptions are placed more directly at risk by Descartes' strategies of hyberbolic doubt. This risk is played down – its threat effectively contained – by Foucault's desire to *make sense* of the

Cartesian episode by presenting it as part of an intelligible narrative sequence. But this is to tranquillize the force of unreason by precisely that kind of recuperative gesture that Foucault attributes to Descartes. A curious compulsion seems to operate here, whereby reason is obliged repeatedly to confront the possibility of madness, only to confirm its own rational status by the *distance* taken up in narrating that experience. Thus the third objection to Foucault's account is that it fails to recognize the oscillating rhythm, the perpetual 'dialogue' (as Derrida describes it) between 'hyperbole and the finite structure, between that which exceeds the totality and the closed totality'.[20] An adequate account of Descartes' text would register the hyperbolic doubt as that which *suspends* the determined opposition of reason and unreason, rather than producing a structured economy which henceforth lends itself to narrative treatment. Thus Foucault's claim to speak on behalf of madness is fatally compromised by his need to make sense of the episode in received (philosophical) terms. 'To all appearances, it is reason that he interns, but, like Descartes, he chooses the reason of yesterday as his target and not the possibility of meaning in general.'[21] It is not so much that Foucault 'misinterprets' Descartes as that he fails to perceive how his own critical strategy repeats the same pattern of predestined blindness and insight.

These two texts of Derrida – 'The Ends of Man' and 'Cogito and the History of Madness' – help toward a better understanding of his recent (so-called) apocalyptic tone. They show that what is in question is *not* some ultimate, decisive leap beyond humanism, 'Western metaphysics' or the principle of reason. In fact they insist that no such leap is possible, that even the most seemingly radical statements of intent – like Foucault's desire to speak the very language of madness – must always at some point rejoin the tradition whose embrace they so fiercely reject. In the same way, it is impossible for thought to give itself over entirely to the kind of 'post-enlightenment' rhetoric of crisis conveyed by the apocalyptic tone. We cannot, Derrida writes, forego the *Aufklärung* – the heritage of critical demystification – to join with those self-appointed *lumières* whose stock-in-trade is the language of premature apocalypse. What is needed, rather, is to see how these age-old antagonists – philosophy and poetry, reason and unreason, enlightenment and vision – exist in a strange solidarity which unites even their most extreme partisans on one or the other side. Hence – as Derrida construes it – the twofold error in Foucault's approach to the

history of madness and civilization. Foucault both *underrates* the genuine threat to reason contained in Descartes' hyperbolical doubt, and
overrates the capacity of his own discourse to break altogether with
normative assumptions and constraints. He thus fails to see how closely
intertwined are the two chief motives of philosophic thinking: the
search for some bedrock rational assurance in the face of a threatening
madness, and the drive to undermine such comforting knowledge by
exposing it to all manner of hyperbolic challenge. What Foucault's
strategy amounts to is 'a Cartesian gesture for the twentieth century',
with the difference that Foucault – unlike Descartes – inherits a
language extensively worked over by the discourse of Cartesian
rationalism. On a deconstructive reading his text offers up a very
different and (for Derrida) more liberating message. 'Crisis of reason,
finally, access to reason and attack of reason. For what Michel Foucault
teaches us to think is that there are crises of reason in strange complicity with what the world calls crises of madness.'[22]

III

It is in relation to these themes in his earlier writing that we can best
understand the position taken up in Derrida's essay 'Of an Apocalyptic
Tone'. What this text strives to articulate is a language 'beyond' the
analytic grasp of traditional philosophy, yet one that would (in some
sense) keep faith with the need to resist all forms of obscurantist or
irrationalist thinking. Such a language might allow us, in Derrida's
words, to 'distinguish a deconstruction from a simple progressive demystification in the style of the enlightenment' (AT, 30). It is precisely
in the space opened up by this distinction that Derrida locates
the radical effects of a deconstructive reading. That is to say,
deconstruction may yet take hold where other forms of critical reason
– belonging to the mainstream 'enlightened' tradition – are compromised by virtue of their long association with instituted structures of
authority. Like the Frankfurt theorists, Derrida perceives a close relation between the rise of 'progressive' (technocratic) reason and the
exercise of power in society at large. The sources of this dialectic of
enlightenment he pinpoints (as we have seen) in the Kantian attempt
to constitute philosophy as a 'parliament of reason' subject only to the
self-imposed laws of rational debate. Any voice that threatens to disrupt

these proceedings – as by taking on the lordly 'apocalyptic tone' – is at once declared irrational, a law unto itself, and hence unfitted to participate. By adopting the accents of that banished tone – in however provisional or guarded a fashion – Derrida is effectively broaching a critique of the parliament, its rules and juridical status.

In his latest writings Derrida has insisted that the strategies of 'textual' deconstruction are of little use unless they can be shown to have a bearing on wider (institutional) structures of authority and power. In particular he has pointed to the close liaison that exists between the new sciences of information technology, the military–industrial complex, and the modern *university* as lineal descendant of Kant's enlightened tribunal.[23] These themes are brought together most strikingly in the text of a paper delivered at a conference on 'nuclear criticism', and rejoicing in the title 'No Apocalypse, Not Now (full speed ahead, seven missiles, seven missives)'.[24] It is the kind of piece that must surely tax patience to the limit for anyone convinced to begin with that deconstruction is just a species of 'textualist' mystification, unconcerned with social or material realities. Such a reader will predictably accuse Derrida of playing games with this most urgent of contemporary issues. He or she will likewise note the very marked 'apocalyptic tone' which might seem to align Derrida's pronouncements with the worst, most dangerous (because potentially self-confirming) kinds of doomsday rhetoric. And indeed, the essay is not without its share of those arch rhetorical locutions that Derrida adopts most often when writing for an American readership, and which might well seem – in such a context – lamentably out of place. But there is more to this rhetoric than mere opportunist play with apocalyptic themes. In fact one could argue – and Derrida claims as much – that the characteristic strategies and aims of deconstruction are closely bound up with this curious hybrid discourse of self-styled 'nuclear criticism'.

One way to make sense of this claim is to start from Derrida's remark that 'a nuclear war has not taken place: one can only talk and write about it'. This makes it preeminently a topic of discourse and, beyond that, 'a utopia, a rhetorical figure, a fantasy . . . even a fabulous specularisation' (p. 23). And to speak in these terms is not, so Derrida would argue, a species of 'irresponsible' word-spinning in the face of terminal catastrophe. Rather it is a plain recognition that nuclear 'reality' is entirely made up of those speech-acts, inventions and projected scenarios which constitute our present knowledge of the future (unthinkable) event. Derrida makes this point effectively enough by examining a handful of 'expert' pronouncements by military strategists and defence correspondents. What emerges from a properly *rhetorical* reading of these texts is the fact that they entail a whole range of imaginary tactics, threats and other such gambits whose complexity far outruns the grasp of any 'rational' decision-making process. Thus there opens up a singular and terrifying gap between the ultra-sophisticated modern technologies of war and the tangle of confused motives and reasons that constitute so-called 'strategic thinking'. So it may be that the 'experts' (scientists and strategists) have no special competence to pronounce on these matters, or at least no authority specifically denied to those who are 'expert' mainly in the reading of texts. 'We can therefore consider ourselves competent,' Derrida writes, 'because the sophistication of the nuclear strategy can never do without a sophistry of belief and the rhetorical simulation of a text' (p. 24).

Opponents will already have seized upon that move by which deconstruction suspends all reference to 'the real' and substitutes a play of seemingly unanchored textual representations. Certainly Derrida invites such a reading when he writes of nuclear war as a 'fabulously textual' non-event, or when he cites Freud as denying that the unconscious makes any distinction between 'reality' and 'a fiction loaded with affect' (p. 23). But it is wrong to suggest – as those opponents often do – that this move amounts to nothing more than a 'textualist' variant of idealist metaphysics or a kind of transcendental solipsism. Derrida is not asking us to doubt for a moment that these technologies are real and their potential effects no less 'material' for existing – as yet – in the realm of pure speculation. What he wants us to consider is the massive shift of balance between matters of *theory* (where technical know-how commands the field) and matters of conjecture, fantasy or *bluff* where strategy becomes a species of extravagant fiction. It is on the basis of this situation, Derrida writes, 'that we have to re-think the relations between knowing and acting, between constative speech acts and performative speech acts' (p. 23). This latter distinction – here at the point of collapse – may remind us of the terms in which Derrida describes the self-imposed limits and powers of Kantian rational critique. It is language in its 'constative' (theoretical) role that properly extends over the full domain of legitimate human knowledge. This principle is materialized by modern technology in the form of a dominant means–end rationality. But the advent of the 'nuclear age' is sufficient to unbalance the whole system of discursive priorities that set reason up in pride of place above mere rhetoric or the arts of persuasion. The line between 'constative' and 'performative' speech-acts is impossible to draw once the arms-race and all its attendant technology hinges on the choice of some novel (and more or less fantastic) projected scenario.

What is more, such shifts of 'policy' may not be a matter of deliberate choice, but may often come about through confused attempts to interpret how 'the enemy' perceives one's intentions, and subsequent (equally confused) adjustments on the basis of that. Thus there develops a series of rhetorical gambits which soon pass beyond the stage of a mere double-bluff to the point where no calculation of interests or motives can possibly dominate the field. One example that Derrida cites is the idea of 'prevailing' in nuclear war, let drop (unsuspectingly, it seems) in a US policy document and thereafter the topic of much debate. The effect of such rhetorical innovations is to strengthen the American sense of 'resolve', but also – as its critics soon pointed out – to undermine any residual belief in the doctrine of deterrence. The issue here had less to do with the *technical* feasibility of 'winning' a nuclear war than with the battle to win over public opinion to *believe* that such a thing might be possible. Thus the single word 'prevail' brings along with it a whole new range of conflicting rhetorical ploys whose ultimate effect – on 'public opinion' as well as on the 'balance of power' – is beyond all rational calculation. Such changes in the currency of nuclear debate possess, according to Derrida, 'at least as much importance as a given set of technological mutations that would, on both sides, be of such a nature to displace the strategic bases of an eventual armed confrontation' (p. 25). And this because the competence of reason itself – both the weapons technology and the thinking which (supposedly) governs its 'strategic' deployment – is rendered obsolete by every shift in the rhetoric of nuclear deterrence.

Derrida glances in passing at the famous dictum of Clausewitz, that diplomacy is only the continuation of war by other means. And 'diplomacy' itself has undergone a shift of meaning as the emphasis passes from the reckoning of calculable interests and motives to a state of play where those ground-rules no longer apply. 'There is only text in the diplomatic moment, that is, sophistico-rhetoric of diplomacy' (p. 26). It is in this sense that deconstruction lends itself to the purposes of 'nuclear criticism': *not* by laying claim to some specialized area of competence, but precisely by acknowledging that no such areas exist any longer. Even those in power – the handful of politicians and military men – assume this role without the least hope of really grasping the strategic situation. There exists, in other words, 'a multiplicity of dissociated, heterogeneous competencies . . . such knowledge is neither coherent nor totalizable' (p. 22). Hence the particular *pertinence* of deconstruction, with its vigilant mistrust of 'totalizing' theories, its alertness to the signs of textual disruption, and its willingness to contemplate an order of discourse without final guarantees of meaning, coherence or truth. It is thus placed *knowingly* in much the same position as those nuclear strategists and decision-makers who have not (presumably) yet caught up with their own incapacity to grasp the situation. All of them, Derrida writes,

> are in the position of inventing, inaugurating, improvising procedures and giving orders where no model . . . can help them at all. Among the acts of observing, revealing, knowing, promising, acting, simulating, giving orders, and so on, the limits have never been so precarious, so undecidable. (p. 22)

It is in this present situation of a radical instability affecting all the discourses of knowledge and power that deconstruction finds itself tactically aligned with the purposes of 'nuclear criticism'.

But to make these points, however forcefully, is not to state anything much beyond the obvious *facts* of this unnerving predicament. Derrida is clearly implying something more when he writes that deconstruction 'belongs to the nuclear age', or that the prospect of terminal warfare 'watches over' deconstruction to the point of pre-empting its every move. Once again, these claims need interpreting carefully in the context of that 'apocalyptic' discourse which Derrida adopts only at risk of being widely and damagingly misunderstood. At one level the text picks up a number of themes familiar from our reading of his essays on Descartes and Kant. The 'unthinkable' event of nuclear war is envisaged as a limit-point of classical reason in much the same way that Cartesian discourse must constantly fend off the demon of madness (or 'hyperbolic' doubt). What we are witnessing now is the generalized spread of a condition that always haunted the parliament of reason, but which currently defeats all strategies of rational containment. ' "Nuclear criticism", like Kantian criticism, is thought about the limits of experience as a thought of finitude' (p. 30). That is to say, it is constrained – like all forms of critique – to keep up the appearances of rational debate, and not to be seduced by that 'apocalyptic tone' that beckons from the far side of progress and enlightenment. But if Kant (like Descartes) could do no more than silence such voices by an act of juridical exclusion, still less can a so-called 'nuclear criticism' hope to keep them at bay. The Kantian ideal – as outlined in *The Conflict of the Faculties* – arose from a faith in the rational community of ends wherein all antinomies could finally in principle be reconciled. Thus the 'faculties' achieve their harmonious coexistence by the same enlightened path that Kant lays down for the future of the European nations. 'As for the history of humanity, that example of finite rationality, it presupposes the possibility of an infinite progress governed according to an Idea of Reason, in Kant's sense, and through a treatise on Perpetual Peace' (p. 30). That this enlightened utopia has receded almost beyond recall is the burden of Derrida's ironic commentary here.

But the question remains: what could come of this attempt to 'think the very limit of criticism'? Especially when, as Derrida writes, this limit can only be glimpsed at the point of a 'remainderless' catastrophe of reason, a moment in which 'the kernel, the nucleus of criticism, itself bursts apart' (p. 30). It might well be argued that such rhetoric is in league with the forces of destruction, that it yields up the last small remnant of hope contained in that Kantian dream of an enlightened *sensus communis*. Derrida's response is to insist once again that we have no choice in this matter. To think the possibility of nuclear war – a very real and present possibility – is to think beyond the limits of reason itself. Lacking all determinate *knowledge* of the subject, and able to project it only as a species of hyperbolic fiction, such thinking necessarily assumes an apocalyptic tone. Hence the most arresting of Derrida's hyperboles: his statement that literature itself belongs to 'the nuclear epoch', in so far as it 'produces its referent as a fictive or fabulous referent', inseparably tied to the 'project of stockpiling, of building a textual archive over and above any traditional oral base' (p. 26). The prospect of this archive's being totally destroyed, beyond hope of memorial reconstruction, is for Derrida the mark of an awareness that imprints itself indelibly on the texts of literary modernism.

This is not to say that all 'serious' literature must nowadays *refer* to the nuclear threat or take it as an explicit theme. Rather it is the case, Derrida writes, that 'the nuclear epoch is dealt with more "seriously" in texts by Mallarmé, of Kafka, or Joyce [and he might have added

Beckett] . . . than in present-day novels that would offer direct and realistic descriptions of a "real" nuclear catastrophe' (pp. 27–8). And this for the reason that a certain *suspension* of 'the referent' is precisely what links the discourse of nuclear criticism to those modalities of language that deconstruction finds insistently at work in 'literary' texts. It is not a question of *abolishing* the referent, as suggested by those who attack deconstruction on grounds of its supposedly idealist character. Derrida has rebutted this charge on numerous occasions, pointing out that there are problems in the notion of 'reference' espoused by its dogmatic or naïve proponents, and that deconstruction attempts to think these problems through in a rigorous and consequent way. It is the process of thus recasting the relation between text, referent and a fictive pseudo-'reality' that Derrida sees as the prime concern of current 'nuclear criticism'.

So the apocalyptic tonings of Derrida's text are best understood as a preemptive move to enlist the full resources of deconstruction for this presently most urgent of tasks: A beginning might be made in terms of the 'constative'/'performative' distinction that Derrida takes over from speech-act philosophy. As we have seen, he extends the scope of that distinction to convey something of the alternating rhythm set up between reason and its strictly 'unthinkable' other, the realm of hyperbole and apocalyptic thinking. And it is this that enables Derrida to write of an opening beyond the logistics of technocratic reason, the 'constative' domain where decisions are taken on the basis of a (henceforth 'incompetent') rational expertise. Thus 'literature belongs to the nuclear age by virtue of the performative character of its relation to the referent, and the structure of its written archive' (p. 28). To rethink the language of nuclear strategy in terms of this performative dimension is to see how delusory is any reliance on a hard-headed 'realist' assessment of the game. Quite simply, the semblances of rational thought have now given way to a fabulous or fictive state of belief where rhetoric creates its own reality-effects. And this applies especially to those key terms in the currency of nuclear debate whose performative force can no longer be reckoned by any straightforward appeal to constative criteria of logic, sense and reference. 'Deterrence' is one such word, a pseudo-concept quite beyond reach of rational accountability.

If there are wars and a nuclear threat, it is because 'deterrence' has neither 'original meaning' nor measure. Its 'logic' is the logic of deviation and transgression, it is rhetorical-strategic escalation or it is nothing at all. It gives itself over, by calculation, to the incalculable, to chance and luck. (p. 29)

Deconstruction can begin this work of undoing the fables, the sophistries and fabulous inventions of current strategic doublethink. And it can best serve this purpose by maintaining an attitude of vigilant scepticism *vis-à-vis* the claims of a 'rational' or 'realistic' wisdom that in fact falls in with the wildest extremes of nuclear-strategic doublethink.

Derrida seeks to persuade us (since *persuasion* must here be the operative mode) that it is possible to raise such questions with regard to the discourse of enlightened reason without thereby lapsing into mere irrationalism. Opponents of deconstruction have assumed too readily that the issue comes down to a straightforward choice between responsible discussion on the one hand and sophisticated 'textual' games on the other. They have misread Derrida's deconstructive strategies as a last-ditch assault on reason itself, and his 'apocalyptic' tone as the symptom of an all-too-Nietzschean contempt for commonplace ethical imperatives. Such a reading might think to find warrant in the opening sentence of 'No Apocalypse, Not Now', where Derrida writes: 'We are speaking of stakes that are apparently limitless for what is still now and then called humanity' (p. 20). But his point in thus raising the apocalyptic stakes is not to endorse a rhetoric of crisis whose effect would be at best to preserve the reign of terror, and at worst to trigger the unthinkable event. On the contrary: what Derrida seeks is a means to *comprehend* that rhetoric, to take full account of its 'performative' aspect, before it achieves the referential status of a discourse whose final guarantee would be catastrophe itself. 'That is why deconstruction, at least what is being advanced in its name today, belongs to the nuclear age' (p. 27). And it is also one reason for not dismissing such claims as just another species of modish rhetorical abandon.

NOTES

Christopher Norris's lecture in the Wolfson series was extemporized on the basis of a typescript essay which proved too long (and too detailed in certain aspects of its argument) for inclusion in this volume. He therefore decided to substitute the present article which treats many of the same themes, but which focuses more broadly on developments in recent postmodernist and post-structuralist thought. Some parts of this chapter draw upon passages in his book *Jacques Derrida* (Fontana 'Modern Masters' series, London, 1987).

1   Michel Foucault, *The Order of Things*, tr. Alan Sheridan (New York, 1970), 387.
2   Gilles Deleuze, *Kant's Critical Philosophy: The Doctrine of the Faculties*, tr. Hugh Tomlinson and Barbara Habberjam (London, 1984).
3   Ibid., 32.
4   Ibid., 32.
5   Gilles Deleuze and Félix Guattari, *Anti-Oedipus: Capitalism and Schizo-phrenia* (New York, 1977).
6   Deleuze, *Kant's Critical Philosophy*, 36.
7   For a powerful argument to this effect see Gillian Rose, *Dialectic of Nihilism: Post-Structuralism and Law* (Oxford, 1984).
8   Jacques Derrida, 'Structure, Sign and Play in the Discourse of the Human Sciences', in *Writing and Difference*, tr. Alan Bass (London, 1978), 278–93; 293.
9   Jacques Derrida, 'Of an Apocalyptic Tone Recently Adopted in Philos-ophy', tr. John P. Leavey, jun., *Oxford Literary Review*, VI, no. 2 (1984), 3–37. All further page-references signalled in the text by 'AT'. For the original work of this title, see Kant, 'Von einem neuerdings erhobenen vornehmen Ton in der Philosophie', in *Immanuel Kants Werke*, ed. Ernst Cassirer (Berlin, 1923), vol. VI.
10 Kant, 'Der Streit der Facultäten', in *Immanuel Kants Werke*, vol. VII.
11 See John R. Searle, 'Reiterating the Differences', *Glyph*, I (1977), 198–208.
12 Jacques Derrida, *La Carte postale de Socrate à Freud et au-delà* (Paris, 1980).
13 See especially Derrida, *Of Grammatology*, tr. Gayatri Chakravorty Spivak (Baltimore, 1976); also *'Speech and Phenomena' and Other Essays on Husserl's Theory of Signs*, tr. D. B. Allison (Evanston, Ill., 1973).
14 Derrida, 'The Ends of Man', in *Margins of Philosophy*, tr. Alan Bass (Chicago, 1982), 109–36; 115.
15 Ibid., 121.
16 Ibid., 123.
17 Michel Foucault, *Madness and Civilization*, tr. Richard Howard (New York, 1965).
18 Derrida, 'Cogito and the History of Madness', in *Writing and Difference*, 31–63; 34.
19 Ibid., 56.
20 Ibid., 60.
21 Ibid., 55.

22 Ibid., 63.

23 See for instance Derrida, 'Où commence et comment finit un corps enseignant', in *Politique de la philosophie*, ed. Dominique Grisoni (Paris, 1976), 55–97.

24 Derrida, 'No Apocalypse, Not Now (full speed ahead, seven missiles, seven missives), *Diacritics*, XIV (Summer, 1984), 20–31. All further references given by page number in the text.

11

Waiting for the End

Frank Kermode

It has all been filed, boys, history has a trend,
Each of us enisled, boys, waiting for the end.
William Empson

A great while ago I wrote a book called *The Sense of an Ending*, in which I suggested that our interest in endings – endings of fictional plots, of epochs – may derive from a common desire to defeat chronicity, the intolerable idea that we live within an order of events between which there is no relation, pattern, mutuality, or intelligible progression. It had struck me that the historiographical patterns proposed by apocalyptic texts, like Daniel and Revelation, were impressive instances of this defence in religious thought, but that it can be discerned in many other situations, certainly in fictional plots, and also in our retrospective and prospective musings on human lives, including our own; and that it might even be present in the way we hear a clock saying tick-tock, tick being a beginning and tock an ending, so constituting a tiny genesis and a tiny apocalypse. The interval between the two seems to be structured and not, as tick-tick would be, merely successive. But I knew that there can be serious doubts about the validity of all such fictions, and conjectured that there exists what I called a 'clerical scepticism', a mental habit developed among people trained to question the *bona fides* of such intellectual devices as I have tried to describe – to distinguish in their own way and according to their own lights, between what they regarded as fact and what they regarded as fiction.

In the interim I have sometimes thought again about these propositions, without noticeably improving or deepening them. However,

I did come upon Viktor Shklovsky's idea of the 'illusory ending', which is brought on by a trick – the reader provides the sense of ending when signalled to do so, perhaps by some terminal remark about the weather or the interminable steppe.[1] That a writer can count on this measure of collusive response shows that he and the reader are ready for what seems the end of a particular small epoch, namely the novel or story or poem. In the same way structural hints are developed by readers who want synchronicity rather than mere chronicity. Perhaps our sense of structure (which requires endings) derives from our notion of well-formedness in sentences; we are predisposed to expect syntax from extended bits of language and could not make sense of them without that structural support. In short, we are programmed to seek not mere sequence but something I like to think of as *pleroma*, fullness, the fullness that results from completion, as when the New Testament incorporates the Old as a set of types it fulfils, and so makes sense of the whole of the book and the whole of history. The effort of the reader may be more or less intensive, and some endings and structures call for what Henry James had in mind when he spoke of interpretations that go beyond 'the simpler forms of attention'.[2] The same powers, it seems, are used in the interpretations of sentences, plots, and lives. We like things to make sense. And although the agreements of teller and auditor may vary in character from one culture to another, it does seem that the desire for consonance and sense is species-specific, not culture-specific. Of course it may be specific to our culture that many will question the interpretations by which sense is made. There are simpler, as well as more exquisite, forms of attention, simpler as well as more complex ends. If there were not, we should hardly find such masses of people living in expectation of them.

The ends of centuries and *a fortiori* of millennia are very convenient *termini*, either of the world or of epochs. Their attraction lies partly in their cyclical character – as we celebrate birthdays and other anniversaries – and partly in the fact that they mark or threaten a linear ending. Yet to attach grave importance to centuries and millennia you have to belong to a culture that accepts the Christian calendar as definitive, despite its incompatibility with other perfectly serviceable calendars. Only if you do so belong need you trouble about the onset of the millennium as an obvious end to something – to an age, or to time. Christianity provided a dating system and also the promise of a spectacular end to time. Its texts also offered the possibility of relatively easy arithmetical predictions as to the possible dates of the end. And interpreters who accept these data can always come up with suitable answers; whenever they happen to live the great moment will come soon enough for them to observe and, if possible, survive it.

Eschatological tension occurs in other traditions, though on different predictive assumptions. The point of the end, or of some vast alteration in history, is preceded by a decadence, and followed, in this world or elsewhere, by a renovation. It is not surprising that even the more sceptical among us associate the nineties of the last century, and probably of this one, with decadence, and decadence is rarely found in isolation from hopes of renovation. In his book *L'An Mil* (1952) Henri Focillon identified the phenomenon he called 'centurial mysticism', a characteristic of which is that people (in our calendar tradition) project their fears and apprehensions on to centurial or millennial dates, thus making of these dates 'a perpetual calendar of human anxiety'. They may also be a perpetual calendar of human hopes.

The early Christians were not alone in looking forward to the end, nor in thinking it imminent. Outside the central Christian tradition there are, for example, those Melanesian cargo cults – the cultists are ever poorer, but will be rich when the cargo arrives, by boat or jumbo jet. A new age will begin. The cargo never does arrive, but it seems to be a general characteristic of apocalyptic or chiliastic thinking that the disappointment of a prophecy does not necessarily dishearten the faithful; there ensues the process called by Leo Festinger in his book *When Prophecy Fails* (1964) 'group reinforcement'. When the prediction turns out to be false, a few more sceptical souls will abandon the group, but most of them stay on and rework the figures. Recently there was news of a Korean sect which expected the end, and their escape from its terrors, on 28 October 1992; they were disappointed, just as another Korean sect had been disappointed in the previous month. Both sects will have to recalculate: the end is certain, only the date is liable to be wrong; the signs of decadence are there for all to see, the renovation is bound to come, and for those who possess the apocalyptic books there are plenty of numbers to work on.

In our culture the Jewish–Christian apocalypses have been, as they remain, the principal means by which investigators map the past and predict the future as it may be discerned from their own temporal situation, which is always, of course, assumed to be a turning point of history; otherwise it wouldn't be worth bothering about. The activities of such students consist largely in the modern application of those ancient texts, written between the end of Old Testament prophecy and about 100 AD.

The *naïveté* of these procedures of course sets these students apart from those of biblical scholarship. They are founded on the presumption that what St John wrote on Patmos has an immediate, direct and unproblematical application to the historical moment of the interpreter. The seven years that separate us from the end of the millennium correspond to the years of Tribulation, and seven appalling years before the end it is predicted that there will occur the phenomenon known as the Rapture, prophesied in 1 Thessalonians 4.17: 'Then we which are alive and remain shall be caught up . . . in the clouds, to meet the Lord in the air: and so shall we ever be with the Lord.' The Rapture, which millions of people, most of them in America, think to be imminent, will be sudden; airliners, their pilots raptured, will crash, the freeways will be a nightmare of driverless cars. The raptured will look down calmly at these events, and at the fearful slaughter that must follow before the general end. There is no shortage of signs that it is about to begin. Middle Eastern conflicts, nuclear assaults on Russia (for confident expectation of these has not been dispelled by the demise of the Soviet Union). The Jews, to more or less everybody's regret, will have to endure another Holocaust.

Paul Boyer, who has made a fascinating study of modern American apocalyptic,[3] emphasizes that its adherents constitute a political force of sufficient strength to exert a real effect on the world, thus affording a cogent illustration of Focillon's thesis. After all, America had for eight years a president who believed that he was living in the end time and rather hoped it might arrive during his administration. America has a history of apocalyptic expectation that goes back to the time of Increase Mather, who prophesied the imminent destruction of the world by fire. Later there was a certain blending of national expectations – America had been chosen to inaugurate the new age – with the desire for personal salvation. The latter now seems to have prevailed, and indeed has done so for a long time. The Millerites expected to be caught up into the air on 22 October 1844, and at least one of them, a businessman, is said to have given away all his property in preparation, a rash career move repeated recently in Korea.

These fundamentalist operations are of course very remote from the learned study of apocalypse; scholars may be interested in popular apocalyptic, but they no longer make their own numerical predictions; though we might remember that John Napier, who invented logarithms, and Newton, who explained the planetary motions, spent much time in that activity. But scepticism has prevailed. The clergy of established ecclesiastical institutions have long found talk of the end-time something of an embarrassment. Since the founding documents proclaimed it, they could hardly deny it, but they took comfort in St Mark's assertion that although in those days there 'shall be affliction, such as was not from the beginning of the creation . . . until this time' (13.19), it must be added that 'the time is not yet'. It was only with difficulty that Revelation was accepted as canonical, but once accepted it was given continuous learned interpretation, which increasingly departed from the literal reading and the apocalyptic sums, and is now often preoccupied with apocalypse simply as a genre characteristic of a particular and distant period. It is not easy for an institution, having moved out of its charismatic phase, to proclaim the imminence of its own demise.

One theological development is of interest because it stresses the large difference between naive and learned interpretation, but also because it shows how the scholars, for all their learning, sense that for them as for the ignorant there is a connection between the idea of apocalypse and the terms and patterns of individual lives. So they repeat, in their own language, Blake's dictum, 'Then the Last Judgment begins, & its Vision is Seen by the imaginative Eye or Every one according to the situation he holds.' Every man imagines his own apocalypse; our sense of endings has its origins in existential anxiety. On this view the end is imm*a*nent rather than imm*i*nent.

Such notions are harder to entertain than that of a general end, literally inferred from an inerrant text; but what animates the holders may be, fundamentally, the same conviction, that to speak of an end is to speak out of an occult desire to make sense of one's own life, its patterns and their completion. Even the clerical sceptics may have anxieties which condition their ideas of history, of crisis, of death. The learned, unlike the ignorant, have learned to mistrust print. But they may still project their ideas of decadence and renovation onto calendar dates; they may see their own moment as a time of transition between them. For the times we live in are always bad enough, or at any rate transitional enough, to qualify for consideration as precedent to an end.

Not everybody has the luck to be given a lifespan that includes the end of a century, much less of a millennium; but the deprived can juggle the figures given in Daniel and Revelation, and come up with some other suitable date, such as 1666 or 1844. There are dozens of them, no longer of great interest to the learned, but the learned can still share in the sense of decadence and transition that tends to accompany the ends of *saecula*, whenever they occur.

It is not difficult to be satirical about popular apocalyptic, and not difficult to ignore the nice speculations of the theologians. It is harder to dismiss consideration of the degree to which the ideas and the literatures we value, and some of the assumptions we ordinarily do not question, are impregnated by an apocalypticism that is neither vulgar nor technical. We need to ask what form this impregnation takes in writers from whom we should only with difficulty withhold respect – who may indeed be in some measure formative of the traditions, creative and critical, in which we still work.

The form in which schematic apocalyptic thought has been most influential in secular circles is probably the one invented by Joachim, Abbot of Fiore, and later developed in various ways, some very fantastic. This is a very large subject, and I can say only a little about it, but that little I must say. Joachim formalized the idea of transition; he found, by studying Revelation, that there would be between his three ages or 'states' – Father, Son and Spirit – a *transitus*. The renovation, in one form or another, will follow the transition from the present 'state'. It might be a millennium of peace, or, as Joachim believed, of monasticism – an age of Grace. His disciples liked to think that there would be an Everlasting Gospel, a new New Testament which would supersede the existing one as that had superseded the Old. The transition at the end of that third age – the end of all time – would presumably be into eternity.

The scheme lent itself to many variations. Like Joachim, his followers thought they were living in the transition between the age of the Son and that of the Spirit, due to begin, according to their calculations, in 1260 (1260 days, or three and a half years, is an important period in both Daniel and Revelation). Joachim's ideas, variously deformed, had wider circulation than his writings, and their strange political and sometimes revolutionary consequences have been described by Norman Cohn[4] and others. More to our purpose is the powerful nineteenth-century secularized revival, now more accessible than formerly because of the work of Marjorie Reeves and Warwick Gould.[5] What would now succeed the ages of Father and Son was to be the age of Humanity.

This surprisingly powerful secular version owed something to Auguste Comte and his three ages, more to Michelet, and most, probably, to Renan and George Sand. Matthew Arnold, a poet of transition, between two worlds, was naturally interested. George Eliot, in *Romola*, correctly represented Savonarola as having been influenced by Joachim's ideas. And it may be that something of what she is usually said to have derived from Comte came instead from the study of Joachim.

Marjorie Reeves temperately remarks that 'Joachimism represents only one current in the stream of nineteenth-century thought about history'; but if, as she has shown, it helped to carry along the thoughts of Renan and George Eliot, Huysmans and J. A. Symonds, Havelock Ellis and Möller van den Bruck, that current was not a negligible force. It united many apparently disparate interests, nestling in the larger context of nineteenth-century occultism in this country, in France and perhaps in Russia also. It may well have contributed more than a little to the thought and feeling of the late-nineteenth-century 'Decadence'.

Decadence is a complicated subject, and many more or less exotic intellectual traditions made their contribution to the form it took in the nineties of the last century. One contribution came from the earlier stirring of interest in Joachim I have been talking about. The strange recrudescence of a thirteenth-century prophet, and his endorsement by the best intellectual society of the age could hardly have happened had there not been a movement of more general opinion that favoured the development. It may be seen as significant that Renan, a scholar of high authority, was greatly taken with what he had heard of these ideas – mostly from George Sand – before he got round to studying them in the Joachimite writings themselves. When he did so he concerned himself not only with their importance to the medieval historian but with their prophetic power in his own day. He believed they supported the ideal of 'a religious state of humanity beyond Christ, corresponding to the Third Age, of the Spirit'.[6]

Such, very generally, was the humanist, optimistic mood of mid-nineteenth-century Joachimism. Later in the century there was a change in the kind of attention accorded to the prophet: *fin-de-siècle* writers saw the scheme as through an occult glass. Yeats welcomed it into his strange syncretic 'System', along with Blake and Nietzsche, alchemy and Rosicrucianism. For him the Third Age was the age of the triumph of the isolated artist over a decadent world – a view which also appealed to Wilde. So Joachim could be adapted to the *fin-de-siècle* myth, or, in Wilde's larger phrase, to the *fin du monde*. Yeats collected prophecies of imminent tribulation, foreseeing a great world war, and at times quite keenly looking forward to it. Excited by news of a skirmish in Venezuela, he invited a friend to 'come and see me on Monday and have tea and perhaps divine for armageddon'.[7] In the usual way he gave various dates for the End, first 1900 and then 1927.

The archetypal Decadent author of the period is doubtless Huysmans, and in *A Rebours* he provided its Evangel, 'the breviary of the Decadence' as Arthur Symons called it.[8] Huysmans, a writer entirely lacking in the optimism or meliorism of Renan or George Eliot, took on Joachim as he took on Rosicrucianism, Satanism, black masses, drug-induced visions and Schopenhauer. He saw his own times, and perhaps life itself, as Tribulation and Decadence; not for him the Mallarméan defence that Decadence was a term properly applied to certain late Latin writers; it applied to human souls and the world they suffered in. Huysmans, or perhaps rather Des Esseintes, hero of *A Rebours*, became a cult, and influenced writers as far apart as Mallarmé and Oscar Wilde. He was a central figure in this new *transitus*, intent on the tribulations of modernity.

D. H. Lawrence, born in the English provinces in 1885, the year after the publication of *A Rebours*, was much given to the construction of systems, and he built Joachim into them. In his own way he gave the Joachimite triad a sexualized interpretation: Law = Woman, Love = Man, Holy Spirit = 'Consummate Marriage'. In the school history book he wrote under a pseudonym he went out of his way to tell the children about Joachim. He expressly saw the years of the 1914–18 war as a time of Tribulation and extreme decadence; the famous tenth chapter of *Kangaroo* contains known apocalyptic symbols, and so does the novella *St Mawr*. Two discarded titles for *Women in Love* – that war novel which does not mention the war – were 'The Latter Days' and 'Dies Irae'.

Lawrence was not alone in seeing the Great War thus. To some it had appeared that the war would abolish a worn-out world and introduce a new one.[9] But the apocalyptic optimism with which many young men, and perhaps especially artists, responded to the prospect of battle could not survive the experience of the following four years, and when hope failed the sense of decadence returned.

In an interesting essay Helmut E. Gerber contends that the 1890s were regularly seen not only as the decadent end of an old epoch but also as the threshold of a new age, seen as the culmination of a long historical process, and a fated moment of transition. 'The basic observation,' as Gerber correctly states it, 'seems to be that at the ends of centuries . . . human beings, artists in particular, are infected by a sense of death, decay, agony, old gods falling, cultural decline, on the one hand, and by a sense of regeneration, at least a newness of some kind, on the other . . . Genuine decadence *is* a renaissance.'[10]

This expresses neatly the triple nature of the phenomenon: transition, with decadence on one side of it and renovation or renaissance on the other. Sometimes decadence and renewal are indistinguishable, or rather contemporaneous; the *fin-de-siècle* decadence was a time of experimentation in the arts, of a desire to find the new. The Vienna of the period offers famous examples of this duality. There were great novelties in the arts and also in psychoanalysis, while all around there was a sense of doom. Karl Kraus wrote about the last days of mankind; Alban Berg remembered what he said as he wrote *Wozzeck*, a dismal enough image of decadence that was nevertheless a new kind of opera.[11]

So it was in the post-war years. Lawrence inherited the nineties sense of doom and possible regeneration and carried it on. Wittgenstein, who came out of turn-of-the-century Vienna, expressed at the outset of his *Philosophical Investigations* his Spenglerian sense that he was writing in 'a time of darkness'. But that sense need not be inherited; it can proceed from personal observation, for the times are always dark enough for independent spirits to have the same kind of perception. Fredric Jameson, evangelist of the postmodern (an idea that nevertheless itself owes something to the tradition of transition) talks about our own *fin-de-siècle* 'loss of affect', yet believes, as so many before him have believed, that he is coming upon something that is happening now for the first time, that it is a consequence of our entering the final phase of capitalism (a view, or hope, at least as old as Engels). A self-confessed utopian Marxist, he probably still expects renovation in due course, a new age. The moral is that however sophisticated our intellectual positions, we are always somehow ready for the end, and for a beginning; we instantly identify our moment as transitional.

So transition is the key term, and we recognize its presence or its onset by the unmistakable signs of decadence. Of course these signs or symptoms will vary with the times; ours will not be quite the same as those of Huysmans. Yet people interested in the arts will often see a certain analogy between deliberate stylistic deliquescence and a more general moral, social or political decadence, as happened in the late nineteenth century. Max Nordau notoriously asserted, in the year of Wilde's disgrace, that what was happening in the arts was a symptom of pathological degeneration in their practitioners. In some ways the artists themselves can be said to have had views that were not dissimilar; the idea of the *poète maudit* took hold; Yeats celebrated his Tragic Generation. There was an avant-garde of artists, haters of science, of the bourgeois, and of the masses, self-alienated from society and associated, in the eyes of the disgusted bourgeoisie and the masses also, with cults of homosexuality, drink, drugs and exotic religions. New styles in art implied new styles in morality. Because of the Wilde trials Arthur Symons changed the title of his most famous book from *The Decadent Movement in Literature* to *The Symbolist Movement in Literature*.[12] He spoke of the literature of his day as 'a new and beautiful and interesting disease', differing from Nordau only in that he liked it. Sometimes he shifted the accusation of decadence onto the enemy – the masses who saw the artists as outsiders. With these *Massenmenschen* one should have no dealings. Yet for a while Decadence was virtually a synonym for modern beauty – Symbolist beauty, for at that time the modern in art was hardly to be distinguished from Symbolism, and Symbolism was Decadent.

Much ostentatiously modernist-decadent behaviour was prudently modified after the Wilde trials of 1895, but much survived them, not least the contempt for the masses. It is partly responsible for the apparent paradox that the avant-garde of the post-war years combined innovation in the arts with political reaction, indeed with fascism, dislike of universal education, and so on, variously expressed by such modern writers as Lawrence, Pound, Eliot and Wyndham Lewis. Evelyn Waugh, too young to have experienced in his own life the apocalyptic hopes and disappointments of the war,[13] called his first novel (1928) *Decline and Fall*; his next, *Vile Bodies* (1930) satirizes decadent behaviour and ends with a global war. The comic treatment of decadent themes continues in *A Handful of Dust* (1934). Lawrence was no less insistent on decadence in the twenties than earlier. Indeed his apocalyptic certainty increased and acquired detail; *Lady Chatterley's Lover* is a profoundly apocalyptic book. And Lawrence's last book was called *Apocalypse*.

We have a different but comparable set of *fin-de-siècle* notions. We think of modernism as a past period, ending about 1939 and having its *anni mirabiles* in the twenties. It was a large and complex affair, embracing the nihilism of Dada as well as the refinements of Mallarmé – the Book as the end of the world – and the cryptic encyclopaedism of Pound. It was experimental in all the arts; the conviction of decadence went together with the sense that the arts and their history were being renewed. Some forms of modernism sought to eliminate decadence by restoring (or inventing) lost traditions; others wanted to achieve it by a clean break with the past.

No doubt there are as many postmodernisms as there were modernisms. What they seem to have in common is a sense of superiority to the modern, indeed to all the past – which can be used at will, often parodically, or ignored. Postmodernists have their own way of recording transition, and celebrate the loss of the delusive *grands récits* which characterized not only modernism but its past or pasts. The older sense of decadence depends on one of those *récits*, and can now be seen through. The end-of-century idea of the artist as *maudit*, in exile from the vulgar community – an idea inherited from romanticism and given more intensive expression – is also under attack. The postmodern is anti-modernist; modernism is the old age out of which we have moved or are moving. Modernists are charged with racism, anti-feminism and other deplorable attitudes. Some of the charges are just, but they are sometimes accompanied by a rancorous egalitarianism, a denial of differential values, which the modernists might with equal justice have dismissed as evidence of decadent mob thinking.

It would be foolish to adjudicate between these periods; what is true is that for all their differences, and the enmity of the new for the old, there are qualities they have in common. Decadence is still formative in *The Waste Land*; a self-consciously apocalyptic poem, it represents the decadence of extreme refinement as well as of a populace sunk in the vulgarities of poverty and promiscuity. Yet there is, in its fragmentary character, and its use of parody, a pre-echo of postmodernist techniques. In its defiance of temporal connection it also anticipates the postmodern questioning of causality and of what is called public time.

What is surely true is that there is repetition, a pattern of response, which might, if we were thorough enough, be found in the latest – the most sceptical and refined – forms of response as well as in the earliest we know about. Foucault impressed the world by announcing the end of man, the death of the epoch in which that conception was entertained. The death of the author, a rather less portentous demise, is now routinely announced. Whether or not one accepts these propositions, they certainly constitute announcements that something erroneous, even decadent – for the idea of the author is a late and unwelcome development – has been superseded; that a transition has occurred, and at the very moment when Foucault, or whoever, happened to be around to witness and explain it. The abandonment of the *grands récits*, which I mentioned a while ago, is another instance of announcing an epoch, the death of an old and the beginning of a new one. To put it another way, when we have achieved what Lyotard calls 'incredulity towards metanarratives' we have surely opened a new epoch. If in addition we deny all end-directed history we have apocalyptically eliminated apocalyptic thinking; if we dispute the validity of traditional philosophical enquiries we have begun a new epoch in philosophy, or are in transition towards it. If we maintain that the long history of capitalism has reached its term, and that we suffer 'loss of affect' in consequence, we are explaining a decadence and, in transition, expecting a renovation.

It isn't difficult to see that whether it is one of transition or not, our period is keenly interested in the idea. The works of Marshall McLuhan, now all but forgotten in the onrush of transitional cultural theories, were concerned almost entirely with transition. A determined postmodernist like Thomas Docherty can deride as fraudulent 'the merely modernist conception of tradition', and argue that postmodernism aims to make unrecognizable 'the always already known';[14] in so saying he is proclaiming, and not in totally original terms, another transition, another way out of decadence.

In a similar but possibly more helpful way the idea of decadence may be seriously used by those who deplore the depredations of technology, the pollution of the atmosphere, the destruction of forests, the risks of nuclear technology. It is indeed remarkable that so many people can ignore these authentic indicators in favour of fundamentalist study of obsolete texts, or reject the discourse of 'greenness' as always already known. We know that those who entertain such worries are no more worried than the medieval observers who saw fighting in the sky and feared an approaching end; but we also know that their fear is real, that from the tribulation they experience there may be no recovery; nevertheless we can list them with those moderns who for other reasons sense transition, and fear an end.

These reversals and alterations of focus cannot prevent us from seeing the pattern – what the present moment, in the last years of the century – that artificial epoch – has in common with the decadence of the last century, indeed with all those in the past who have recognized transition and feared or welcomed an end. All through history those who have marked epochs – ages of gold, silver, brass, iron – have known what it is to live at a time of crisis. Whether this sense has intensified – whether it has grown more acute with modernity, so that to write its history you might have to speak of Kierkegaard, of Sartre, of Jaspers – I do not certainly know. But the sense exists, and a failure of scepticism may make it keener for all of us as century and millennium come to a close. It seems, after all, that it is in our own lives that we are waiting for, and sensing, the end.

NOTES

1 'La construction de la nouvelle et du roman' – the translation by Tzvetan Todorov in his *Théorie de la littérature* (Paris, 1966), 170–96.

2 The argument of this paragraph is developed in my 'Sensing Endings', *Nineteenth-Century Fiction*, 33 (1978), 144–58.

3 P. Boyer, *When Time Shall be no More* (Cambridge, Mass., 1992).

4 *The Pursuit of the Millennium*, 2nd edn (London, 1961).

5 Marjorie Reeves, *The Influence of Prophecy in the Later Middle Ages* (Oxford, 1969); *Joachim of Fiore and the Prophetic Future* (London, 1976); Marjorie Reeves and Warwick Gould, *Joachim of Fiore and the Myth of the Eternal Evangel* (Oxford, 1987). Also Bernard McGinn, *The Calabrian Abbot: Joachim of Fiore in the History of Western Thought* (New York, 1985).

6 Reeves and Gould, *Joachim of Fiore*, 139.

7 Ibid., 139.

8 *The Symbolist Movement in Literature* (New York, 1958), 76.

9   See Modris Eksteins, *Rites of Spring: The Great War and the Birth of the Modern Age* (Boston, 1989).

10 'The Nineties: Beginning, End or Transition?', in R. Ellmann, ed., *Edwardians and Late Victorians*, English Institute Essays (New York, 1959 (1960)), 50–79.

11 David P. Schroeder, 'Opera, Apocalypse and the Dance of Death', *Mosaic* 25/1 (Winter, 1992), 91–105.

12 R. K. R. Thornton, ' "Decadence" in Later Nineteenth-Century England', in *Decadence and the 1890s*, ed. I. Fletcher (London, 1979), 15–29.

13 See Eksteins' *Rites of Spring*, n. 9.

14 *After Theory: Postmodernism/Post-Marxism* (London, 1990), 198.

12

Adorno as Lateness Itself

Edward W. Said

Beginnings of course stand at the first moment of any undertaking and in most cases express hopefulness and a sense of forward-looking expectation. Beginnings are usually associated with youth, not with age, although literature, music and art are full of examples of renewal, beginning-again, that are found in the work of older artists. Verdi, for instance, is justifiably described as having started again with *Othello* and *Falstaff*, both of them operas written when he was well into his late seventies, nearly eighty. Cyclical thinkers like Vico and Ibn Khaldun (and in our own time Northrop Frye) associate endings with beginnings. The decrepitude of a dynasty in Ibn Khaldun's *Muqaddimah*, the terminal despair and barbarism of reflection that Vico describes in his account of civil wars, these finally bury an old state of affairs in order that a new one might begin again. The cycles of autumn and winter that Frye talks about in *The Anatomy of Criticism* inevitably give rise to spring and summer, more or less unendingly.

In all these instances beginnings can either be recovered or somehow returned to. There is absolutely no finality implicit in the idea: hence its optimism and hopefulness which, to speak as someone whose feelings about mornings are much more enthusiastic than they are about evenings, is very much the same sort of rise in energy and expectation some of us feel at the dawning of a new day, its prospects seeming to raise one up from the darkness and gloom of even the unhappiest night.

As opposed to endings of that generally cyclical type, that is, endings that are part of a recurring pattern of birth, death and rebirth, there are endings of an altogether, more or less terminal, finality. They too occur after some earlier beginning, obviously enough, but we sense in them much more of the conclusiveness of death, of an absolute and irrevocable cadence for which beginnings have at best only a very distant and even ironic appeal. It is these that I want to talk about here.

Few writers to my knowledge have focused so severely and unrelentingly on the difficulties of life at the ending than Swift. In Book III of *Gulliver's Travels*, the peculiar race of Struldbruggs at first opens up an extremely pleasing prospect for Gulliver, who believes that the immortality of these rare creatures guarantees them all sorts of privileges and insights: rather vainly he then proceeds to imagine how such miraculous beings will make it possible for him to derive many advantages. Together, he dreams, they will oppose the corruption of time and the 'degeneracy of human nature' and quite without any justification except his own gullibility and egotism, he also starts to imagine how well he would live if, like the Struldbruggs, he could be released from the threat of death. When at last he is told the truth about those miserable creatures he is sadly disillusioned. Far from immortality bringing salvation and insight it brings the Struldbruggs an apparently unending catalogue of woes. They lose their teeth and hair, as well as memory and desire. Past the age of ninety, because the language changes from generation to generation, they can no longer communicate with anyone. And all this is preceded by a disastrous process of physical, mental and moral decrepitude that is awful to read about:

> they had not only all the Follies and Infirmities of other old Men, but many more, which arose from the dreadful Prospect of never dying. They were not only opinionative, peevish, covetous, morose, vain, talkative; but uncapable of Friendship, and dead to all natural Affection, which never descended below their Grandchildren. Envy and impotent Desires, are their prevailing Passions. But those Objects against which their Envy seems principally directed, are the Vices of the younger Sort, and the Deaths of the old.[1]

One can easily imagine Swift, with his fierce conservatism and Christian fatalism, rather enjoying his quite horrendous demystification of age. But although both the Struldbruggs and Gulliver actually long for death as a result of these appalling circumstances, it is, I think, Swift's portrait of age itself that concentrates the modern secular reader's mind so acutely. When you are old there really is no escaping the fact that you are approaching the end, and at the end there is, properly speaking, nothing but the end without in the end any real, or alleged satisfactions. It is the peculiar power of that realization that is compressed in Swift's portrait of the dying Struldbruggs, who remain at the end without experiencing the conclusiveness of death. This terrifying, but potentially comic situation is what appealed to one of Swift's modern disciples, Samuel Beckett, many of whose characters are in effect equivalents of the Struldbruggs. To be old in these circumstances is to lose contact with the beginning, to be left in a place and time without recourse either to hope or enthusiasm. Hence *Endgame*.

Swift's tactic is transparent. Endings are bad enough without trying to postpone them, he seems to be saying, and therefore the more readily we accept what is inevitable the less painful it will seem. Yet by giving the Struldbruggs too much life without any of the legendary attributes of immortality (eternal youth, for example) he also affords his readers, in a kind of sadistic slow-motion, a glimpse of what waiting for the end is like. The result, almost by inadvertence, is an unpleasant anatomy of ending, which is enacted for Gulliver in the reports he hears about the Struldbruggs and confirmed when he meets them. As I said, Beckett seems to have seized on this experience for his plays and novels, and extended it with remarkable ingenuity. Like Swift, Beckett is severe and minimalist: endings are comic because at such moments human struttings and posturings have a lucid futility to them that can be entertaining.

Besides Beckett there is a whole roster of modern writers who are fascinated by endings. This includes *fin-de-siècle* figures like Wilde and Huysmans, as well as writers like Mann, Eliot, Proust, Yeats, for whom mortality carries with it considerable sadness and nostalgia. Nevertheless these writers differ from Swift and Beckett in that *their* sense of an ending is mitigated by some glimmer of redemption, that in growing old one achieves insight, or some new and rounded sense of life's wholeness, or as in Proust's case, through art one can perhaps survive death. A book that deeply impressed me when I read it about twenty years ago – David Grene's *Reality and the Heroic Pattern: Last Plays of Ibsen, Shakespeare, and Sophocles*[2] – puts forth a version of this argument very convincingly. Ibsen, Grene says, uses his last plays to understand the mistakes, failures, and wounds of a person's life, allowing backward vision to provide a new, integrative vision of the whole. In this Ibsen's *John Gabriel Borkman*, and *When we Dead awake* recall *The Tempest*, *Cymbeline* and *The Winter's Tale*, which in turn send us back to the *Ajax* and the *Philoctetes*. Drama is the vehicle enabling this final vision in ways, Grene says, that are not available intellectually but only aesthetically. Here too art is redemptive.

For Ibsen, as for the other modernist writers to whom I have referred, personal time corresponds to the general time. Personal exhaustion and failing health to the insufficiencies, dangers, threats and debasements of modernity itself. A great deal (perhaps too much) of what has been written about the modernist movement has emphasized this traffic between the individual and the general. Modernism has therefore come to seem paradoxically not so much a movement of the new but rather a movement of aging and ending, a sort of Age masquerading as Juvenility, to quote Hardy in *Jude the Obscure*. For indeed the figure in that novel of Jude's son, Little Father Time, does seem like an allegory of modernism with its sense of accelerated decline and its compensating gestures of recapitulation and inclusiveness. Yet for Hardy the little boy is hardly a symbol of redemption, any more than the darkling thrush is. This is evident in Little Father Time's first appearance riding the train to be met by Jude and Sue.

> He was Age masquerading as Juvenility, and doing it so badly that his real self showed through crevices. A ground swell from ancient years of night seemed now and then to lift the child in this his morning-life, when his face took a back view over some great Atlantic of Time, and appeared not to care about what it saw.
>
> When the other travellers closed their eyes, which they did one by one – even the kitten curling itself up in the basket, weary of its too circumscribed play – the boy remained just as before. He then seemed to be doubly awake, like an enslaved and dwarfed Divinity, sitting passive and regarding his companions as if he saw their whole rounded lives rather than their immediate figures.[3]

Little Jude represents not so much a premature senescence but a montage of beginnings and endings, an unlikely jamming together of youth and age whose divinity – the word has a sinister sound to it here – consists in being able to pass judgement on himself and on others. Later, when he performs an act of judgement on himself and his little siblings, the result is collective suicide, which is to say, I think, that so scandalous a mixture of extreme youth with extreme age cannot survive for very long.

But there is ending *and* surviving together and this is what I want to spend the rest of the time discussing here. For reasons that will become clear in a moment, I have given this rather peculiar modern aesthetic mode the name of *late style*, a phrase whose meaning has given a fascinating range of references to Theodor Adorno: he uses it most memorably and most powerfully in an essay fragment entitled 'Spätstil Beethovens' dated 1937, but included in a 1964 collection of Adorno's musical essays *Moments musicaux*.[4] For Adorno, far more than for anyone who has ever spoken of Beethoven's last works, those compositions that belong to what is known as his third period (the last five piano sonatas, the Ninth Symphony, the *Missa Solemnis*, the last six string quartets, a handful of bagatelles for the piano), Beethoven's late-style works constitute an event in the history of modern culture: a moment when the artist who is fully in command of his medium nevertheless abandons communication with the bourgeois order of which he is a part and achieves a contradictory, alienated relationship with it. One of Adorno's most extraordinary essays included in the same collection with the late-style fragment is on the *Missa Solemnis*,[5] which he calls an alienated masterpiece (Verfremdetes Hauptwerke) by virtue of its difficulty, its archaisms, and its strange subjective revaluation of the Mass.

What Adorno has to say about late Beethoven throughout his voluminous writings (Adorno died in 1969) is clearly a construction that serves him as a sort of beginning point for all his analyses of subsequent music. The American musicologist Rose Subotnik has done an extended analysis of this late-Beethoven construction and shown its astonishing influence within Adorno's work, from beginning to end of his career.[6] So convincing a cultural symbol to him was the figure of the aging, deaf and isolated composer that it even turns up as part of Adorno's contribution to Thomas Mann's *Doctor Faustus* in which early in the novel young Adrian Leverkuhn is impressed by a lecture on Beethoven's final period given by Wendell Kretschmer:

> Beethoven's art had overgrown itself, risen out of the habitable regions of tradition, even before the startled gaze of human eyes, into spheres of the entirely and utterly and nothing-but personal – an ego painfully isolated in the absolute, isolated too from sense by the loss of his hearing; lonely prince of a realm of spirits, from whom now only a chilling breath issued to terrify his most willing contemporaries, standing as they did aghast at these communications of which only at moments, only by exception, they could understand anything at all.[7]

This is almost pure Adorno. There is heroism in it, but also intransigence. Nothing about the essence of the late Beethoven is reducible to the notion of art as a document, that is, to a reading of the music that stresses 'reality breaking through' in the form of history or the composer's sense of his impending death. For 'in this way,' by stressing the works as an expression of Beethoven's personality, Adorno says 'the late works are relegated to the outer reaches of art, in the vicinity of document. In fact, studies of the very late Beethoven seldom fail to make reference to biography and fate. It is as if, confronted by the dignity of human death, the theory of art were to divest itself of its rights and abdicate in favour of reality.'[8]

Impending death is there of course, and cannot be denied. But Adorno's stress is on the formal law of Beethoven's final compositional mode, by which he means to stress the rights of the aesthetic. This law reveals itself to be a queer amalgam of subjectivity and convention, evident in such devices as 'decorative trill sequences, cadences and fiorituras'. In an immensely powerful formulation of the relationship between convention and subjectivity Adorno says the following:

> This law is revealed precisely in the thought of death . . . Death is imposed only on created beings, not on works of art, and thus it has appeared in art only in a refracted mode, as allegory . . . The power of subjectivity in the late works of art is the irascible gesture with which it takes leave of the works themselves. It breaks their bonds, not in order to express itself, but in order, expressionless, to cast off the appearance of art. Of the works themselves it leaves only fragments behind, and communicates itself, like a cipher, only through the blank spaces from which it has disengaged itself. Touched by death, the hand of the master sets free the masses of material that he used to form; its tears and fissures, witnesses to the powerlessness of the ego confronted with Being are its final work (der endlichen Ohnmacht des Ichs vorm Seienden, sind ihr letztes Werk).[9]

It is very easy to be impatient with this sort of writing but, as with nearly everything in Adorno, the dense and extremely involuted style is always based on a remarkably fresh and direct sensuous insight, and will usually yield up considerable interpretive capital if one is patient with it. What has gripped Adorno in Beethoven's late work is its episodic character, its apparent carelessness about its own continuity.

Compare the development sections of such works as the *Eroica* or the Third piano concerto on the one hand with, on the other, the opus 110 or the *Hammerklavier* and you will be struck with the totally cogent and integrative logic of the former and the somewhat distracted, often extremely slapdash-seeming character of the latter. The opening theme in the thirty-first sonata is spaced very awkwardly and when it gets going after the trill its accompaniment – a student-like, almost clumsy repetitive figure – is, Adorno correctly says, 'unabashedly primitive'. And so it goes in the late works, massive polyphonic writing of the most abstruse and difficult sort alternating with what Adorno calls 'conventions', which are often seemingly unmotivated rhetorical devices like trills, or appoggiaturas whose role in the work seems unintegrated into the structure. 'His late work still remains process, but not as development; rather as a catching fire between extremes, which no longer allow for any secure middle ground or harmony of spontaneity.'[10] Thus, as Kretschmer says in Mann's *Doctor Faustus*, Beethoven's late works often communicate an impression of being unfinished, something that the energetic teacher of Adrian Leverkuhn discusses at great and ingenious length in his disquisition about the two movements of opus 111.

Adorno's thesis is that all this is predicated upon two facts of mortality: first, that when he was young, Beethoven's work had been vigorous and *durchcomponiert*, whereas now it has become more wayward and eccentric; and second, that as an older man facing death Beethoven realizes, as Subotnik puts it, that his work cannot even achieve 'a Kantian duality, for which no synthesis is conceivable, [but is in effect] the remains of a synthesis, the vestiges of an individual human subject sorely aware of the wholeness, and consequently the survival, that has eluded it forever'.[11] Beethoven's late works therefore communicate a tragic sense in spite of their irascibility; quoting Adorno on the *Missa* directly, Subotnik reminds us that 'the sorrow he detects in Beethoven's last style, [is] where "failure [becomes] in a supreme sense the measure of success"'.[12] How exactly and poignantly Adorno discovers this is readily evident at the end of his fragment on Beethoven's late style. Noting that in Beethoven, as in Goethe, there is a plethora of 'unmastered material', he goes on to observe that in the late sonatas, conventions, for instance, are 'splintered off', the main thrust of the composition left to stand, fallen away and abandoned, like the odd recitations that precede the fugues in opus 106 and 110. As for the great unisons (in the Ninth Symphony or the *Missa*), they stand next to huge polyphonic ensembles. Adorno then adds:

> It is subjectivity that forcibly brings the extremes together in the moment, fills the dense polyphony with its tensions, breaks it apart with the *unisons*, and disengages itself, leaving the naked tone behind; that sets the mere phrase as a monument to what has been, marking a subjectivity turned to stone. The caesuras, the sudden discontinuities that more than anything else characterize the very late Beethoven, are those moments of breaking away; the work is silent at the instant when it is left behind, and turns its emptiness outward.[13]

What Adorno describes here is the way that Beethoven seems to inhabit the late works as a lamenting, or somehow feeling personality, and then seems to leave the work or phrase in it incomplete, suddenly, abruptly left behind, as in the opening of the F Major Quartet, or the various pauses in the slow movement of opus 106. The sense of abandonment is peculiarly acute in comparison with the driven and relentless quality of second-period works such as the Fifth Symphony, where at moments like the ending of the fourth movement Beethoven can't seem to tear himself away from the piece. Thus, to conclude, Adorno says that the style of the late works is both objective and subjective:

> Objective is the fractured landscape, subjective the light in which – alone – it glows into life. He does not bring about their harmonious synthesis. As the power of dissociation, he tears them apart in time, in order, perhaps, to preserve them for the eternal. In the history of art late works are the catastrophe.[14]

The crux of this, as always in Adorno, is the problem of trying to say what it is that holds the works together, makes them more than just a collection of fragments. Here he is at his most paradoxical: you cannot say what connects the parts other than by invoking 'the figure they create together'. Neither can you minimize the differences between the parts, and, it would appear, you cannot actually *name* the unity, or give it a specific identity, which would then reduce its catastrophic force. Thus the power of Beethoven's late style is negative, or rather, it *is* negativity: where one would expect serenity and maturity, one finds a bristling, difficult and unyielding – perhaps even inhuman challenge. 'The maturity of the late works,' Adorno says, 'does not resemble the kind one finds in fruit. They are . . . not round, but furrowed, even ravaged. Devoid of sweetness, bitter and spiny, they do not surrender themselves to mere delectation.'[15] Beethoven's late works remain unco-opted: they do not fit any scheme, and they cannot be reconciled or resolved, since their irresolution and un-synthesized fragmentariness are constitutive, not ornamental or symbolic of something else. Beethoven's late compositions are about, are in fact 'lost totality', and therefore catastrophic.

Here we must return to the notion of lateness. Late for what? we are inclined to ask. The American critic Harold Bloom has evolved an interesting theory about poetic creation which is based on what he calls belatedness.[16] All poets, he says, are haunted by their great predecessors, as Wordsworth was by Milton, and Milton by Homer and Virgil. Poetry is therefore an antithetical art, since what poets do is to write against their antecedents: *The Prelude* is a rewriting, and a distortion of *Paradise Lost*. By the same token criticism is misreading too, since critics come after poets. There is some similarity here between Bloom and Adorno, except that for Adorno *lateness* includes the idea of surviving beyond what is acceptable and normal; in addition, lateness includes the idea that one cannot really go beyond lateness at all, not transcending or lifting oneself out of lateness but rather deepening the lateness, as in his book *The Philosophy of Modern Music*, Adorno says Schoenberg essentially prolonged the irreconcilabilities, negations, immobilities of the late Beethoven.[17]

Two further points. The reason Beethoven's late style so gripped Adorno throughout his writing is that in a completely paradoxical way Beethoven's immobilized and socially resistant final works are at the core of what is new in modern music. In *Fidelio* – the quintessential middle-period work – the idea of humanity is manifest throughout, and with it an idea of a better world. Similarly for Hegel irreconcilable opposites were resolvable by means of the dialectic. Late-style Beethoven keeps the irreconcilable apart, and in so doing, 'music is transformed more and more from something significant into something obscure – even to itself'.[18] Thus late-style Beethoven presides over music's rejection of the new bourgeois order, and forecasts the totally authentic and *novel* art of Schoenberg, whose 'advanced music has no recourse but to insist on its own ossification without concession to that would-be humanitarianism which it sees through . . . Under the present circumstances [music] is restricted to definitive negation.'[19] Secondly, far from being simply an eccentric and irrelevant phenomenon, late-style Beethoven, remorselessly alienated and obscure, becomes the prototypical aesthetic form, and by virtue of its distance from and rejection of bourgeois society acquires an even greater significance.

And in so many ways the concept of lateness, as well as what goes with it in these astonishingly bold and bleak ruminations on the position of an aging artist, comes for Adorno to seem *the* fundamental aspect of aesthetics, and of his own work as critical theorist and philosopher. One of the best recent books on Adorno – Fredric Jameson's *Late Marxism: Adorno or the Persistence of the Dialectic*[20] – goes further than any in reclaiming Adorno for lateness, even though Jameson finally does situate (and to a certain degree instigate) the man's lateness within Marxist thought. My reading of Adorno, with his reflections about music at its centre, sees him as injecting Marxism with a vaccine so powerful as to dissolve its agitational force almost completely. Not only do the notions of advance and culmination in Marxism crumble under his rigorous negative scorn, but so too does anything that suggests movement at all. With death and senescence before him, with a promising start years behind him, Adorno is, I think, prepared to endure ending in the form of *lateness* but *for itself*, its own sake, not as a preparation for or obliteration of something else. Lateness is being at the end, fully conscious, full of memory, and also very (even preternaturally) aware of the present. Adorno as lateness itself, not as Swiftian Struldbrugg but as scandalous, even catastrophic commentator on the present.

No one needs to be reminded that Adorno is exceptionally difficult to read, whether in his original German or in any number of translations. Jameson speaks very well about the sheer intelligence of his sentences, their incomparable refinement, their programmatically complex internal movement, the way they have of almost routinely foiling a first, or second, or third attempt at paraphrasing their content. Adorno's style violates various norms: he assumes little community of understanding between himself and his audience, he is slow, unjournalistic, unpackageable, unskimmable. Even an autobiographical text like *Minima Moralia* is an assault on biographical, narrative, or anecdotal continuity; its form exactly replicates its subtitle – Reflections from Damaged Life – a cascading series of discontinuous fragments, all of them in some way assaulting suspicious 'wholes', fictitious unities presided over by Hegel whose grand synthesis has derisive contempt for the individual. 'The conception of a totality harmonious through all its antagonisms compels him to assign to individuation, however much he may designate it a driving moment in the process, an inferior status in the construction of the whole.'[21]

Adorno's counter to false totalities is not just to say that they are inauthentic but in fact to write, to *be* an alternative through subjectivity, albeit subjectivity addressed to philosophic issues. Moreover, he says, 'Social analysis can learn incomparably more from individual experience than Hegel conceded, while conversely the large historical categories . . . are no longer above suspicion of fraud.'[22] In the performance of individual critical thinking there is 'the force of protest'. Yes, such critical thought as Adorno's is very idiosyncratic and often very obscure, but, he wrote in 'Resignation', his last essay 'the uncompromisingly critical thinker, who neither superscribes his conscience nor permits himself to be terrorized into action, is in truth the one who does not give up'.[23] To work through the silences and fissures is to avoid packaging and administration, and is in fact to accept and perform the *lateness* of his position. 'Whatever was once thought however, can be suppressed, it can be forgotten and can even vanish. But it cannot be denied that something of it survives. For thinking has the momentum of the general [here Adorno means both that individual thought is part of the general culture of the age, and that because it is individual, it has its own momentum generated, and veers or swerves off on its own, from the general]. What has been cogently thought must be thought in some other place and by other people. This confidence accompanies even the loneliest and most impotent thought.'[24]

Lateness therefore is coming after, and surviving beyond what is generally acceptable. Hence Adorno's evaluation of the late Beethoven and his own lesson for his reader today. The catastrophe represented by late style for Adorno is that in Beethoven's case the music is episodic, fragmentary, riven with the absences and silences that can neither be filled by supplying some general scheme for them, nor ignored and diminished by saying 'poor Beethoven, he was deaf, he was approaching death, these are lapses we shall overlook'. Years after the first Beethoven essay appeared, and in a sort of counterblast to his book on new music, Adorno published an essay called 'Das Altern der neuen

Musik', the aging of the new music.[25] He spoke there of advanced music, which had inherited the discoveries of the second Viennese School and had gone on 'to show symptoms of false satisfaction' by becoming collectivized, affirmative, safe. New music was negative, 'the result of something distressing and confused': Adorno recalls how traumatic to their audiences were the first performances of Berg's *Altenberg Songs* or Stravinsky's *The Rite of Spring*. That was the true force of new music, fearlessly drawing out the consequences of Beethoven's late-style compositions. Today, however, so-called new music has simply aged beyond Beethoven: 'where once an abyss yawned, a railroad bridge now stretches, from which the passengers can look comfortably down into the depths. The situation of [aged modern] music is no different.'[26]

Just as the negative power of late Beethoven derives from its dissonant relationship with the affirmative developmental thrust of his second-period music, so too the dissonances of Webern and Schoenberg occur 'surrounded by a shudder'; 'they are felt as something uncanny and are introduced by the author only with fear and trembling'.[27] To reproduce the dissonances academically or institutionally a generation later without risk or anything at stake emotionally or in actuality, says Adorno, is completely to lose the shattering force of the new. If you just line up a bunch of tone rows happily, or if you hold festivals of advanced music, you lose the core of, for instance, Webern's achievement, which was to juxtapose 'twelve tone technique . . . [with] its antithesis, the explosive power of the musically individual'. Now, an aging, as opposed to a late art, modern music amounts to little more than 'an empty, high-spirited trip, through thinkably complex scores, in which nothing actually occurs'.[28]

There is therefore an inherent tension in late style which abjures mere bourgeois aging, with its geriatric therapies, relatively comfortable circumstances, and well-funded programmes. One has the impression reading Adorno from the aphoristic essays on such things as punctuation marks and book covers collected in *Noten zur Literatur*, to the grand theoretical works like *Negative Dialectics* and *Aesthetic Theory*, that what he looked for in style was the evidence he found in late Beethoven of sustained tension, unaccommodated stubbornness, lateness and newness next to each other by virtue of an 'inexorable clamp that holds together what no less powerfully strives to break apart'.[29] Above all, late style as exemplified by Beethoven and Schoenberg, the former in the past, the latter in the present, cannot be replicated by invitation, or lazy reproduction, or by mere dynastic or narrative reproduction. There is a paradox: how essentially unrepeatable, uniquely articulated aesthetic works written not at the beginning but at the end of a career can nevertheless have an influence on what comes after them. And how does that influence enter and inform the work of the critic whose whole enterprise stubbornly prizes its own intransigence and untimeliness?

Philosophically Adorno is unthinkable without the majestic beacon provided by Lukács's *History and Class Consciousness*, but also unthinkable without his refusal of the earlier work's triumphalism and implied transcendence. If for Lukács the subject–object relationship and its antinomies, the fragmentation and the lostness, the ironic perspectivism of modernity were supremely discerned, embodied, and consummated in narrative forms such as the rewritten epics both of the novel and the proletariat's class consciousness, for Adorno that particular choice was, he said in a famous anti-Lukács essay, a kind of false reconciliation under duress. Modernity was a fallen, unredeemed reality, and new music, as much as Adorno's own philosophic practice, took its task to be a ceaselessly demonstrated reminder of that reality.

Were this reminder to be simply a repeated *no* or *this will not do*, late style and philosophy would be totally uninteresting and repetitive. There must be a *constructive* element above all, and this animates the procedure. What Adorno finds so admirable about Schoenberg is his severity as well as his invention of a technique that provides music with an alternative to tonal harmony, and to classical inflection, colour, rhythm. Adorno describes the twelve-tone method of Schoenberg in terms taken almost verbatim from Lukács's drama of the subject–object impasse, but each time there is an opportunity for synthesis Adorno has Schoenberg turn it down. What we see is Adorno constructing a breathtakingly regressive sequence, an endgame procedure by which he threads his way back along the route taken by Lukács; all the laboriously devised solutions volunteered by Lukács for pulling himself out of the slough of modern despair are just as laboriously dismantled and rendered useless by Adorno's account of what Schoenberg was really about. Fixated on the new music's absolute rejection of the commercial sphere, Adorno's words cut out the social ground from underneath art. For in fighting ornament, illusion, reconciliation, communication, humanism and success, art becomes untenable.

Everything having no function in the work of art – and therefore everything transcending the law of mere existence is withdrawn. The function of the work of art lies precisely in its transcendence beyond mere existence. . . . Since the work of art, after all, cannot be reality, the elimination of all illusory features accentuates all the more glaringly the illusory character of its existence. This process is inescapable.[30]

Are late-style Beethoven and Schoenberg actually like this, we finally ask, and is their music so isolated in its antithesis to society? Or is it the case that Adorno's descriptions of them are models, paradigms, constructs intended to highlight certain features and thereby give the two composers a certain appearance, a certain profile in and for Adorno's own writing? What Adorno does is theoretical, that is, his construction isn't supposed to be a replica of the real thing, which had he attempted it would be little more than a packaged and domesticated copy. The location of Adorno's writing is theory, a space where he can construct his demystifying negative dialectics. Whether he writes about music or literature or abstract philosophy or society, Adorno's theoretical work is always in a strange way extremely concrete, that is, he writes from the perspective of long experience rather than revolutionary beginnings, and what he writes about is saturated in culture. Adorno's position as a theorist of late style and of endgames is an extraordinary *knowingness*, the polar opposite of Rousseau's. There is also the supposition (indeed the assumption) of wealth and privilege, what today we call elitism, and more recently, political incorrectness. Adorno's world is the world of Weimar, of high modernism, of luxury tastes, of an inspired if slightly sated amateurism. Never was he more autobiographical than in the first fragment, entitled 'For Marcel Proust', of *Minima Moralia*:

The son of well-to-do parents, who whether from talent or weakness, engages in a so-called intellectual profession, as an artist or a scholar, will have a particularly difficult time with those bearing the distasteful title of colleagues. It is not merely that his independence is envied, the seriousness of his intentions mistrusted, and that he is suspected of being a secret envoy of the established powers. *Such suspicions*, though betraying a secret resentment, *would usually prove well-founded*. But the real resistances lie elsewhere. The occupation with things of the mind has by now itself become 'practical', a business with strict division of labour, departments and restricted entry. The man of independent means who chooses it out of repugnance for the ignominy of earning money will not be disposed to acknowledge the fact. For this he is punished. He is not a 'professional', is ranked in the competitive hierarchy as a dilettante no matter how well he knows his subject, and must, if he wants a career, show himself even more resolutely blinkered than the most inveterate specialist.[31]

The dynastic fact of importance here is that his parents were wealthy. No less important is the sentence where having described his colleagues as being envious as well as suspicious of his relationship with 'the established powers' Adorno adds that these suspicions are well founded. Which is to say that in a contest between the blandishments of an intellectual Faubourg St Honoré and those afforded by the moral equivalent of a working-class association Adorno would end up with the former not the latter. On one level his elitist predilections are of course a function of his class background. But on another what he likes in it well after his defection from its ranks is its sense of ease and luxury; this, he implies in the *Minima Moralia*, allows him a continuous familiarity with great works, great masters, great ideas, not as subjects of professional discipline but rather as the practices indulged in by a well-frequented habitué at a club. Yet this is another reason why Adorno is impossible to assimilate to any system, even that of upper-class sensuousness: he literally defies predictability, turning his disaffected, but rarely cynical eye, on virtually everything within range.

Nevertheless Adorno, like Proust, lived and worked his entire life next to, and even as a part of, the great underlying continuities of Western society: families, intellectual associations, musical and concert life, philosophical traditions, as well as any number of academic institutions. But always to one side, never fully a part of any. He was a musician who never had a career as one, a philosopher whose main subject was music. And Adorno never pretended to an apolitical neutrality, unlike many of his academic or intellectual counterparts. His work is like a contrapuntal voice intertwined with fascism, bourgeois mass society, and communism, inexplicable without them, always critical and ironic about them.

I have spoken about Adorno in this way because around his amazingly peculiar and inimitable work a number of general characteristics of endings have coalesced. First of all, like some of the people he admired and knew – Horkheimer, Thomas Mann, Steuermann – Adorno was a worldly person, worldly in the French sense of *mondain*.

Urban and urbane, deliberate, incredibly able to find interesting things to say about even so unassuming a thing as a semicolon or an exclamation mark. Along with this goes the late style – that of an aging but mentally agile European man of culture absolutely not given to ascetic serenity or mellow maturity: there isn't much fumbling for references, or footnotes, or pedantic citations, but always a very self-assured and well-brought-up ability to talk equally well about Bach as about his devotees, about society as about sociology.

Adorno is very much a late figure because so much of what he does militates ferociously against his own time. Although he wrote a great deal in many different fields he attacked the major advances in all of them, functioning instead like an enormous shower of sulphuric acid poured over the lot. He opposed the very notion of productivity by being himself the author of an over-abundance of material, none of it really compressible into an Adornian system or method. In an age of specialization he was catholic, writing on virtually everything that came before him. On his turf – music, philosophy, social tendencies, history, communication, semiotics – Adorno was unashamedly mandarin. There are no concessions to his readers, no summaries, small talk, helpful roadsigns, convenient simplifying. And never any kind of solace or false optimism. One of the impressions you get as you read Adorno is that he is a sort of furious machine decomposing itself into smaller and smaller parts. He had the miniaturist's penchant for pitiless detail: the last blemish is sought out and hung out to be looked at with a pedantic little chuckle.

It is the *Zeitgeist* that Adorno really loathed and that all his writing struggles mightily to insult. Everything about him to readers who came of age in the 1950s and 1960s is pre-war and therefore unfashionable, perhaps even embarrassing, like his opinions on jazz or on otherwise universally recognized composers like Stravinsky or Wagner. Lateness for him equals regression, from *now* to *back then*, when people discussed Kierkegaard, Hegel and Kafka with direct knowledge of their work, not with plot summaries or handbooks. The things he writes about he seems to have known since childhood, and were not learned at university or by frequenting fashionable parties. As I said earlier, there is a practised knowingness in Adorno that seems unfazed by the dizzying variety of subjects and fields.

What is particularly interesting to me about Adorno is that he is a special twentieth-century type, the out-of-his-time late-nineteenth-

century disappointed or disillusioned romantic who exists almost ec-
statically detached from, yet in a kind of complicity with, new and
monstrous modern forms − fascism, anti-Semitism, totalitarianism,
bureaucracy, or what Adorno called the administered society and
the consciousness industry. Unlike Benjamin, Adorno is very much a
secular figure; and like the Leibnizian monad he often discussed with
reference to the art work, he − along with rough contemporaries like
Richard Strauss, Lampedusa, Visconti − is unwaveringly Eurocentric,
unfashionable, resistant to any assimilative scheme, and yet he oddly
reflects the predicament of ending without illusory hope or manufac-
tured resignation.

Perhaps in the end it is Adorno's unmatched technicality that is so
significant. His analyses of Schoenberg's method in *The Philosophy of
Modern Music* give words and concepts to the inner workings of a
formidably complex new outlook in another medium, and he does so
with a prodigiously exact technical awareness of both mediums, word
and tones. A better way of saying it is that Adorno never lets technical
issues get in the way, never lets them awe him by their abstruseness
or by the evident mastery they require. He can be more technical
by elucidating technique from the perspective of lateness, seeing
Stravinskian primitivism in the light of later fascist collectivization.

Late style is *in*, but oddly *apart* from, the present. Only certain artists
and thinkers care enough about their *métier* to believe that it too ages,
and it too must face death within failing senses and memory. As
Adorno said about Beethoven, late style does not admit the definitive
cadences of death; instead, death appears in a refracted mode, as irony.
But with the kind of opulent, fractured, and somehow inconsistent
solemnity of a work such as the *Missa Solemnis*, or in Adorno's own
essays, the irony is how often lateness as theme and as style keeps
reminding us of death.

NOTES

Edward Said's lecture was prepared for publication by the editor of this
volume, who is solely responsible for any errors it may contain.

1 Jonathan Swift, *Gulliver's Travels* (Oxford, 1971), 212.
2 David Grene, *Reality and the Heroic Pattern: Last Plays of Ibsen, Shakespeare,
   and Sophocles* (Chicago, 1976).

3 Thomas Hardy, *Jude the Obscure* (Harmondsworth, 1978), 342–3.

4 Theodor W. Adorno, *Moments musicaux* (Frankfurt/Main, 1964), 13–17.

5 Ibid., 167–85.

6 Rose Rosengard Subotnik, 'Adorno's Diagnosis of Beethoven's Late Style: Early Symptoms of a Fatal Condition', *Journal of the American Musicological Society*, 29 (1976), 242–75.

7 Thomas Mann, *Doctor Faustus*, tr. H. T. Lowe-Porter (London, 1949), 52.

8 Adorno, *Moments musicaux*, 13.

9 Ibid., 15–16.

10 Ibid., 17.

11 Subotnik, 'Adorno's Diagnosis', 270.

12 Ibid.; Adorno, *Moments musicaux*, 183.

13 Adorno, *Moments musicaux*, 17.

14 Ibid.

15 Ibid., 13.

16 Harold Bloom, *The Anxiety of Influence* (New York, 1973).

17 Theodor Adorno, *The Philosophy of Modern Music*, tr. A. G. Mitchell and W. V. Blomster (London, 1973).

18 Ibid., 19.

19 Ibid., 20.

20 Fredric Jameson, *Late Marxism: Adorno or the Persistence of the Dialectic* (London, 1990).

21 Theodor Adorno, *Minima Moralia*, tr. E. F. N. Jephcott (London, 1974), 17.

22 Ibid.

23 Theodor Adorno, 'Resignation', tr. W. Blomster, *Telos*, 35 (1978), 168.

24 Ibid.

25 Theodor Adorno, 'Das Altern der neuen Musik', *Gesammelte Schriften*, 20 vols, ed. R. Tiedemann et al. (Frankfurt/Main, 1970–86), vol. 14, pp. 143–67.

26 Ibid., 146.

27 Ibid., 148.

28 Ibid., 151.

29 Ibid., 149.

30 Adorno, *Philosophy of Modern Music*, 70.

31 Adorno, *Minima Moralia*, 21, emphases added.

Index